The Guru Guide™
to Money Management

The Guru Guide™ to Money Management

The Best Advice from Top Financial Thinkers on Managing Your Money

Joseph H. Boyett

and

Jimmie T. Boyett

WILEY

John Wiley & Sons, Inc.

Published by John Wiley & Sons, Inc., Hoboken, New Jersey.
Published simultaneously in Canada.

Designations used by companies to distinguish their products are often claimed as trademarks. In all instances where John Wiley & Sons, Inc., is aware of a claim, the product names appear in initial capital letters. Readers, however, should contact the appropriate companies for more complete information regarding trademarks and registration.

Limit of Liability/Disclaimer of Warranty: While the publisher and author have used their best efforts in preparing this book, they make no representations or warranties with respect to the accuracy or completeness of the contents of this book and specifically disclaim any implied warranties of merchantability or fitness for a particular purpose. No warranty may be created or extended by sales representatives or written sales materials. The advice and strategies contained herein may not be suitable for your situation. The publisher is not engaged in rendering professional services, and you should consult a professional where appropriate. Neither the publisher nor author shall be liable for any loss of profit or any other commercial damages, including but not limited to special, incidental, consequential, or other damages.

For general information on our other products and services, please contact our Customer Care Department within the U.S. at (800) 762-2974, outside the United States at (317) 572-3993 or fax (317) 572-4002.

Wiley also publishes its books in a variety of electronic formats. Some content that appears in print may not be available in electronic books. For more information about Wiley products, visit our web site at www.Wiley.com.

Library of Congress Cataloging-in-Publication Data
Boyett, Joseph H.
  The guru guide to money management / Joseph H. Boyett and Jimmie T. Boyett.
    p. cm.
  Includes bibliographical references and index.
  ISBN 0-471-21889-8 (cloth)
    1. Finance, Personal. 2. Money. I. Boyett, Jimmie T. II. Title.

HG179.B66 2003
332.024- dc21   2003049658

Printed in the United States of America.
10 9 8 7 6 5 4 3 2 1

To our grandson,
David Augustine Luongo,
who gave us reasons to smile when we needed them most.

Contents

Introduction

There are over 8,000 personal finance and investment books in print. More than 300 were published in 2002 alone. They come in every shape and form, from quick "how-to" paperbacks to academic tomes to "get-rich-quick" treatises to detailed explanations of the "secrets" of the millionaires and the rich dads who live next door. They are written by predictable writers—financial advisors, CPAs, and investment counselors—as well as the highly unusual: motivational speakers, psychotherapists, and at least one who bills himself as a windsurfer, inventor, and prison fellowship ministry volunteer. Almost every nonfiction best-seller list contains at least one money management book, and frequently more than one. Some money management gurus, like Suze Orman, described as the "queen of money advice," are sufficiently popular to have multiple books on the nonfiction best-seller lists at the same time. Some stay on the best-seller list for months, even years.

The financial gurus offer a wide range of advice that is often conflicting. For example, some argue that you should maximize your earnings, minimize your expenses, meet your obligations, and at the same time, make sure you have some sort of nest egg to provide for your old age and to pass along to the kids. Others say that wealth is to be spent while you're alive, either on yourself or your loved ones, and that your goal in life should be to LIVE RICH and DIE BROKE. Whether you believe that consumption is the path to grace or that saving is the way to salvation, you will find at least one guru who supports your position.

Readers are confused about where to turn for reliable information, whose financial advice they should seek, and even what questions they should ask. When they do find answers to their questions, they are perplexed because they can't be sure the answers are correct. After all, what are they to make of the financial gurus' promises that their readers will learn how to "build a million-dollar portfolio on $3.50 a day," "increase their income by 10 percent in nine weeks," "earn an extra million in their lifetime," "earn up to a 50 percent return on their investments—guaranteed," "double their money in the stock market—FAST," and become wealthy on as little as a dollar a day?

The volume and confusing range of advice the financial gurus offer makes them perfect candidates for the synthesis and sense making in the Guru Guides™. *The Guru Guide to Money Management* will dissect the advice of America's top personal finance management gurus, expose their conflicts, and separate the practical from the theoretical.

This *Guru Guide™ to Money Management* has been designed to provide you with a clear, concise, and informative digest of the best thinking about money management today. You are holding in your hands a highly opinionated but informative guide to ideas of the world's top financial advisors. Like the original *Guru Guide*™ (Wiley, 1998), we have designed this guide to be more than just an overview of current thinking. We go further to link and cross-link the ideas to show where the experts agree and disagree. Finally, we provide an evaluation of their strengths and weaknesses.

OUR GURUS

In selecting our gurus, we began by making a list of established money management authorities and media personalities, such as Clark Howard, Jane Bryant Quinn, and Suze Orman. We added authorities on the rich, such as Thomas Stanley, who wrote *The Millionaire Mind,* and investment wizards such as Arthur Levitt, Peter Lynch, and the Motley Fools, David and Tom Gardner. Then we went looking for the newcomers. We browsed the online and offline bookstores. We consulted with our friends and associates, asking them whose advice they listened to. We searched the mainstream press to find out what journal articles and books on money management people were reading and talking about. We asked who the popular media—TV, radio, business periodicals—were citing on money management and investing issues. Who was widely recognized as THE authority in personal finance management and investing? Who was getting recognized? Who was being quoted? Whose ideas were being discussed?

Because the economy has changed so dramatically in the last few years, we focused our search primarily on the most significant books and articles that have been published recently. We ultimately narrowed our list down to the 80 gurus listed here:

Robert Allen, author of *Multiple Streams of Income*
Ginger Applegarth, author of *Wake Up and Smell the Money*
Murray Baker, author of *The Debt-Free Graduate*
Gary Belsky, coauthor of *Why Smart People Make Big Money Mistakes and How to Correct Them*
Stacie Zoe Berg, author of *The Unofficial Guide to Managing Your Personal Finances*
Jacqueline Blix, coauthor of *Getting a Life*
Mark Bryan, coauthor of *Money Drunk, Money Sober*
Julia Cameron, coauthor of *Money Drunk, Money Sober*
David Caruso, coauthor of *Let's Talk Money*
Nancy Castleman, coauthor of *Invest in Yourself*
Jean Chatsky, author of *Talking Money*
Jonathan Clements, author of *25 Myths You've Got to Avoid If You Want to Manage Your Money Right*

Amy Dacyczyn, author of *The Complete Tightwad Gazette*

William Danko, coauthor of *The Millionaire Next Door*

Gerri Detweiler, coauthor of *Invest in Yourself*

Joe Dominguez, coauthor of *Your Money or Your Life*

Ric Edelman, author of *New Rules of Money* and *The Truth about Money*

Marc Eisenson, coauthor of *Invest in Yourself*

Debra Englander, author of *How to Be Your Own Financial Planner*

Ron Gallen, author of *The Money Trap*

David Gardner, coauthor of *The Motley Fool Investment Guide* and *You Have More Than You Think*

Tom Gardner, coauthor of *The Motley Fool Investment Guide* and *You Have More Than You Think*

Thomas Gilovich, coauthor of *Why Smart People Make Big Money Mistakes and How to Correct Them*

Ilyce Glink, author of *50 Simple Things You Can Do to Improve Your Personal Finances*

Neale S. Godfrey, author of *Making Change*

Andrew Hacker, author of *Money: Who Has How Much and Why*

Bob Hammond, author of *Life after Debt*

Christopher L. Hayes, coauthor of *Money Makeovers*

Christy Heady, coauthor of *The Complete Idiot's Guide to Managing Your Money*

Robert Heady, coauthor of *The Complete Idiot's Guide to Managing Your Money*

David Heitmiller, coauthor of *Getting a Life*

Napoleon Hill, author of *Think and Grow Rich*

Bambi Holzer, author of *Retire Rich*

Clark Howard, author of *Get Clark Smart*

Mary Hunt, author of *Mary Hunt's Debt-Proof Living* and *Mary Hunt's The Complete Cheapskate*

Mary Ivins, author of *Financial Security for Women*

Azriela Jaffe, coauthor of *The Complete Idiot's Guide to Beating Debt*

Jason Kelly, author of *The Neatest Little Guide to Personal Finance*

Mike Kidwell, coauthor of *Get Out of Debt*

George Kinder, author of *The Seven Stages of Money Maturity*

Robert Kiyosaki, author of *Rich Dad's Guide to Investing* and *Rich Dad's Cashflow Quadrant*

Deborah Knuckey, author of *The Ms. Spent Money Guide*

Phil Laut, author of *Money Is My Friend*

Dee Lee, coauthor of *Let's Talk Money*

Dwight Lee, coauthor of *Getting Rich in America*

Mark Levine, coauthor of *Live Rich* and *Die Broke*

Arthur Levitt, coauthor of *Take on the Street*

Nancy Lloyd, author of *Simple Money Solutions*

Marshall Loeb, author of *Marshall Loeb's Lifetime Financial Strategies*
Peter Lynch, coauthor of *Learn to Earn*
Richard McKenzie, coauthor of *Getting Rich in America*
Deborah McNaughton, coauthor of *The Insider's Guide to Managing Your Credit*
Olivia Mellan, coauthor of *Money Shy to Money Sure* and *Overcoming Overspending*
Mark Miller, author of *The Complete Idiot's Guide to Being a Cheapskate*
Ted Miller, author of *Kiplinger's Practical Guide to Your Money*
Edward Mrkvicka, author of *Your Bank Is Ripping You Off*
Stephen Nelson, author of *The Millionaire Kit*
Maria Nemeth, author of *The Energy of Money*
Holly Nicholson, author of *Money and You*
James O'Shaughnessy, author of *How to Retire Rich*
Suze Orman, author of *The 9 Steps to Financial Freedom, Suze Orman's Financial Guidebook,* and *The Courage to Be Rich*
Greg Pahl, author of *The Unofficial Guide to Beating Debt*
Stephen Pollan, coauthor of *Live Rich* and *Die Broke*
Jonathan Pond, author of *Your Money Matters*
Jane Bryant Quinn, author of *Making the Most of Your Money*
Dave Ramsey, author of *Financial Peace* and *More Than Enough*
Steve Rhode, coauthor of *Get Out of Debt*
Vicki Robin, coauthor of *Your Money or Your Life*
Terry Savage, author of *The Savage Truth on Money*
Charles Schwab, author of *Charles Schwab's Guide to Financial Independence* and *You're Fifty—Now What?*
Robert Sheard, author of *The Unemotional Investor*
Don Silver, author of *The Generation Y Money Book*
Thomas Stanley, author of *The Millionaire Mind* and coauthor of *The Millionaire Next Door*
Barbara Stanny, author of *Prince Charming Isn't Coming*
Julie Stav, author of *Fund Your Future*
Brooke Stephens, author of *Wealth Happens One Day at a Time*
Steven Strauss, coauthor of *The Complete Idiot's Guide to Beating Debt*
Howard Strong, author of *What Every Credit Card User Needs to Know*
David Teitelbaum, author of *The Procrastinator's Guide to Financial Security*
Eric Tyson, author of *Personal Finance for Dummies*

Our gurus include the best and most popular personal finance management and investment writers and thinkers. You won't agree with everything they have to say, but we are confident that they will stimulate your thinking, point you in new directions, and challenge many of your best-loved assumptions about what it takes to effectively manage your money and invest for success.

ORGANIZATION OF THE BOOK

We have designed this book to be your reference manual for the current challenges we all face in managing our personal finances. It is organized around key money management issues. We cover each issue in a separate chapter and present a summary of the best thinking of a panel of money management gurus about that issue. We show where the gurus agree and disagree. When our gurus offer different approaches—such as a different sequence of steps to follow in addressing an issue or solving a financial problem—we use charts and exhibits to illustrate the similarities and differences.

We have organized our gurus' ideas into nine chapters.

Chapter 1, Understanding Your Relationship with Money, provides an overview of our gurus' recommendations about how to root out any dysfunctional thoughts you might have about money and replace them with healthier attitudes and beliefs. With our gurus' help, we show you how to start feeling like a million when it comes to managing your money and thinking like the rich.

Chapter 2, Getting Your Finances in Order, provides step-by-step guidance from our gurus on how to calculate your net worth and cash flow. We show you how to read and evaluate your net-worth and cash-flow statements and how to develop financial and life goals. We conclude this chapter with our gurus' advice on how to determine if you need professional advice and assistance in managing your money and how to select the right financial planner.

In **Chapter 3, Making Money and Protecting Your Income,** we present our gurus' advice on the right and wrong ways to make money and show you four strategies for boosting your income. We conclude this chapter with some sage advice on cutting your taxes and show you how to find a bank that's right for you.

Chapter 4, Spending and Saving, shows you how to determine if you are overspending and presents nine strategies for getting your spending under control. We then review our gurus' step-by-step guidance for developing a spending plan (a.k.a., a budget) that works. We conclude this chapter with five money-saving ideas from our gurus that will help you simplify your life and start living happily as a conscious spender.

In **Chapter 5, All about Insurance,** we review our gurus' recommendations for how to get the best deals on life, disability, health, long-term care, homeowner's/renter's, and auto insurance. We share our gurus' guidance on determining the amount and type of insurance you need and how to find an insurance company.

In **Chapter 6, Debit and Credit,** we present our gurus' advice on how to determine if you are carrying too much debt. We then outline a rapid debt reduction program that our gurus praise as an effective and painless way to pay off your debt and explain why they say quick-fix schemes such as using a home equity loan to pay off debt are bad ideas. We conclude this chapter with an overview of our gurus' advice on selecting and using credit and debit cards and the tips they offer for using credit cards wisely.

Chapter 7, Borrowing for Big-Ticket Items, covers our gurus recommendations for getting the best deals on auto loans, student loans, and home mortgages.

Finally, in **Chapter 8, Investment Basics,** and **Chapter 9, Investing for Retirement,** we turn to the topic of investing. In Chapter 8, we discuss what our gurus say are the pros and cons of different types of investments (stocks, bonds, real estate, and so on) and tell you the investments they say to avoid. We then look at what our gurus have to say about the advantages and disadvantages of investing through mutual funds and summarize their advice for picking a mutual fund that suites your investment style.

Chapter 9 shows you methods our gurus recommend for calculating how much you will need for retirement and reviews five essential strategies our gurus name for minimizing market risk and maximizing return when it comes to managing your retirement investments.

We include an appendix in which we provide biographies for all of the gurus, including in many instances postal addresses where they can be reached.

SOME GUIDANCE ON WHAT FOLLOWS: HOW THE CHAPTERS ARE ORGANIZED

Throughout the *Guru Guide™ to Money Management,* we have tried to summarize as clearly, succinctly, and objectively as possible the gurus' key ideas.

At the beginning of each chapter, we use the following icon to identify the gurus whose ideas are covered in that chapter:

    Our Gurus

At the end of each chapter, we provide a summary of the key ideas presented in that chapter. Key ideas are identified by the following icon:

 KEY POINTS   Key Points

In addition, look for the following icons as clues to important points or guru warnings concerning financial risks:

    Good Idea

    Bad Idea

    Caution! Warning!

    Pros and Cons

    Notes of Interest

Rule of Thumb

  Tips

We wish you good reading and success in achieving your personal financial goals. If you have comments about *The Guru Guide™ to Money Management* or would like to learn about other *Guru Guides*™ as they become available, please visit our Web site at http://www.jboyett.com or e-mail us at Boyett@jboyett.com.

Joseph H. Boyett

Jimmie T. Boyett

OUR GURUS

Mark Bryan, coauthor of *Money Drunk, Money Sober*

Julia Cameron, coauthor of *Money Drunk, Money Sober*

Nancy Castleman, coauthor of *Invest in Yourself*

Gerri Detweiler, coauthor of *Invest in Yourself*

Marc Eisenson, author of *Invest in Yourself*

Napoleon Hill, author of *Think and Grow Rich*

Mary Hunt, author of *Mary Hunt's Debt-Proof Living*

Azriela Jaffe, coauthor of *The Complete Idiot's Guide to Beating Debt*

George Kinder, author of *Seven Stages of Money Maturity*

Phil Laut, author of *Money Is My Friend*

Olivia Mellan, coauthor of *Money Shy to Money Sure*

Suze Orman, author of *The 9 Steps to Financial Freedom* and *The Courage to Be Rich*

Thomas Stanley, author of *The Millionaire Mind* and coauthor of *The Millionaire Next Door*

Brooke Stephens, author of *Wealth Happens One Day at a Time*

Steven Strauss, coauthor of *The Complete Idiot's Guide to Beating Debt*

Understanding Your Relationship with Money

We begin this book where most of our gurus begin theirs. It is not with having you calculate your assets and liabilities and prepare a financial plan—that will come later. Instead, we start with your relationship with money. Maybe you didn't realize that you have a relationship with money, but our gurus say you do, and they add that the relationship may be dysfunctional. In this chapter, we examine our gurus' recommendations for steps you can take to root out any dysfunctional money thoughts and replace them with healthier money attitudes and beliefs. With their help, we will get you feeling like a million and thinking like a millionaire.

YOUR MONEY THOUGHTS

In her best-seller *The Courage to Be Rich,* Suzie Orman writes that "when it comes to money, what you think will direct what you say, what you say will direct what you do, and what you do will create your destiny."[1] Fundamentally, says Orman, true riches are a product of mind-set. Think rich thoughts, and you just might become rich. Think thoughts of poverty, and you might become poor, if you aren't already. Most of our gurus make the same argument.

According to Orman and our other gurus, you need to root out your dysfunctional money thoughts, beliefs, and attitudes because they are the cause of your dysfunctional money behaviors. Once you have identified the money thoughts that are standing in the way of your prosperity, our gurus explain, you have to replace them with alternative "rich" thoughts that will aid you in your journey to financial independence and well-being.

> The road to financial freedom begins not in a bank or even in a financial planner's office . . . but in your head. It begins with your thoughts.
>
> *Suze Orman*[2]

The gurus offer a wide range of exercises for helping you to uncover your deepest money thoughts and beliefs. For convenience in discussing them, we have grouped the exercises into three complementary approaches:

- Examine your past to uncover your beliefs, or *The Blame-Mom-and-Dad Approach*
- Examine your relationship with money, or *The Money-as-a-Person Approach*
- Getting at your beliefs by analyzing the words you use to talk about money, or *The Language-of-Poverty Approach*

Each of these approaches, as you might imagine, has its own special appeal. We invite you to peruse all of the approaches and try at least some of the exercises.

The Blame-Mom-and-Dad Approach

The blame-Mom-and-Dad approach is perhaps the most popular method for uncovering your money thoughts, beliefs, and attitudes. Essentially, it involves thinking back on your earliest experiences with money and reflecting on how those experiences shape your current money behaviors. Orman explains the approach this way:

> [T]he first step toward financial freedom is a step back in time to the earliest moments you can recall when money meant something to you, when you truly understood what it could do. When you began to see that money could create pleasure—ice-cream cones, merry-go-round rides; and also to see that it could create pain—fights between your parents, perhaps, or longings of your own that couldn't be fulfilled because there wasn't enough money or even because there was too much. When you first understood that money was not just a shiny object or something to color on. When you understood that money was money. I want you to think back and see that your feelings about money today (fearing it, enjoying it, loving it, hating it) can almost certainly be traced to an incident, possibly forgotten until now, from your past.[3]

Orman reports that she has done this exercise with hundreds of people and that it almost always opens up a floodgate of emotions. Most people, even those who grew up in the wealthiest families, find themselves recalling a least one painful money memory that they come to realize is shaping their money behaviors.

Orman provides a number of questions to help you get started. We include them in Exercise 1.1, along with questions posed by other gurus. Take a moment and read through these questions. What kinds of memories do they illicit? What kinds of money habits or ways of thinking about financial matters did they teach you? Can you see a connection between what you learned back then and what you do, or don't do, today when it comes to managing your money? Remember that no answer is necessarily right or wrong. What you want to accomplish is uncovering feelings, memories, and attitudes that may be impacting your relationship with money. Finally, don't try to overanalyze each answer as you work through the exercise. We will explore the significance of your answers later in this chapter.

The Money-as-a-Person Approach

Our gurus say that another way of getting at your underlying thoughts, beliefs, and feelings about money is to think of money as a person and ask yourself what type of relationship you have with it.

Orman offers another series of questions for you to answer. As you answer the questions in Exercise 1.2, think about what your answers tell you about your relationship with money.

The Wallet Exercise

Tired of answering questions? Well, here are two alternative exercises to help you unravel your relationship with money. The first is what Orman calls the "Wallet Exercise." (See Exercise 1.3.)

Orman suggests that if your wallet is a mess, you should complete a "wallet checklist" each morning. Before you leave the house, take out your wallet, arrange all the bills in order, and make sure they are all facing the same way. Also, if you find you are carrying old, wrinkled, and limp-to-the-touch bills, you should stop at a bank the first chance you get and exchange the old bills for nice, crisp, new ones.[4]

The Language-of-Poverty Approach

Finally, say our gurus, you can get at your thoughts and beliefs about money by examining the words and phrases you use when speaking about money matters. Orman believes that the words you use when talking your financial affairs are important because, "just as your destiny begins with your thoughts, your words bring you closer to your destiny."[5] She argues that there are both words of poverty and words of wealth. In fact, she says, the words you speak, hear, and exchange each day are predictive of your financial future. "Speak poor," she writes, "and you will be poor. Speak rich, true words, on the other hand, and you start to change your entire outlook."[6] She says you should watch out for the following words and phrases because they are the words of poverty:

- **I'm broke.** The words "I'm broke" suggest, in fact, that you're broken, at rock bottom, unable to function, unable to meet your responsibilities. Is that the message you want to send to the world?

EXERCISE 1.1. **Your Money Memories**

Instructions: Read through these questions. What kinds of memories do they illicit? What kinds of money habits or ways of thinking about financial matters did they teach you? Remember that no answer is right or wrong. The purpose of this exercise is to uncover feelings, memories, and attitudes that may impact your relationship with money.

1. Did your mother have to work when others didn't, or not have to work when others did?

2. Did you feel like your friends had nicer clothes than you did? Did your friends' parents have more expensive cars than yours did?

3. Do you remember the very first wallet you ever had? Was it given to you empty, or with a penny in it, or a dollar?

4. Did you get less of an allowance than your friends or siblings? Did you have to work for it, or was it given to you as your right? What did you do with it?

5. What did your parents tell you about money that made you feel good? What did they tell you that made you feel bad?

6. What are the feelings attached to your three earliest memories of money: elation, satisfaction, humiliation, shame, guilt?

7. When and how did money first enter your relationship with your mother? How did it change the emotional tone between the two of you? What about your father?

8. When did you first discover that you were richer than some people and poorer than others? How did that discovery feel?

9. As you were growing up, did you ever make a vow about money ("Someday I'll have piles and piles of money and they'll have to respect me")? What incident gave rise to these vows? What feelings flowed through you at the time? How long did you keep repeating those vows? Did your feelings change over time in relation to the vows? What feelings come up in you now as you recall these incidents and the vows you made?

10. What were your parents' actions regarding money? Was it a source of constant worry? Did they avoid talking about it? Did they always argue about it? Did they blame each other or you and your siblings for money problems? Did they act as if they never had enough, or maybe as if they had more than they really had? What did this teach you?

11. What did you know about your family's financial situation? Was it ever discussed? If it was a secret, why do you think that was so? Was money a source of pride or embarrassment? What did you learn from this?

12. Did you have to work as a teen? What happened to the money you earned?

13. When did you first go into debt to get something that you wanted? How did you feel going into debt? Was this the beginning of a pattern?

14. Did money influence your choice of careers? Was that a good idea?

Sources: Adapted from George Kinder, The Seven Stages of Money Maturity: Understanding the Spirit and Value of Money in Your Life *(New York: Delacorte Press, 1999), pp. 77–78; Suze Orman,* The 9 Steps to Financial Freedom: Practical and Spiritual Steps So You Can Stop Worrying *(New York: Three Rivers Press, 2000), pp. 14–15; and Steven D. Strauss and Azriela Jaffe,* The Complete Idiot's Guide to Beating Debt *(Indianapolis, IN: Alpha Books, 2000), pp. 35–37.*

EXERCISE 1.2. **Do You Respect Your Money?**

Instructions: Answer the following questions and think about what your answers tell you about your relationship with money.

1. Do you spend more money on your friends than you can afford to? Why?
2. Do you find yourself buying more presents for your children for the holidays or their birthdays than feels right to you? Why?
3. Will you spend money on others but never a penny on yourself? Why?
4. Do you send things Federal Express or next-day air because they'll come pick it up, rather than going to the post office to mail it far more cheaply? Why?
5. Have you ever bought a dress and decided, when you got it home, that it really didn't suit you, then neglected to return it to the store in time to get your money back? Why?
6. Do you give to charities because you really believe in the cause or to impress people? Why?
7. Do you put away as much money as you possibly can for retirement each year? Why not?
8. Do you sometimes "forget" to pay off personal loans from friends with the same regularity that you'd pay off a credit card? Why?
9. Do you constantly return videos a day late and have to pay the late fee, even though you've already watched them? Why?
10. Do you send your clothes out for dry cleaning when all they need is a quick once-over with an iron? Why?
11. Do you often go out to dinner simply because you don't feel like cooking? At what cost over time? Why?
12. Do you sometimes pay your bills late when you didn't have to? Why?

Source: Suze Orman, The 9 Steps to Financial Freedom: Practical and Spiritual Steps So You Can Stop Worrying (New York: Three Rivers Press, 2000), pp. 119–120.

EXERCISE 1.3. **The Wallet Exercise**

Instructions: Take out your wallet and look at the way you are carrying your folding money.

- Are the bills all facing the same direction?
- Are they arranged in order by denomination: ones then fives then tens, and so on?
- Are the bills smooth or crumpled and dog-eared?
- Are the bills new, neat and crisp or are they old, rumpled and limp to the touch?
- What does the way you carry your money tell you about the respect or lack of respect you have for it?

Source: Suze Orman, Suze Orman's Financial Guidebook: Putting the 9 Steps to Work (New York: Three Rivers Press, 2002), p. 89.

- **I know I should . . .** Anything that you "should" be doing is something you're clearly not doing. "Should" is another way of absolving yourself of responsibility. Any sentence that contains the word is not even close to a statement of intent.
- **It's only money.** There's nothing "only" about money. Money matters, plain and simple. If this is your attitude toward money, . . . your money will take the same apathetic attitude toward you.
- **I need a new . . .** Do you really *need* it? Is "need" the right word? Elevating desires to needs is destructive—to ourselves and to those around us. Let's say you saw a new suit and you thought, I would like to own that—you were able to keep need out of it. Isn't that statement more accurate and therefore truer to the language of wealth?
- **Never.** Never say "never," when it comes to money. "Never" cuts off tomorrow, and tomorrow holds the possibility of always. "I'll never be rich." "I'll always be rich." One word makes a world of difference.
- **I could start investing if . . .** When I get a raise, things will be different. "If" and "when" take us away from the here and now to a place that exists only conditionally.
- **Poor Bill,** or whoever. The words evoke someone who is bankrupt, not necessarily financially, perhaps, but certainly emotionally and spiritually. A pitiful case, a person who must be treated with extra sensitivity, a person who's weak. The words evoke poverty. They also enforce poverty. Either Bill, through his thoughts, words, and actions, is soliciting pity, or else poverty is being thrust upon him by what other people think and say about him. Either way, the poorer the thoughts, words, and actions are, the harder it is to rise above them.[7]

Marc Eisenson, Gerri Detweiler, and Nancy Castleman, coauthors of *Invest in Yourself: Six Secrets to a Rich Life,* add excuse words and phrases like the following to the list:[8]

- If only.
- Can't.
- Won't.
- It's their fault.

See Exhibit 1.1 for some of the 55 famous alibis that Napoleon Hill lists in his classic book *Think and Grow Rich.*

Orman suggests that you listen carefully to the language you are using to see if poverty words and phrases have crept into your vocabulary. What do you do if you find them? When you find yourself about to say one of these poverty words, Orman says that you should stop and ask yourself if what you are about to say is what you really want to come true. "For example," she writes, "if you are about to say, 'I will never get out of debt,' ask yourself: Is that what I want to be true?"[9] Then don't say it, or better yet, rephrase it into a positive statement. Change your poverty language into wealth language. See Exhibit 1.2 to learn how.

EXHIBIT 1.1. Classic Alibis of Failures

In *Think and Grow Rich,* Napoleon Hill identified what he called the 55 most common alibis that people who do not succeed use to justify their failure. We list a number of them here:

IF I didn't have a wife and family . . .

IF I had a good education . . .

IF I could get a job. . . .

IF I only had time . . .

IF times were better . . .

IF other people understood me . . .

IF conditions around me were only different . . .

IF I could live my life over again . . .

IF I did not fear what "they" would say . . .

IF I now had a chance . . .

IF I were only younger . . .

IF I could only do what I want . . .

IF I had been born rich . . .

And the greatest of them all—

IF I had the courage to see myself as I really am, I would *find out what is wrong with me and correct it.* Then I might have a chance to profit by my mistakes and learn something from the experience of others, for I know that there is something wrong with me, or I would now be where I would have been if I had spent more time analyzing my weaknesses, and less time building alibis to cover them.

Source: Napoleon Hill, Think and Grow Rich *(New York: Fawcett Crest, 1960), pp. 250–253.*

How did you do? Are you treating your money with respect? What about your money language? Did you detect some poverty words in your vocabulary? We hope these exercises gave you some new insights into your relationship with money.

So far we have explored the money thoughts, beliefs, and attitudes of typical Americans like us. We do some things right and some things wrong when it comes to our money. We practice some money habits that our gurus would applaud and think some money thoughts that our gurus say are dysfunctional. Now let's take a different tack. Instead of talking about Mr. and Ms. Typical American, let's talk about the rich.

THINKING LIKE A MILLIONAIRE

What makes millionaires different from the rest of us? Do the rich harbor money thoughts, attitudes, and beliefs that are unique? Yes, our gurus say, they do, and we could all benefit by learning to think like a millionaire.

EXHIBIT 1.2. From Poverty Language to Wealth Language

POVERTY LANGUAGE	WEALTH LANGUAGE
"I'll never get around to investing."	"I am finally beginning to learn about investing.'
"I just know the market is going to crash."	"I believe the stock market is a good investment over time."
"My husband will probably leave me with nothing."	"If I get divorced, I will take every measure to get what's fair."
"I'll never get out from under."	"Slowly but surely, I am putting my finances in order."
"I'm an impulse spender. I can't help it."	"I spend only what I can afford to spend."
"I just can't save money."	"I'm beginning to save a little from every paycheck."

Source: Adapted from Suze Orman, The Courage to Be Rich: Creating a Life of Material and Spiritual Abundance (New York: Riverhead Books, 1999), p. 32.

We turn to guru Thomas Stanley, author of the best-seller *The Millionaire Mind*, to examine some of the millionaire money thoughts and beliefs. Stanley's book is based on national surveys of American millionaires.

See Exhibit 1.3 for a brief summary of Stanley's findings concerning the thoughts, attitudes and money beliefs of millionaires. As you review these results, ask yourself to what extent the money thoughts, beliefs, and attitudes you identified for yourself as a result of the exercises covered earlier in this chapter match those of the millionaires. What changes do you need to make to start thinking like a millionaire?

Let's revisit that last attitude in Exhibit 1.3: Millionaires believe that becoming wealthy is a mind game and that before you can become a millionaire, you have to learn to think like one.

"The rich are different from us."

F. Scott Fitzgerald

"Yes, they have more money."

Ernest Hemingway

If you're like most people, you have beliefs and attitudes from both the poverty and the millionaire schools of thought. How do you rid yourself of your poverty

---

EXHIBIT 1.3. **Millionaire Thoughts, Beliefs, and Attitudes**

According to Stanley in *The Millionaire Mind,* millionaires have the following spending strategies, attitudes toward work and money, and approach toward success. (References to appropriate page numbers in Stanley's book follow each item.)

- **Millionaires believe in being frugal.** Most millionaires have never spent more than $41,000 for an automobile or $38 for a haircut (including tip). They have their shoes resoled and always develop a shopping list before going shopping. Many millionaires are price sensitive when purchasing products such as automobiles and clothes that lose all or most of their initial value after the date of purchase. They also believe in buying quality products and in making them last and in living below their means (pp. 7, 26, 288, 290).
- **Millionaires believe in owning their home but seek to have a small outstanding mortgage.** Many millionaires believe in purchasing an existing home rather than building a new one and that one should never pay the asking price. They look to purchase a home that is likely to appreciate in value, reasoning that the quality of the public schools in the area is a good predictor of the likelihood that the house will appreciate in value (pp. 8, 28).
- **They believe in living a comfortable but not extravagant lifestyle.** For example, they don't indulge in fancy and expensive vacations (p. 11).
- **They believe in doing work that they love and that people's choice of a vocation has much to do with their success in life** (p. 10).
- **These millionaires believe in working hard, but they also think it is important to spend time with family and friends.** They don't feel that one has to be a workaholic to succeed. They avoid "do-it-yourself" activities, preferring instead to work hard at their main vocation and spend the rest of their free time doing what is enjoyable (pp. 10, 29).
- **They strive to balance their financial goals and their lifestyles.** They feel that there is a positive correlation between the number of activities people take part in and their net worth (p. 10).
- **The millionaires believe that the best things in life are free, or at least reasonably priced** (p. 1).
- **They think that luck has little to do with success and have little regard for gambling or playing the lottery.** They believe that their "luck" is a product of hard work and that the harder they work, the "luckier" they will become (pp. 11, 83, 376).
- **The millionaires know that there is a strong correlation between one's willingness to take financial risk and one's level of wealth.** They see economic risk taking as a requirement for becoming financially independent (pp. 12, 134).
- **Millionaires look for opportunities to provide a product or service that has strong demand but few suppliers to fulfill that demand.** They don't follow the crowd when it comes to deciding what to sell or how to invest. They think that success comes at the price of *not* being one of the gang, one of the good old boys (pp. 12, 50).

(continued)

EXHIBIT 1.3. (continued)

- **The millionaires don't consider themselves "intellectually gifted."** In fact, they question the relationship between intellect, academic performance, and economic success. They think that hard work is more important than genetic high intellect in achieving success (pp. 14, 106).
- **They believe that it is risky *not* to be self-employed** (pp. 18, 135).
- **They think success, not failure.** And they believe that by studying the probable outcomes of an endeavor, they can enhance the odds of success (p. 19).
- **The millionaires believe that success requires mental toughness and an athlete's heart and that competitive sports provide an important training ground for both** (p. 19).
- **They discount criticism.** They view negative comments such as "you will never succeed" or "that's the dumbest idea for a business I've ever heard" as theories to be disproved. They don't allow negative evaluations or forecasts to weaken their resolve. They don't take rejection personally (pp. 46, 48, 50).
- **They don't see the stock market as something that an individual investor can control or influence.** They invest in the stock market, but they diversify their investments, especially with endeavors like real estate (pp. 74, 337).
- **Finally, the millionaires think that becoming wealthy is a mind game and that before you can become a millionaire, you have to think like one** (p. 135).

Source: Thomas J. Stanley, The Millionaire Mind *(Kansas City, MO: Andrew McMeel, 2000).*

---

thoughts and reinforce your wealthy thoughts? Our gurus have a suggestion: positive affirmation.

THE POWER OF THE POSITIVE AFFIRMATION

Remember the book from your childhood titled *The Little Engine That Could*—"I think I can. I think I can"? Our gurus recommend that you use the power of positive affirmation to convert your negative, poverty thoughts into positive, wealthy ones. They say that you should take one or more of your poverty thoughts—such as "I want it now!"— and turn it into a wealthy thought, such as "waiting builds character." Then repeat the positive thought over and over.

Write it down. Post it on the mirror in your bathroom. Read it out loud every morning while you are shaving or putting on your make-up.

Record it on a tape and play it over and over as you commute to and from work.

Write it on a card, and carry the card in your pocket or purse. Take the card out several times a day and read what you have written

You'll have to come up with your own affirmations. Go back and look at the results of the exercises you completed earlier in this chapter. Read over the list of millionaire thoughts we just covered, and pick a few positive, wealthy thoughts to drum into your brain. If you're still having trouble, then see the list of affirmations in Exhibit 1.4 that reflect the recommendations of several of our gurus.

The gurus guarantee that in a few days or weeks of such activity, you will be banishing your dysfunctional money thoughts and replacing them with healthy new ones. You'll be feeling and thinking like a million, and you'll be ready to tackle the job of getting your money house in order, our next topic. But first, let's review the key ideas from this chapter.

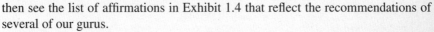

KEY POINTS

- True riches are a product of mind-set. Think rich thoughts, and you just might get rich. Think thoughts of poverty, and you are likely to become poor.

- There are three complementary approaches to uncovering your thoughts and beliefs about money:
    - Examine your past to uncover your beliefs, or *The Blame-Mom-and-Dad Approach*
    - Examine your relationship with money, or *The Money-as-a-Person Approach*
    - Analyze the words you use to talk about money matters, or *The Language-of-Poverty Approach*

- Most people, even those who grew up in the wealthiest families, have at least one painful money memory that they come to realize is shaping their money behaviors.

- Money behaves like a person. It is attracted to people who are strong and powerful, respectful of it, and open to receiving it.

- The way you carry your money—neat and orderly or disorganized and messy—says much about your respect, or lack of respect, for your money.

EXHIBIT 1.4. **Positive Money Thoughts**

The following is a list of positive affirmations as suggested by several of our gurus:

1. I am so thankful for a regular paycheck.
2. This is not difficult; it is challenging!
3. I work too hard to let money leak out of my life.
4. Waiting builds character.
5. I'd rather save $5 a week than throw it away on the lottery.
6. Even the little things add up.
7. More money is not the answer—managing what I have is!
8. I choose to be happy regardless of my present circumstances.
9. I have the confidence to make my own financial decisions.
10. I spend in appropriate ways and only as I need.
11. I allow myself to shop moderately.
12. I buy wisely.
13. Money serves me, and I use it wisely.
14. I accept financial good and let go my fears of abundance.
15. I allow abundance in my life.
16. I accept comfort in my life.
17. My finances are mine to control.
18. I think clearly in financial dealings.
19. I choose wisely in financial matters.
20. No matter how much money I have, I am making my money grow.
21. I am learning to take more intelligent risks, and I am confident that sensible risk taking will help me build my financial future.
22. It's not a bit selfish to take good care of myself financially. It's self-respecting and self-caring and ultimately makes my relationship with others richer and more satisfying.
23. My loved ones enjoy, respect, and appreciate my financial knowledge, power, and success.
24. I have abundance in all things; my needs are met easily and effortlessly. I now give and receive money easily.
25. I now have a perfect, satisfying, well-paying job.
26. I now have enough money to do whatever I want.
27. I commit to do whatever it takes and make whatever sacrifices are necessary to achieve and maintain solvency.
28. I can achieve financial well-being.
29. Money is my friend.

Sources: Mark Bryan and Julia Cameron, Money Drunk, Money Sober: 90 Days to Financial Freedom *(Los Angeles: Lowell House, 1992), pp. 205–208; Mary Hunt,* Mary Hunt's Debt-Proof Living *(Nashville, TN: Broadman & Holman, 1999), p. 149; Mary Hunt,* Mary Hunt's The Complete Cheapskate: How to Get Out of Debt, Stay Out, and Break Free from Money Worries Forever *(Nashville, TN: Broadman & Holman, 1998), pp. 26–30; Phil Laut,* Money Is My Friend *(New York: Ballantine Wellspring Books, 1999), p. 15; Olivia Mellan and Sherry Christie,* Money Shy to Money Sure: A Woman's Road Map to Financial Well-Being *(New York: Walker, 2001), p. 261; Brooke Stephens,* Wealth Happens One Day at a Time: 365 Days to a Brighter Financial Future *(New York: Harper Books, 1999), p. 9; and Steven D. Strauss and Azriela Jaffe,* The Complete Idiot's Guide to Beating Debt *(Indianapolis, IN: Alpha Books, 2000), p. 47.*

- There are words of poverty and words of wealth. The words you speak, hear, and exchange each day when you talk about your financial affairs are predictive of your financial future.

- You can use the power of positive affirmation to convert your negative, poverty thoughts into positive, wealthy ones.

Ginger Applegarth, author of *Wake Up and Smell the Money*

Jean Chatzky, author of *Talking Money*

William Danko, coauthor of *The Millionaire Next Door*

Ric Edelman, author of *The Truth about Money*

Ilyce Glink, author of *50 Simple Things You Can Do to Improve Your Personal Finances*

Christopher L. Hayes, coauthor of *Money Makeovers*

Mary Hunt, author of *Mary Hunt's Debt-Proof Living*

Azriela Jaffe, coauthor of *The Complete Idiot's Guide to Beating Debt*

Jason Kelly, author of *The Neatest Little Guide to Personal Finance*

George Kinder, author of *The Seven Stages of Money Maturity*

Mark Levine, coauthor of *Die Broke*

Olivia Mellan, coauthor of *Money Shy to Money Sure*

Maria Nemeth, author of *The Energy of Money*

Holly Nicholson, author of *Money and You*

Suze Orman, author of *Suze Orman's Financial Guidebook*

Stephen Pollan, coauthor of *Die Broke*

Jane Bryant Quinn, author of *Making the Most of Your Money*

Dave Ramsey, author of *More Than Enough*

Thomas Stanley, coauthor of *The Millionaire Next Door*

Barbara Stanny, author of *Prince Charming Isn't Coming*

Brooke Stephens, author of *Wealth Happens One Day at a Time*

Steven Strauss, coauthor of *The Complete Idiot's Guide to Beating Debt*

Eric Tyson, author of *Personal Finance for Dummies*

2

Getting Your Finances in Order

I n the previous chapter, you learned how to dig out the poverty thinking that has been getting in the way of your building a secure financial future for yourself and your family. You learned how to use positive affirmation to banish those nasty, negative thoughts from your mind and replace them with healthy, wealthy thoughts. As a result, the gurus consider you mentally ready to take stock of your financial situation and to take the first steps to getting your financial affairs in order. So, sharpen your pencils, locate those financial records, and fire up your computer or calculator. It's time for you to develop a financial plan.

TAKING STOCK

In their best-seller *The Millionaire Next Door,* Thomas Stanley and William Danko distinguish between people they call "prodigious accumulators of wealth" (PAWs) and "under accumulators of wealth" (UAWs). PAWs are extremely effective in building their net worth compared with others in their income and age group. In fact, PAWs typically have a net worth that is four times that of UAWs. So, what do PAWs do when it comes to accumulating wealth?

- PAWs devote much more time and energy to managing their finances than UAWs.
- PAWs operate their households on a well-thought-out annual budget.
- Most important, PAWs are much more likely than UAWs to develop and execute a written financial plan.

Stanley and Danko conclude from their research that people who devote time and effort to planning are much more likely to accumulate wealth. In fact, they write, "*Planning and wealth accumulation are significant correlates even among investors with modest incomes*" (our emphasis).[1] In short, say the gurus, the best answer to the question of who should have a financial plan is "everyone."

The first step in developing your financial plan involves calculating two things: (1) your net worth and (2) your cash flow. We will begin with your net worth.

CALCULATING YOUR NET WORTH

You probably already know the formula:

Your Net Worth = Your Assets
(what you own) − Your Liabilities (what you owe)

Your Assets

Your assets could include any or all of the following:

- Cash in your checking account(s), savings account(s), and money market fund(s)
- The value of your certificates of deposit (CDs), bonds, treasuries, stocks, IRA accounts, 401(k) or 403(b), Keogh accounts, annuities, and other similar investments
- The value of your house, car(s), boat(s), investment real estate, art and antiques, clothing, jewelry, furniture, and so on

Your Liabilities

Your liabilities are things for which or on which you owe and may include any of the following:

- Credit card debt
- Medical and dental bills
- Outstanding automobile, educational, personal, business, and home equity loans
- The mortgage and property taxes on your primary residence, vacation home, and rental property
- Any other outstanding bills and/or debts

(See Exhibit 2.1 for an example of a net-worth statement.)

EXHIBIT 2.1. Sample Net-Worth Statement

Assets	Sample	Actual
Cash	$ 2,450	
Savings account	$ 4,500	
CDs	$ 12,000	
Money market	$ 6,500	
Stocks	$ 25,000	
Bonds	$ 48,000	
Individual Retirement Account	$ 55,000	
401(k) plan	$ 34,500	
Vehicles	$ 12,000	
Home	$350,000	
Real estate investment	$ 45,000	
Other Assets	$ 38,000	
Total Assets	$633,000	
Liabilities		
Mortgage	$150,000	
Installment/auto loans	$ 8,000	
Credit card debt	$ 4,350	
Life insurance/pension loan	$ 2,000	
Unpaid taxes	$ 1,850	
Other liabilities	$ 6,000	
Total liabilities	$172,200	
Net Worth (Assets–Liabilities)	**$460,800**	

Our gurus generally suggest that you recalculate your net worth at least annually to see how it is changing. Also, see Exhibit 2.2 for some suggestions on the types of information about your financial life you can derive from looking at your net worth and how it is changing.

EVALUATING YOUR NET WORTH

When you totaled your assets and subtracted out your liabilities, did you come out with a positive net worth? If you didn't, don't despair—turning your situation around is probably one of the reasons you are reading this book. If your net worth

---

EXHIBIT 2.2. Analyzing Your Net Worth

Jane Bryant Quinn, author of *Making the Most of Your Money*, says that you can learn a lot of interesting things about your financial well-being by examining your net-worth calculation. Among other things, you can learn the following:

- **Whether your debts are under control:** Is your indebtedness growing faster than the money you're saving?
- **How well you're investing the money you save:** Does your investment account generally rise in value? Or are you losing money faster than you're putting it away?
- **How much money you could lay your hands on in an emergency:** Do you have enough readily salable assets to help you through a bad patch, or are too many of your assets tied up?
- **Whether you need more life and disability insurance:** What income could you get from your assets compared with how much you need to live on?

In addition to looking to see whether your net worth is growing from year to year, Bryant recommends that you also examine your assets to ensure that you have "a good balance between assets that are tied up, like your house, and assets that can quickly be turned into cash." You should not load up on *slow assets* until you have plenty of *quick assets* you can tap for cash in an emergency.

Source: Jane Bryant Quinn, Making the Most of Your Money (New York: Simon & Schuster, 1997), pp. 27–28.

---

is positive, congratulations. You are probably wondering, however, if your net worth is positive enough given your age and situation. Of course, the answer to that question is highly personal. What is enough net worth to one person falls far short of enough for others. But you might like some rules of thumb by which you can gauge the value of your net worth. Here are three offered by our gurus.

Net Worth #1: The Millionaire Formula

Thomas Stanley and William Danko provide the following formula for comparing your net worth to that of the millionaires they studied: "Multiply your age times your pretax annual household income from all sources except inheritances. Divide by ten. This, less any inherited wealth, is what your net worth should be."[2]

For example, if you are 40 years old and your pretax income from all sources is $150,000 then your net worth should be $600,000 (40 × $150,000 = $6,000,000 ÷ 10 = $600,000).

Net Worth #2: The Tyson Annual Income Method

Eric Tyson, author of *Personal Finance for Dummies,* evaluates net worth based on three conditions of annual income:[3]

1. **Your net worth is less than half of your annual income:** If your net worth is less than half your annual income or even negative, then your situation is like that of the majority of Americans. Tyson says you shouldn't be too concerned if this describes your net worth, but you still have work to do. You need to get rid of your debt, build a safety reserve of three to six months living expenses, reduce your spending, and learn more about tax-saving ways to invest.

2. **Your net worth is greater than your annual income but less than a few years' income:** Tyson says that if you are under the age of 40 and especially if you own your own home, you should consider yourself in good shape if your net worth is greater than your annual income. If you are over 40 and still renting, you are okay for now, but you should take this as a sign to reduce your spending and do a better job of investing.

3. **Your net worth is more than a few years' income:** Tyson considers this a sign that you are doing quite well, especially if you are still under the age of 40.

Net Worth #3: The Kelly Annual Income Method

Jason Kelly, author of *The Neatest Little Guide to Personal Finance,* evaluates net worth based on four conditions of annual income:[4]

1. **Your net worth is less than your annual income:** Kelly says that this is the net worth most people have, particularly when they are young and first starting out. If you find yourself in this category, you need to concentrate on reducing your spending, getting out of debt, and investing more wisely.

2. **Your net worth is between one and three years' annual income:** If you fall in this category, Kelly says you have some financial stability. You should feel good that you have socked away some funds to see you through the bad times, and you should now be looking at financial strategies to make you truly prosperous.

3. **Your net worth is more than three years' annual income:** If you have this level of net worth, then you should consider yourself well on your way to financial independence and the good life, especially if your net worth is growing each year.

CALCULATING YOUR CASH FLOW

As we just saw, your net worth is defined as the difference between what you own and what you owe.

$$\text{Net Worth} = \$ \text{You Own} - \$ \text{You Owe}$$

Your cash flow is defined as what you earn minus what you spend.

Cash Flow = $ Earned − $ Spent

The gurus tell us that one of the most important things you can do to get your financial house in order is calculate your cash flow because, as we will see in a moment, your cash flow significantly impacts your net worth. If you earn more than you spend, then you have excess cash you can use either to increase what you own and/or to decrease what you owe, either of which increases your net worth. On the other hand, if you spend more than you earn, you have to increase what you owe (through borrowing) and/or decrease what you own (by selling off assets) to cover your excess spending. Either way, your net worth declines. In short, your net worth is largely determined by how effectively you manage your cash flow. (See Exhibits 2.3 and 2.4.)

Your Income

Your income is the easiest of the two numbers—income and expenses—to obtain. Pull out your pay stubs, tax records, dividend statements, and so on, and come up with the total you earned from all sources last year. Include in your total any or all of the following:

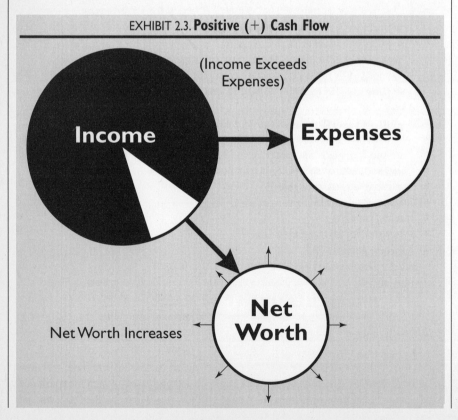

EXHIBIT 2.3. **Positive (+) Cash Flow**

(Income Exceeds Expenses)

Income

Expenses

Net Worth Increases

Net Worth

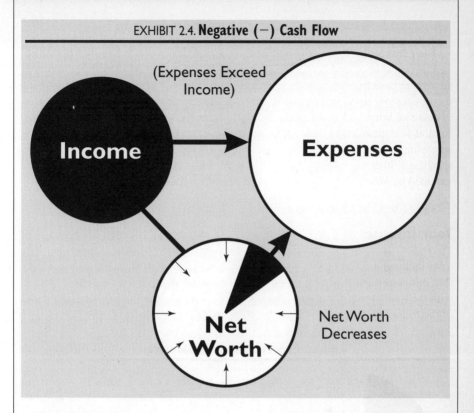

EXHIBIT 2.4. **Negative (−) Cash Flow**

(Expenses Exceed Income)

Income

Expenses

Net Worth

Net Worth Decreases

- Your salary
- Your spouse's salary
- Social Security receipts
- Pensions
- Child-support payments
- Income from rental property
- Investment dividends
- Interest income
- Income from capital gains
- Business income
- All the taxable income you reported to Uncle Sam
- Any and all nontaxable income you didn't report to Uncle Sam

Your Expenses

Now comes the tough part. To get a handle on your cash flow, you have to know how much you are spending, and you can't just guess. Suze Orman's experience with clients has convinced her that when the average person is asked to estimate what it costs them to live, they *underestimate* their spending by $1,000 to $1,500 *per month.* She says it doesn't matter how much or little a client is actually spending, their estimate falls short about the same amount. Orman believes this is the result of our failure to include many expenses that don't occur every month. For example, we forget about those insurance premiums that we pay quarterly or twice a year or those cash expenses that just crop up, such as batteries for our flashlight or the popcorn we bought at the movies. She adds that this almost-unconscious spending accounts for much of the discrepancy between what we think we spend and what we actually spend.[5] To avoid this underestimating, the gurus direct us to track ALL of our spending.

How to Track Your Spending

Mary Hunt, author of *Mary Hunt's Debt-Proof Living,* recommends tracking your daily expenses on three-by-five-inch index cards. Each morning, you (and your spouse) take out a new card, date it, and use it to record what you purchase and how much you spend, item by item, throughout the day.

She warns that you must be complete in your record keeping. As she says, "You cannot be selective—you must be brutally honest. Just write it down one day at a time. Write down the cash you spend, the checks you write, the credit purchases you make. I really do mean everything—even those things you may think are too trivial to track."[6]

At the end of the day, you should toss the spending card in a box or drawer. At the end of the week, take out the cards, spread them on a table, and look at them. Do you find any surprises? Do you see any patterns to your spending? Hunt suggests grouping your spending by categories, such as groceries, your daily coffee, meals eaten outside the house, and so on.[7] (See Exhibit 2.5 for some possible spending categories).

Hunt advises you to keep filling out your spending cards for at least one month and predicts that if you do this honestly and faithfully, you will be amazed at what you discover about your spending habits. If fact, she says, this simple exercise will be like turning on a floodlight in a dark cave.

If you think recording all of your spending on index cards will be too difficult and time consuming, here are three alternative ways of collecting information on your spending habits, suggested by Jean Chatzky.[8]

■ **Pencil and paper:** Get a receipt for everything and put them all in an envelope or in your wallet (whenever you receive one of those nondescript, flimsy paper receipts, jot a note on the back to remind you what you bought). Then sit down once a week and record them by category (you'll find a list of categories in Exhibit 2.5). Use a calculator to figure out how much you've spent on, say, food or entertaining. Don't underestimate the shock value of this exercise. Seeing that you spent $160 last month on substandard take-out Chinese is enough to send many people back into the kitchen.

EXHIBIT 2.5. **Spending Categories**

HOUSING

Property insurance
Property taxes
Utilities (gas, electric, oil, water)
Home repairs
Lawn care
House cleaning
Garbage pickup
Pest control
Baby-sitter
Other (pet-related expenses, house sitter, etc.)

TRANSPORTATION

Car/lease payments
Car repair and maintenance
Car insurance
Gasoline
Commuting costs (train tickets, bus passes, etc.)
Tolls
Other transportation (buses, taxis, subways, etc.)
Parking

FOOD/SUNDRIES

Groceries
Drugstore expenses
Take-out meals
Restaurant meals
Habits (alcohol, cigarettes, etc.)

CLOTHING

Clothes*
Shoes
Dry cleaning, laundry expenses
Tailoring

EDUCATION

Tuition
Room and board
Books
School-related expenses (class dues, parties, fund-raisers, etc.)

HEALTH

Nonreimbursed visits to doctors**
Health insurance
Nonreimbursed pharmaceuticals
Health-club dues, at-home equipment

RECREATION

Vacations
Entertainment (cost of going out to movies, theater, etc.)
Entertaining (cost of parties, dining in your home)
Books, newspapers, magazine subscriptions
Country-club, social-club dues

GIFTS

Charitable contributions
Gifts to friends, family, and so on.***

OTHER REGULAR PAYMENTS

Insurance (life, disability, etc.)
Contributions to your house of worship
Maintenance, child support
Child care
Credit card, loan payments
Retirement contributions
Savings account contributions
Investments

---

*You may want to break these expenses down by family member.

**These medical expenses can break down by type: doctors, dentists, eye care, psychiatrists, physical therapists, nutritionists , massage therapists, and so on.

***You may want to break this down by holiday and nonholiday expenses, particularly if you feel you're overspending in December.

Sources: Jean Chatzky, Talking Money: Everything You Need to Know about Your Finances and Your Future (New York: Warner Business Books, 2001), pp. 49–51; and Steven D. Strauss and Azriela Jaffe, The Complete Idiot's Guide to Beating Debt (Indianapolis, IN: Alpha Books, 2000), p. 66.

- **Credit card:** If you charge every possible item (even those $3 lightbulbs you bought at the hardware store), your bill automatically becomes a tool to help you track your spending. The key to making this work is spending as little in actual cash as possible and, when you do, making sure you save receipts. The bonus is the frequent-flyer miles (or bonus points) that anyone on this system ought to be racking up. The risk is interest. Only people who are completely sure they'll pay off their credit card bills every month without fail should go this route. (If you like the idea, but your confidence isn't high, give it a test drive with the American Express card, which forces you to pay it off, or a debit card that pulls money out of your checking account each time you make a purchase, rather than sending you a bill at the end of the month.)

- **Computer:** Just as you can enter your expenses into a log you keep by hand, you can enter them into a computer program like Quicken or Microsoft Money. The benefit of going electronic is the ease of running "what-if" scenarios (e.g., "What if I switched from Starbucks to the local deli?" or "What if I spent less on shoes?") and of charting proportionately how much of your take-home pay you are spending on clothes, entertainment, housing, and so on. Plus, you can keep tabs on your investment portfolio, downloading the most current stock prices with just a few keystrokes.

You want to end up with a cash-flow statement that looks like the one in Exhibit 2.6.

It may seem like a lot of work to get your financial house in order; however, remind yourself of the following advice:

> If you're looking for a magic formula that will make you rich beyond your wildest dreams, here it is: Spend less than you earn. It's the only way to start accumulating true wealth.
>
> *Ilyce Glink*[9]

PLANNING FOR THE FUTURE

Now that you have a handle on your net worth and cash flow, you probably have already developed some ideas about things you need to change. Maybe your net worth is a lot less than you thought it was, or maybe your cash is flowing but in the wrong direction. Perhaps you're shocked at just how much those lattes are costing you each month. Maybe you are ready to slash some expenses here, build up some investing there, or even ask for a raise. Before you start making changes, our gurus recommend that you reflect for a moment. Ask yourself: What do you really want?

EXHIBIT 2.6. Sample Monthly Cash-Flow Statement

Income	Sample	Planned	Actual	Difference
Salaries	$5,450			
Interest income	$ 230			
Dividends	$ 600			
Rental property	$ 450			
Other				
Total Income	$6,730			
Expenses				
Child care	$ 425			
Clothing/dry cleaning, etc.	$ 320			
Eating out	$ 325			
Entertainment	$ 190			
Gifts	$ 100			
Groceries	$ 475			
Health care	$ 430			
Home repairs	$ 50			
House cleaning	$ 85			
Household supplies	$ 80			
Housing	$1,317			
Lawn care	$ 45			
Life insurance	$ 95			
Other	$ 350			
Personal care	$ 75			
Transportation	$1,500			
Utilities	$ 285			
Vacations	$ 500			
Total Expenses	$6,647			
Income–Expenses	$ 83			

What are your financial and life goals? If, like many of the rest of us, you've been meaning to sit down and sort out what you wanted to do with the rest of your life but haven't, the gurus say it's time for you to set some goals.

DEVELOPING YOUR FINANCIAL AND LIFE GOALS

Dave Ramsey, author of *More Than Enough,* cites the following statistics when explaining the importance of setting and documenting specific financial goals:[10]

- Only 8 percent of Americans have clearly defined financial goals.
- Only 3 percent of Americans have written financial goals.
- Only 3 percent of Americans retire wealthy.

Do you see anything interesting about Ramsey's statistics? Could those 3 percent with clearly defined and written financial goals be the same 3 percent who are wealthy? Ginger Applegarth, author of *Wake Up and Smell the Money,* cites a survey of a Harvard Business School class from the early 1950s. When they graduated, only 3 percent of the class had developed specific financial goals for themselves. When resurveyed 25 years later, the 3 percent of Harvard graduates who said they had financial goals when they graduated owned 97 percent of the class's total wealth.[11]

Make 'Em S.M.A.R.T.

Not only do you need clearly defined and written financial goals, but your goals must be S.M.A.R.T., says Maria Nemeth, in her book *The Energy of Money:*

- **S is for specific.** Is your goal explicit and precise? For example, "I want to be happy" is not a goal. It is not specific. "I want to learn scuba diving by next summer" or "I want to buy a house" is specific.
- **M is for measurable.** How will I know that I have learned scuba diving? One way is by getting my certificate. "I want to get my scuba-diving certificate" is measurable. I will either have it or not. Similarly, "I want a two-bedroom home with a swimming pool" leaves no wiggle room. Pin down your goals.
- **A is for attainable.** A goal needs to be a stretch for you but not impossible. For example, to say that you are going to save $600 a year when you are already saving $50 a month is not a stretch. It's predictable. At the same time, "pie-in-the-sky" goals are a setup for failure. Make the goal worth planning for, yet attainable.
- **R is for relevant.** This is where we take care of the Whim Factor. In other words, is it relevant to who you are and what you want to be? Next, does proceeding with this goal demonstrate one or more of your

Standards of Integrity? For example, one of my standards is "courageous." If I learn to scuba dive, whether or not I am afraid, I demonstrate courage.

- **T is for time-based.** You must anchor your goal in time by giving it a date by which it'll be accomplished. As you do this you are making a promise to yourself and demonstrating that you are earnest about getting it.[12]

> Ask some people what their goal is and they'll say, "I want to be rich!" This is not a goal but a fantasy, like winning the lottery or having the Easter Bunny slip you a fortune. Money by itself is not a goal—you have to know what you want to do with it.
>
> Brooke Stephens[13]

You may already have some specific S.M.A.R.T. goals in mind based on your review of your net-worth and cash-flow calculations. If not, or if you just would like some help in coming up with your goals, try the three goal exercises recommended by George Kinder, author of *The Seven Stages of Money Maturity*. (See Exercises 2.1, 2.2, and 2.3.)

EXERCISE 2.1. Big Bucks and Then

Instructions: Imagine yourself in the following three situations, and work your way through these scenarios in the order presented.

1. You may not be as wealthy as Bill Gates or the Sultan of Brunei, but you do have all the money you need, now and in the future. What will you do with it? From this moment forward, how will you live your life?
2. You have just come back from a visit to a doctor who has discovered from your lab reports that you have only 5 to 10 years to live. In a way you're lucky. This particular disease has no manifestations, so you won't feel sick. The bad part is that you will have no warning about the moment of your death. It will simply come upon you in an unpredictable instant, sudden and final. Knowing death is waiting for you sooner than you expected, how will you change your life? And what will you do in the uncertain but substantial period you have remaining?
3. Again, you've gone to the doctor, but this time you learn you'll be dead within 24 hours. What regrets and longings do you have? What are your unfulfilled dreams? What do you wish you had completed, been, had, or done in this life that is just about to end?

The first scenario is meant to help you understand your material desires. The second helps you unlock dreams and wishes that you may never have expressed and helps you sort out the things in life that are superficial and that are central. The final scenario, says Kinder, taps into your most powerful longing.

Source: Adapted from George Kinder, The Seven Stages of Money Maturity: Understanding the Spirit and Value of Money in Your Life (New York: Delacorte Press, 1999), pp. 154–169.

EXERCISE 2.2. **Beyond Death and Taxes**

Instructions: Fill in the boxes as follows. In the row labeled "Have," list the possessions you feel you have "got to" have, "should" have, and would "like to" have. In row 2, list the things you have "got to" do in you life, "should" do, and would "like to" do. Finally, in row 3, list what you have "got to" be, "should" be, and would "like to" be.

	Got to	Should	Like to
Have			
Do			
Be			

Kinder finds this exercise quite revealing. His experience is that people typically put things like family and career in the "got to" column and items like vacations, sports cars, and second homes in the "like to" column. But the "should" column tends to fill up with a combination of practical issues and obligations, including obligations to parents and children. You may even find financial issues like budgets, tax preparation, and bill paying in the "should" column.

Source: Adapted from George Kinder, The Seven Stages of Money Maturity: Understanding the Spirit and Value of Money in Your Life *(New York: Delacorte Press, 1999), p. 163.*

HIRING A FINANCIAL PLANNER

Take a step back and assess your progress. How did you do? Were you able to pull together your net-worth and cash-flow statements and make sense of them? Were you able to come up with some goals? Did the exercises suggested by Kinder and the others help, or do you think you need some more advice and assistance? Don't feel bad if you think you could use some help in crunching the numbers and sorting through your life choices. Many others feel the same. That's what financial planners are paid to do. We'll conclude this chapter with some advice from our gurus on how to know when you need a financial planner and how to hire one who is right for you. But first, some words of caution about using financial planners.

EXERCISE 2.3. **Time Flies**

Instructions: Create a chart with columns representing time frames (one week, one month, six months, 1 year, 5 years, 10 years, 20 years, lifetime) and rows representing categories of things that are important to you—your career, health, family, relationships, and so on. Then fill in the cells of the chart with your goals, in any order that you choose. Here's an example:

	1 Week	1 Month	6 Months	1 Year	3 Years	5 Years	10 Years
Promoted to vice president				X			
Lose 15 pounds			X				
Zero credit card balance					X		
Dinner with family three nights per week			X				
Kick my latte habit	X						
Complete financial plan		X					

Kinder believes that the order in which you fill in your goals on this chart and the time frames you pick can be very revealing. He says most people fill in their most important goals first. These are the goals you think you can accomplish easily and are those you are likely to devote attention and effort to accomplishing. He adds that you should focus your financial planning on the first 10 goals you record on your chart. The time frame you pick for your goals should assist you in making investment decisions because, as we will show later in this book, the length of time you have to invest is a critical factor in determining your choice of investment vehicle.

Source: Adapted from George Kinder, The Seven Stages of Money Maturity: Understanding the Spirit and Value of Money in Your Life *(New York: Delacorte Press, 1999), p. 168.*

Some Words of Caution

Before we begin discussing what our gurus say about the process of hiring a financial advisor, we would like you to take a look at the warnings offered by several of our gurus, starting with Jane Bryant Quinn.

From Jane Bryant Quinn

There's a lot of bad advice out there.

The majority of planners are delivery systems for prepackaged financial products. They make their living selling insurance policies, tax deferred annuities, unit trusts, loaded mutual funds, and other high commission investments. They may give you very good advice. On the other hand, they cannot escape the taint of bias. Most planners have to sell or starve.[14] (Emphasis ours.)

From Eric Tyson

[T]he financial planning and brokerage fields are *mine fields for consumers.* The fundamental problem is the *enormous conflict of interest* that is created when "advisors" sell products that earn them sales commissions to people who believe they are getting unbiased advice. Selling ongoing money management services . . . creates *conflicts of interest* as well. . . .

In its review of the financial planning industry, *Consumer Reports* said, "Financial planners often end up being *wolves in sheep's clothing* with hidden agendas to sell mutual funds, for example, or life insurance." (Emphasis ours.)[15]

If these words of caution frighten you, that's good. They are intended to. Pay close attention, and proceed with utmost care when choosing a financial planner. Your financial life may be at stake. With these cautions having been duly stated, let's look at what our gurus have to say about financial planners, starting with the basic question of how you know if you need a financial planner.

How to Know If You Need a Financial Planner

Barbara Stanny, author of *Prince Charming Isn't Coming*, says that any of the following may be a sign that you need a financial planner:

1. You are in debt and can't seem to get out.
2. You are so busy you don't have time to manage money.
3. You have gotten involved with some bad investments and are concerned.
4. You keep trying to learn about money but don't seem to be getting anywhere.
5. You want to take charge of your money but don't have any confidence in yourself.
6. You and your spouse/partner constantly argue about what to do with your money, so you end up doing nothing.
7. You don't have a cent in savings and can barely make ends meet.
8. You don't have a retirement plan.
9. You have a 401(k) plan, but you don't understand what's in it or if it is invested well.
10. You don't have insurance, or you are unsure whether you have enough.
11. You don't have an estate plan or a will, or you are not sure that you have adequately prepared for your heirs.
12. You have a specific goal in mind, such as buying a new car or a second house, but you don't know how to achieve it.
13. You want to make a major change in your life, such as beginning a new career or starting a family, but you don't know if you can afford it.
14. You see a change in lifestyle looming, such as a divorce, marriage, or cross-country move, and you don't know if you are financially prepared for it.
15. Someone else, such as your spouse, takes care of your money, and you feel left in the dark.
16. You expect to come into money as a result of an inheritance, bonus, or pay raise.
17. You have all of your money in a savings account.[16]

Eric Tyson adds that you should turn to a financial planner to do any or all of the following:

- Help you identify your financial problems and goals
- Help you identify financial strategies to meet your goals
- Help you set priorities by suggesting the key changes in your financial affairs that would probably have the greatest value

- Save you time and trouble in getting access to information on financial topics that you need to make informed decisions about managing your money
- Provide objective advice when you are about to make a major decision such as whether and how much house to buy or where to invest a windfall
- Mediate between you and your spouse/partner in the case of a disagreement the two of you have over money matters
- Make you money and provide you with peace of mind[17]

Choosing a Financial Planner

By now you may have decided that you need a financial planner, but you still aren't sure how to go about choosing one. The first step, according to the gurus, is to decide what type of financial planner is right for you.

Types of Financial Planners

Generally, say our gurus, financial planners can be distinguished by the way they are paid and the credentials they possess. Financial planners are compensated in four basic ways. Here are the pros and cons of each, according to Jean Chatzky.[18]

Fee-Only Planners

Fee-only planners charge an hourly or per-plan fee for their advice. You can expect to pay between $100 to $300 per hour or $1,000 to $5,000 per plan. The advantages of these types of planners is that they have no financial incentive to push you to buy a particular financial product, such as insurance, or make an investment that might not be right for you. Their major disadvantage, says Chatzky, is that they get paid regardless of whether you implement their suggestions—therefore, they have no incentive to push you to actually implement the financial plan they help you develop. Many of our gurus prefer fee-only planners for the simple reason that these planners don't have any obvious conflict of interest when making their recommendations. In addition, says Eric Tyson, you have the option of using this type of planner as a sounding board for your ideas or as someone to consult about a specific investment strategy or financial product. You pay for only the advice you need when you need it and save money by doing the implementation on your own.[19]

Commission-Only Planners

Commission-only planners make their money from commissions on the investments and financial products you purchase from them. Obviously, the advantages and disadvantages of these types of planners are just the opposite of those of fee-only planners. Commission-only planners have every reason to push you to make purchases and investments because they don't earn their fees until you do. On the other hand, they can't be objective. For example, says Chatzky, whereas fee-only planners might encourage you to consider a no-load (no sales charge) mutual fund, commission-only planners probably won't because they would receive no commission from your investment in such a fund.

Eric Tyson warns that many people who call themselves commission-only planners aren't really planners at all but *salespeople:* "Many stock brokers and insurance brokers . . . are now called financial consultants or financial service representatives in order to glamorize the profession and obscure how the planners are compensated. Ditto for insurance salespeople calling themselves estate planning specialists."[20]

Fee-Based Planners

Fee-based planners are paid fees in some situations and commissions in others. For example, says Chatzky, you may pay a fee-based planner a fee for working with you to develop your financial plan and then a commission on any investments you make or financial products you purchase when implementing that plan. The major advantages of working with fee-based planners are that their fees are generally less than those charged by fee-only planners, and their commissions may be less than those charged by commission-only planners. Their chief downside is the potential for a conflict of interest when they are recommending products or investments from which they generate commissions.

Wealth/Asset/Money Managers

Wealth/asset/money planners design and manage your entire investment plan for a fee that is equal to a percentage (e.g., 2 percent) of the assets they manage for you. The biggest advantage of these types of planners, says Chatzky, is also their biggest disadvantage. They take you out of the loop—that is, they save you time and effort by managing your assets for you. Of course, the risk is that you lose control of a major part of your financial affairs and can wake up one day to find yourself broke because of the planner's poor performance or outright criminal behavior. Tyson adds that these types of planners have their own kind of conflict of interest:

> [S]uppose that you're trying to decide to invest in stocks, bonds, or real estate. A planner who earns her living managing your money likely won't recommend real estate because that would deplete your investment capital. The planner also won't recommend paying down your mortgage for the same reason—she'll claim that you can earn more investing your money (with her help, of course) than it will cost you to borrow.[21]

Finally, as Tyson notes, most of these types of planners are only interested in working with people who have $100,000 or more in assets to invest.

Alphabet Soup: The Credentialing Game

When a financial planner hands you a business card, the chances are that his or her name will be followed by some initials—CFP, CFA, RIA, and so on—but do they offer you any guarantee of competence? Here are some of the titles, initials, and qualifications you are likely to see most often:

Certified Financial Planner (CFP®): To earn this designation, the financial planner must pass an examination administered by the Certified Financial Planner Board of Standards and agree to abide by the CFP Board's Code of Ethics and Professional Responsibility. For more information, consult http://www.cfp-board.org.

Chartered Financial Analyst (CFA®): To earn this designation, the financial planner must pass three levels of examinations covering investment valuation and portfolio management administered by The Association for Investment Management and Research (AIMR). For more information, consult http://www.aimr.com/cfaprogram/.

Chartered Financial Consultant (ChFC) or Chartered Life Underwriter (CLU): To earn one of these designations, the financial planner must have completed a course of study in insurance and financial planning offered by The American College in Bryn Mawr, Pennsylvania. The ChFC is the insurance industry's financial-planning designation. The CLU designation is for life insurance agents who do insurance planning. Ric Edelman says you should expect financial planners with these designations to emphasize insurance when offering recommendations.[22]

Personal Financial Specialist (PFS): To earn this designation, the financial planner must be a certified public accountant (CPA) with financial-planning experience and must pass an exam administered by The American Institute of CPAs.

Registered Investment Advisor (RIA): To earn this designation, the financial planner must be registered with either the Securities and Exchange Commission (SEC), if they manage more than $25 million in client assets, or their state's securities division if they manage less than $25 million in client assets.

Warning! Credentials Aren't Everything

Do the financial planner's credentials tell you anything about the competency of the person to advise you in financial matters? The answer, say our gurus, is maybe and maybe not. The registrations, testing, and so on all sound good and 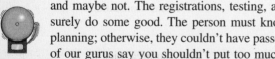 surely do some good. The person must know something about financial planning; otherwise, they couldn't have passed the exams. However, many of our gurus say you shouldn't put too much faith in the testing and credentialing processes. Take, for example, what Eric Tyson has to say about the CFP certification, one of the most common designations you are likely to see.

[T]ens of thousands of people have earned the Certified Financial Planning credential. This is basically a home-study course that, unlike gaining entrance into medical, law, or business school, virtually anyone can undertake. The test itself isn't difficult to pass—an astounding 74 percent of people recently enrolled in the College for Financial Planning passed the CFP test. . . .

The CFP Board of Standards, which licenses the CFP credential, claims that the combination of passing a test and meeting continuing education requirements ensures that their profession is doing the best that it can. . . .

- The CFP tests nothing of a planner's business ethics or how the planner earns income.
- The CFP exam covers arcane financial details, which are rarely encountered by consumer-oriented planners and could easily be contained in a handy reference book.
- The CFP curriculum has little practical information on the important topics of asset allocation and mutual fund selection.
- And the few individuals who don't pass the CFP exam on the first try are told what answers they got wrong so that they can focus their time memorizing the trivial details and pass the exam on the second try.[23]

Selecting a Financial Planner

Credentials aren't everything; however, there are many solid ways to find a great financial planner. Our gurus recommend that you start your search for a financial planner by asking friends, neighbors, associates, your lawyer, your CPA, and/or your tax advisor who they use or would recommend. You can also check the local yellow pages under the heading "financial planners" or "financial planning consultants." In addition, you can go to the Web sites of the following professional associations to get listings of financial planners in your area:

Financial Planning Association at http://www.fpanet.org/plannersearch/
National Association of Personal Financial Advisors at http://www.napfa.org/
American Institute of Certified Public Accountants at http://www.aicpa.org/
American Society of Financial Service Professionals at http://www.financialpro.org/
International Association of Registered Financial Consultants at http://www.iarfc.org/

Once you have compiled a list of planners in your area, pick five or six, contact them by telephone, and ask them to send you some information about their services. Holly Nicholson, author of *Money and You,* recommends that you try to get answers to the following questions from your telephone conversations and review of the brochures and other printed material that the planners send you:[24]

- What are the planner's education background and credentials (CFP, CFA, etc.)?
- What type of services does the planner provide—tax planning, investment planning, estate planning, retirement planning, and so on? What is his or her area of expertise?
- What are the planner's fees? How is the planner paid—commission, fee, or both? Nicholson notes that some planners may resist disclosing their fee structure over the phone. If they resist, says Nicholson, be prepared to be subject to some high-pressure sales tactics when and if you do meet with them.
- Is the planner accepting new clients? If so, is there a minimum asset value or other criteria that you must meet for the planner to work with you?

Use the answers to these questions to narrow your list to at least three possibilities and arrange a meeting with each planner you are considering. Nicholson says that if you are married, both you and your spouse should attend these meetings. Your goal at these meetings is to get to know more about the planner and how he or she works with clients. Most important, you need to decide if you (and your spouse) would be comfortable working with this person.

Tyson cautions to be wary of "free" consultations; they may turn into nothing more than high-pressure sales pitches.[25]

Here are some questions our gurus suggest that you ask the planners during the course of the meetings:[26]

- How long have you been in this business? How long has your firm been in this business?
- What experience do you have as a financial planner?
- What did you do before you became a financial planner?
- What professional organizations do you belong to? Are you actively involved with them? How?
- Are you registered with any regulatory agencies such as the U.S. Securities & Exchange Commission? If so, how would I contact them to determine if they have any outstanding complaints against you or your firm?
- How do you keep abreast of changes in the financial planning field?
- Will you provide a list of references of clients you have with needs similar to mine?
- Will you be the person working directly with me, or will an associate be assigned to me? If I will be working with someone else, can I meet that person?
- How often will you review my portfolio?
- Is planning done in-house, or do you send my information elsewhere?
- May I see a sample of the kind of plan you will prepare for me?

- Will you recommend specific financial (investment or insurance) products and assist in the implementation of my plan? Can I implement your recommendations on my own or do I have to implement them through you or your firm?
- Do you receive any compensation from any persons or firms to whom I may be referred for tax, legal, insurance, or other advice?
- How are you compensated? What percentage of your compensation comes from fees paid by your clients versus commissions from the products that you sell?
- How do I pay for planning work? How much of the cost must I pay in advance?
- What is your investment philosophy? What do you think does and does not constitute "a lot" of risk?
- Who will make decisions to buy or sell investments? Will I have prior approval before you execute transactions?
- Must I sign a contract to work with you? If so, do I have the right to cancel the contract within 30 days or less if I decide to do so?
- Do you carry liability insurance?
- How will I know whether you're doing a good job?

Let's assume that you are happy with your prospective financial planner's answers to your questions. You hire the planner. Now you can relax, right? Wrong, say our gurus. Now you have to be ever vigilant. You had better watch your planner like a hawk, for there is great potential for things to go wrong and for your money to suffer.

Working with a Financial Planner: The Dos and Don'ts

Here are some dos and don'ts and things to watch for in your relationship with a financial planner, courtesy of Ric Edelman and Eric Tyson.

Taboos between You and Your Planner

Edelman says the following are strictly taboo:[27]

- Never write a check made payable to your planner other than for your planner's fees.
- Never allow your planner to be listed as a beneficiary or joint owner on your accounts.
- Never lend your planner money.
- Never give your planner discretionary authority to execute financial or investment transactions without your prior knowledge or consent; this would be equivalent to a license to steal from you.
- Never let your planner sign your name to anything. That's forgery and a felony.

- Never let your planner allow you to sign a blank form or contract, and when you sign any contract, strike out any sections that don't apply.
- Never let your planner use his or her address on account statements instead of yours. You want all the statements to come directly to you.
- Never let your planner sell you an investment that isn't available from others.
- Never let your planner share in your investment profits unless your planner is equally prepared to share in your investment losses.
- Never let your planner assign any agreement with you to another advisor.

Your Financial Planner and Conflicts of Interest

In addition to biases toward products that pay commissions, Tyson warns you to keep a sharp eye out for the following conflicts of interest that may keep a financial planner from giving you good advice.[28]

- **Not recommending that you save through your employer's retirement plan:** Your employer's retirement savings plan may be one of your best investment options because it is tax deductible, but many planners may be reluctant to encourage you to take full advantage of it; when you invest in the retirement plan, you have less funds available to invest in the planner's products that generate high commissions.
- **Ignoring debts:** Sometimes your best financial strategy may be to pay off debts rather than make investments, but many planners won't recommend that you do so because then you would have less money for purchasing commission-laden investments and financial products.
- **Selling legal services:** More planners are offering to help you with legal documents for such things as setting up trusts and estate planning. Even if they are competent to perform such services, you may be able to get the legal work done elsewhere cheaper.
- **Scaring you unnecessarily:** Although one of your financial planner's jobs is to make you see reality—even bleak reality—some planners go to the extreme. Instead of helping you face reality, they may just be using scare tactics to get you to buy financial products and investments you don't need.
- **Creating dependency:** Financial planners have a tendency to make things sound more complicated than they really are so that their clients end up feeling that they could never possibly manage their finances on their own.

YOU'RE ON YOUR WAY

If you have worked through the exercises and run the calculations our gurus suggested, you've calculated your net worth and cash flow, developed some S.M.A.R.T. personal and financial goals, and hired an honest and competent financial advisor. Still, you may need more advice. Maybe you are thinking about buying a house but aren't sure if you should. After examining your expenses, you may be troubled by how much you are spending for insurance and need some help in deciding if you are spending too much or too little. Or perhaps you found that cutting back on your spending is a tad more difficult than you imagined, or you feel you need some help with shopping smarter and becoming more thrifty. Don't worry. Help is on its way. For now, we need to pause and assess where we have been by listing this chapter's key points.

KEY POINTS

- Everyone needs a financial plan.

- People who devote significant time to planning their finances are much more likely to accumulate wealth.

- To understand your financial situation, you need to know your net worth and your cash flow.

- Your net worth = Your assets (what you own) − Your liabilities (what you owe).

- Your cash flow impacts your net worth. If your cash flow is positive, then you have funds to purchase additional assets and/or reduce your liabilities and thus increase your net worth.

- If you are like most people, you probably underestimate your monthly spending by as much as $1,000 to $1,500.

- Your financial goals should be S.M.A.R.T. goals—specific, measurable, attainable, relevant, and time-based.

- Use extreme caution when hiring a financial planner.

- There is no relationship between the number of credentials a financial advisor has earned and his or her level of competence.

- When working with a financial planner, you should never do any of the following:
  - Write a check make payable to your planner other than for his or her fee
  - Lend money to your planner
  - Let your planner sign your name on any document
  - Give your planner discretionary authority to execute financial or investment transactions without your prior knowledge and consent.

Robert Allen, author of *Multiple Streams of Income*

Stacie Zoe Berg, author of *The Unofficial Guide to Managing Your Personal Finances*

Jean Chatzky, author of *Talking Money*

Joe Dominguez, coauthor of *Your Money or Your Life*

Ric Edelman, author of *The New Rules of Money*

Christy Heady, coauthor of *The Complete Idiot's Guide to Managing Your Money*

Robert Heady, coauthor of *The Complete Idiot's Guide to Managing Your Money*

Clark Howard, author of *Get Clark Smart*

Jason Kelly, author of *The Neatest Little Guide to Personal Finance*

Robert Kiyosaki, author of *Rich Dad's Cashflow Quadrant*

Dwight Lee, coauthor of *Getting Rich in America*

Mark Levine, coauthor of *Live Rich*

Nancy Lloyd, author of *Simple Money Solutions*

Richard McKenzie, coauthor of *Getting Rich in America*

Edward Mrkvicka, author of *Your Bank Is Ripping You Off*

Stephen Pollan, coauthor of *Live Rich*

Jane Bryant Quinn, author of *Making the Most of Your Money*

Vicki Robin, coauthor of *Your Money or Your Life*

Brooke Stephens, author of *Wealth Happens One Day at a Time*

Eric Tyson, author of *Personal Finance for Dummies*

3

Making Money and Protecting Your Income

I n the last chapter, we noted that there are only two ways to increase your net worth: You can increase your income or you can cut your expenses. We discuss methods for increasing your income in this chapter and will cover cutting expenses in the next. Also in this chapter, we discuss steps our gurus say you should be taking to protect your income from taxes and how you should go about selecting a bank or other financial institution. We start with some myths about earning a living. According to our gurus, what you have been taught about making a living may be all wrong.

THE RIGHT AND WRONG WAYS TO MAKE MONEY

When you were growing up, your mother probably said to you, "Study hard, get good grades, go to school, graduate, and get yourself a good, secure job." And as Stephen Pollan and Mark Levine remark, your dad probably gave you some advice that went something like this:

> If you do your work you'll keep your job.
>
> If you do your work *well* you'll be promoted.
>
> If you keep your job you'll get regular pay raises.
>
> If you get promoted you'll get a sizable pay raise.
>
> If you're loyal to the company the company will be loyal to you.[1]

What is wrong with the advice you got from Mom and Dad? Everything, say some of our gurus. Joe Dominguez and Vicki Robin describe the typical scenario for Americans who followed their parents' advice:

Grab commuter mug and briefcase (or lunch box) and hop in the car for the daily punishment called rush hour. On the job from nine to five. Deal with the boss. Deal with the coworker sent by the devil to rub you the wrong way. Deal with Suppliers. Deal with clients/customers/patients. Act busy. Hide mistakes. Smile when handed impossible deadlines. Give a sigh of relief when the ax known as "restructuring" or "downsizing"—or just plain getting laid off—falls on other heads. Shoulder the added workload. Watch the clock. Argue with your conscience but agree with the boss. Smile again.[2]

If that sounds a lot like your life, say Dominguez, Robin, and most of our other gurus, you aren't making a living, you're "making a dying," and you are not alone in thinking that your way of making a living is much less than ideal. Here are some additional realities about the modern workplace as reported by Dominguez and Robin:

- Some workers feel underemployed.
- Others feel overworked.
- The . . . baby-boom generation is discovering that . . . a smaller percentage [of them] will make it to the top of the corporate ladder.
- Job security ain't what it used to be.
- Retirement security is no longer secure.[3]

Earning Money the Rich Dad's Way

Fine, you say, things are tough all over, but what choice does the average person have? You have to make a living, which means getting a job, right? Wrong, say our gurus. Sure, you have to make a living, but that doesn't mean you have to work for a paycheck. In fact, our gurus argue that working for someone else and drawing a regular paycheck is the *worst* way to make a living if you ever expect to be financially independent or even financially secure. No one makes that argument more forcefully than Robert Kiyosaki, author of *Rich Dad's Cashflow Quadrant*.

Kiyosaki begins his argument by noting that there are three types of income:

- **Earned income:** income that comes in the form of a paycheck
- **Portfolio income:** income from stocks, bonds, mutual funds, CDs, and so on
- **Passive income:** income that comes from things you own, such as real estate, patents, license agreements, and businesses

He adds that there are four legal ways you can earn this income:

- You can be someone's employee.
- You can be self-employed.

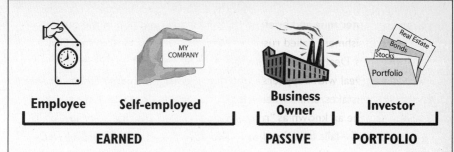

Employee	Self-employed	Business Owner	Investor
EARNED		PASSIVE	PORTFOLIO

EXHIBIT 3.1. **Three Types of Income**

- You can own a business or businesses.
- You can be an investor.

Employees and the self-employed receive earned income. Business owners receive passive income. Finally, investors receive portfolio income. (See Exhibit 3.1.)

Kiyosaki notes that if you want to be rich or even financially independent, you want as much portfolio and passive income as you can get because, he argues, "income from a paycheck . . . is the highest-taxed income, so it is the hardest income with which to build wealth."[4] He adds that "for people who earn their income, . . . there are virtually no tax breaks left. Today in America, being an employee means you are a 50/50 partner with the government. That means the government ultimately will take 50 percent or more of an employee's earnings, and much of that even before the employee sees the paycheck."[5]

What you want to happen, say Kiyosaki and many other gurus, is eventually to have enough passive and/or portfolio income so you no longer need earned income at all. You become "financially independent" or "financially free." You could quit your job tomorrow, never work again for a paycheck, and still live comfortably. Joe Dominguez and Vicki Robin call this the "Crossover Point." "At the Crossover Point, where monthly [passive and portfolio] income crosses over monthly expenses, you will be financially independent in the traditional sense of that term. You will have a safe, steady income for life from a source other than a job." (See Exhibit 3.2.)[6]

Becoming Self-Employed

If working for a paycheck puts you at a disadvantage taxwise, as Kiyosaki says, you might ask whether you would be better becoming self-employed. Although Kiyosaki might admire your gumption for the attempt, he doesn't think much of self-employment as a wealth-building strategy. He explains that although self-employment may be rewarding, it is also risky. To make matters worse, says Kiyosaki, being successful can be worse than failing because you will have to work

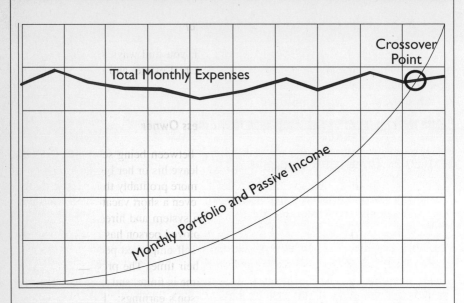

EXHIBIT 3.2. **The Crossover Point**

harder to sustain your success. The self-employed take on responsibilities ranging from answering the telephone to handling customers to hiring and firing employees, and they face daunting odds against success. Consider these statistics from Kiyosaki:

> Nationally, nine out of 10 of these types of businesses fail in five years. Of the one that is remaining, nine out of 10 of them fail in the next five years In other words, 99 out of 100 small businesses ultimately disappear in 10 years. . . .
>
> [T]he reason most fail in the first five years is due to the lack of experience and lack of capital. The reason the one survivor often fails in the second five years is not due to lack of capital, but lack of energy. The hours of long, hard work finally get to the person. Many . . . just burn out.[7]

Achieving Financial Independence

If being an employee means you get taxed to death and being self-employed means you work yourself to death, you may ask: What is the path to financial independence? Kiyosaki offers three paths, which as you might expect, all involve finding ways to make more portfolio and passive income.

Path #1: Employee or Self-Employed to Investor

When moving from employee to an investor, you find ways to acquire stocks, bonds, mutual funds, interest-earning accounts, real estate, and so on in order to begin making money with money.

Path #2: Employee or Self-Employed to Business Owner

Kiyosaki explains that there is a difference between being self-employed and being a business owner. A business owner can leave his or her business for a year or more and return to find it running better and more profitably than ever. If a self-employed person leaves his or her business for even a short vacation, the business comes to a standstill. A business owner owns a system and hires other people to employ that system to make money. A self-employed person has an expertise and uses that expertise to make money. Generally, self-employed people are paid for their time much like employees are paid for their time. The problem with tying one's income to time, writes Kiyosaki, is that time is finite, and that finite amount of time puts a ceiling on the self-employed person's earnings: "For example, if a person charges $50 an hour for his or her time and puts in an eight-hour day, that person's maximum earning potential is $400 per day, $2,000 per week, for a five-day week, and $8,000 per month. The only way this person can increase that amount is to work more hours."[8]

Business owners aren't similarly constrained. If they want to serve more customers and make more money, they simply hire more people to use their system.

> Most entrepreneurs own businesses that are nothing more than glorified monkey traps, . . . sweatshops that simply provide jobs for the owners. They don't have freedom to come and go as they wish. They are tied to their one-person businesses. That is not my idea of fun.
>
> *Robert Allen*[9]

Path #3: Employee or Self-Employed to Business Owner to Investor

Kiyosaki says he prefers and recommends the path from employee to business owner to investor most often for two reasons. First, he says, if you become a business owner before you become a heavy investor, you will develop the knowledge and experience to recognize good business owners who are worthy of your investment. Second, says Kiyosaki, if you own a successful business that is up and running on its own, you will have the free time you need to research potential investments and the positive cash flow you will need to take advantage of good investment opportunities when you identify them.[10]

Kiyosaki says if you are an overtaxed employee or overworked self-employed professional, your path to income nirvana is first to become a business owner and then an investor. While you might be skeptical of your ability to follow his preferred path to financial freedom, Kiyosaki has every faith that you can accomplish just what he advocates. "The good news," he writes, "is that it is now easier than ever before to [become a business owner.]"[11]

We should note that when Kiyosaki was writing those reassuring words, it was the late 1990s, and we were still in a period of unbridled optimism about a "new economy," where everything was possible and everyone could get rich. Even then, a few gurus were much less enthusiastic about the ability of most of us to start our own business. Take, for example, these sobering words of Dwight Lee and Richard McKenzie, coauthors of *Getting Rich in America,* at about the same time Kiyosaki was writing. Lee and McKenzie caution that if you want to follow Kiyosaki's advice and start your own business, then do so, but keep the following in mind:

> The potential for high profit from business ownership is partly explained as a return to the considerable risk involved. There is a high probability that you will incur heavy losses from starting and running your own business. Starting and running a business is much riskier than investing some of your salary in an index mutual fund. You will not lose everything you invest in such a fund, even in the event of a major downturn in the market, and all you have to do to recoup the short-run losses you do experience occasionally is wait. Losing almost everything is a real possibility when starting a business, and the greater that possibility the larger the potential return will be.
>
> One reason researchers have found that most millionaires are business owners is that they are reporting on the owners who actually "made it" in business. If you start a business with the prospect of a high rate of return and if you actually make it in the business, then it stands to reason that you will likely end up with a lot of wealth. However, the researchers often ignore all those would-be successful business owners who tried but failed, and many people who start their own businesses fall into that category.[12]

So who is right? Can just about everybody become a business owner, as Kiyosaki seems to think? Unfortunately, it is extremely hard to be a successful entrepreneur even in the United States (which is perhaps the easiest country in the world in which to become an entrepreneur). We learned that lesson when we wrote *The Guru Guide™ to Entrepreneurship,* which we refer you to if you want to learn more about what it takes.[13]

We think Kiyosaki is right when he says that few people are ever going to become financially independent with earned income alone. We are all going to have to become investors. The trick is coming up with some extra money to invest. There are only two ways that is going to happen if we stay in a salaried job: We have to make our paycheck bigger or we have to cut our spending so that our current paycheck goes further. We'll cover spending in the next chapter. For now, let's look at the paycheck issue. Are there any ways to pump up your earned income in the short run? At least one guru thinks so.

Boosting Your Income

Nancy Lloyd is a personal finance commentator for National Public Radio and ABC television. In her book *Simple Money Solutions,* she outlines four strategies to enhance your earned income.[14]

1. **Make the most of employer-paid benefits.** Lloyd says that one way "to boost your net worth is to stop paying for things out of your own pocket if someone else (namely your employer) is offering to pay them for you."[15] She argues that the average employee could treat themselves to the equivalent of a 30 to 40 percent raise by simply taking full advantage of benefits and tax breaks that their employer offers. If you are like most employees, she says, you are probably missing out on any number of benefits and tax breaks simply because you don't review your benefit and tax choices on a regular basis. Your employer may have changed plans, your personal situation may have changed, and/or your tenure with the company may entitle you to additional benefits.[16]

Lloyd recommends that you do the following to make sure you are getting all of the benefits and tax breaks to which you are entitled as a salaried worker:

- Fully fund your **flexible spending account** that lets you set aside *pretax* dollars to pay for a range of things such as child care, attorney's fees, health care deductibles, and so on.
- Make the maximum contribution to your company's **401(k) retirement savings plan,** particularly if your company will match some or all of your contribution.
- Load up on "free" **company-offered life insurance.**
- Sign up for any **disability insurance** that your company may offer.
- Take full advantage of **health insurance** choices your company offers.
- Take advantage of any **training or tuition reimbursement plans** your company may offer.
- Ask if your employer will pick up some of the **cost of adoption.**
- Ask if your employer will match your **charitable contributions.**
- Take full advantage of any **stock options** your employer offers.

2. **Get yourself a pay raise.** Lloyd says you shouldn't expect just to be able to walk up to your boss and ask for a raise out of the blue and get it. You have to position yourself for a raise months (or even years) in advance. Here is how she recommends you accomplish that positioning:

- **Pick the right time to ask for a raise.** Just after you have accomplished something good for the organization is a good time; just after the company has announced the next round of downsizing isn't.
- **Let your boss know you are serious.** Point out your accomplishments, but don't try to convince your boss that you deserve a raise by citing what someone else is making, pleading that you need a raise because you have kids to feed and can't pay the bills, or threatening to leave the company if your request isn't granted. Instead, focus on your achievements and your demonstrated value to the company.
- **Become your own publicist.** Don't expect your boss to remember what you have accomplished. You have to remind him or her. Lloyd says one way to do that is to keep your boss informed by sending a one-page "Highlights List" each month summarizing your accomplishments and updating your boss on the progress you are making on your assigned projects.
- **Prepare your boss for your appraisal.** Three to four weeks *before* your next scheduled performance appraisal, Lloyd says you should have a friendly, casual meeting to remind your boss of all that you have accomplished since your last appraisal. Make the chore of writing up your appraisal easy for your boss by suggesting some of the nice things he or she might say about you.
- **Understand what is expected of you.** Lloyd says that if at all possible, you should get this in writing and don't accept vaguely written objectives. Make sure you understand what you are being asked to do. In addition, says Lloyd, find out how your objectives tie into your boss's. Find out what your boss needs to accomplish to succeed. Let your boss know that you want to succeed by helping your boss to succeed.
- **Tell your boss what you expect in return.** Lloyd says that you should meet with your boss at least twice per year so that your boss can tell you what is expected from you *and* you can tell your boss what you expect from him or her. What would you like? Additional responsibility? A raise? A promotion? A special assignment?

Finally, says Lloyd, once you get that hard-earned raise, don't squander it by buying a bunch of trinkets or increasing your spending. Instead, use all or most of your raise to acquire assets (stocks, bonds, mutual funds, investment real estate) or reduce your liabilities by, for example, making extra payments on your mortgage or paying off your credit card debt.

3. **Land a better-paying job.** Go for greener pastures. Even if you get a raise in your present job, you may find more money and/or better benefits elsewhere. Lloyd believes that you should be on the lookout for something better even if things seem to be going great with your current employer. Here are some things Lloyd says you can do to land a better job:

- **Target your job search; don't just apply anywhere and everywhere.** You want to find companies where your skills are needed. Network. Join professional associations and alumni groups. Do some volunteer work. Use all of these contacts to begin identifying a small handful of companies that might serve as your next green pasture, and then do research to find out as much as you can about them.

■ **Write a focused resume.** Lloyd says that your resume should be short and that you should think of it as a sales pitch in which you are the product. What are the features and benefits you have to offer? What problems or challenges is the target company facing that you could help solve? And, says Lloyd, make sure that you send your resume to the person who will make the hiring decision. For example, instead of responding to the name listed in an ad, call the company and get the name of the person who heads the department doing the hiring.

■ **Use the Internet with caution.** Realize, says Lloyd, that posting your resume to the Internet is like tacking it to a tree in the town square. You don't know who is going to read it or where it is going to end up. To protect yourself, Lloyd says that you should include your e-mail address and perhaps your home phone number on resumes you post to the Internet but that you should *not* include your home address, salary history, or Social Security number. In fact, she warns, your Social Security number should never appear on any resume, whether paper or electronic.

4. **Get a better severance package.** There is a good chance given the turmoil in corporate America today that you will face a layoff at some point in your career. When that happens, Lloyd suggests several things you can do to make it less financially painful.

■ **Ask for more severance pay.** Who knows, you might just be able to turn the one to two weeks pay per year of employment they are probably offering into three or four weeks or even more.

■ **Ask for benefits to help you in the transition,** such as office space, secretarial services, access to copiers and fax machines, and outplacement assistance.

■ **Make sure your health insurance coverage doesn't lapse.**

■ If you are eligible for retirement, **make sure you fully understand your pension, be wary about lump-sum payments, and understand the tax consequences for everything you do.** (Read Chapter 9, which deals with retirement, 401(k)s, company pensions, and related topics.)

■ **Don't leave the building without a good reference.** Don't count on your former boss to write you a letter of reference. Write one yourself and send it to your boss for his or her signature along with an up-to-date resume and summary of your accomplishments.

If you are not retiring but will be looking for another job, Lloyd suggests that you give yourself a short mourning period before beginning your new job search. Once you start looking, she cautions, don't take just anything that comes along. Sure, you're anxious to land something new, but in the long term, it is better to hold out for a good fit than to take a job you're really not right for or that you will not enjoy.

CUTTING YOUR TAXES

Let's look at other ways to boost your income immediately without having to ask your boss for a raise or look for a higher-paying job. If you are like most people, you probably pay a lot more in taxes than you realize. Take a guess. What do you think that the average person pays in combined federal, state, and local taxes in the United States?

[ ] 20% [ ] 25% [ ] 30% [ ] 35% [ ] 40% [ ] Over 40%

If you chose over 40 percent, you're right. And according to Ric Edelman, if you include federal income taxes, social security and other payroll taxes, sales taxes, property taxes, gasoline taxes, and all the other taxes that most people have to pay, your total tax burden is very likely close to 50 percent of your gross income.[17]

Given that you are sacrificing so much of your income to taxes, it makes sense to try to reduce your tax burden whenever you can. As our gurus point out, every dollar you save in taxes is an automatic and effortless boost to your income. Here are some tax-saving tips from Eric Tyson:[18]

Focus on Reducing Your Total Taxes, Not on Maximizing Your Income Tax Refund
Tyson says that most people focus on whether they get a federal income tax refund. Instead, he says, you should focus on reducing your *total tax*. In fact, say Tyson and other gurus, if you get an income tax refund, you've already paid too much in taxes. To find out how much you currently pay in *total* tax, look for the lines on your last year's federal and state income tax returns labeled *total tax* (line 54 on IRS form 1040) and add together those two numbers. You want to reduce the combined total of those two numbers.

Robert Heady and Christy Heady note that if you are self-employed, it is critical that you carefully monitor your estimated tax payments throughout the year to make sure you are not over- or underpaying your estimated taxes.[19] Likewise, they say, if you have an employer, you should periodically review your withholding to make sure the right amount is being taken out of your check each month.

Take Maximum Advantage of Retirement Plan Contributions Make the maximum contribution you can to your 401(k) or 403(b) account at work, as well as to your IRA account and other tax-sheltered retirement accounts. (For more information on these accounts, see our discussion on investing for retirement in Chapter 9.)

Use Income or Deduction Shifting to Reduce Your Tax Burden If you have a choice about when to receive some income, take it in the year in which it will have the most favorable impact on your total taxes. For example, explains Tyson, if you have the option of taking a year-end bonus in December of one year or January of the next, consider how the extra income would impact your total tax obligation. You would want to take the bonus in December if you expect to be in a higher tax bracket next year. You may be able to make similar choices when it comes to deductions. For example, if you usually make a charitable contribution late in the calendar year, consider the tax consequences if you delayed your contribution until January of the next year. Figure out which year the deduction would offer you the greatest tax advantage.

 Invest in Tax-Free Money Market Funds and Bonds Tax-free investments such as municipal bonds will have a lower return than taxable investments, but you may come out ahead if you are in a high tax bracket. See our discussion in chapter 8.

 Consider the Tax Consequences of Your Mutual Fund Investments Mutual funds can create tax liabilities for you through dividends and capital gains. You should take such tax consequences into account when you are deciding where to invest your money. See our discussion in Chapter 8 on mutual fund investing.

Take Advantage of Real Estate Deductions As Tyson notes, the tax code is extremely friendly to real estate investments. In addition to deductions on mortgage interest and property taxes you pay on your home, you can also get a deduction for wear and tear and losses on rental property. If you own such property or are considering such an investment, make sure you take advantage of all of the tax benefits.

Organize to Itemize It is getting more difficult for most people to itemize deductions because the standard deduction keeps getting raised. Still, say our gurus, you should keep track of any deductible expenses just in case. A shoebox or set of clearly labeled file folders work nicely. Tyson says that if you own your own business or are a self-employed professional, it is absolutely essential that you devise some method to keep track of your expenses.[20] Otherwise, you stand to lose significant opportunities to reduce your taxes. In particular, say our gurus, keep track of charitable contributions (including expense you incur for work you do for a charity), auto registration and state disability insurance fees, educational expense, job search expenses, unreimbursed expenses related to your job, and any and all expenses you have if you are self-employed. Their advice is to keep all of your receipts. Even little things add up.

Trade Consumer Debt for Mortgage Debt Mortgages not only offer a lower interest rate than credit card and other consumer debt, but they also come with a tax deduction. Therefore, you may be able to get some tax benefit by taking out a home equity loan and paying off your credit card and other nondeductible consumer debt. However, be careful. Such loans can be extremely dangerous if used incorrectly.

Recognize When You Need Help   Robert Heady and Christy Heady declare that not getting help when they need it is one of the top 10 mistakes people make in preparing their taxes.[21] You may be able to prepare your tax return yourself with the help of tax preparation software such as TurboTax, but if you have doubts about a tax issue, you should seek professional advice. As Tyson notes, you have four choices when finding tax-preparation help:[22]

1. **Tax preparer:** These people have the least amount of training. Many work part-time for a tax preparation firm such as H&R Block. They are also the least expensive. Tyson notes that a tax preparer makes sense if you have a simple return, are budget minded, and want help primarily because you hate doing tax returns.
2. **Enrolled agent:** These people hold a license from the Internal Revenue Service that allows them to represent you in an audit. They have more training than a tax preparer but less than a CPA. Tyson considers enrolled agents to be suitable for people with moderately complex returns who don't necessarily need ongoing financial advice. To find an enrolled agent, contact the National Association of Enrolled Agents, 200 Orchard Ridge Drive, Suite 302, Gaithersburg, MD 20878-1978, telephone: (301) 212-9608, Fax: (301) 990-1611; or go to their Web site at http://www.naea.org/eadirectory.cfm/; or call their referral line at (800) 424-4339.
3. **Certified public accountants:** CPAs have significant training and must pass a rigorous exam. Their fees vary by location but can be several hundred dollars per hour. According to Tyson, you only need a CPA if your tax situation is complex or if you are self-employed and don't want to deal with filing lots of forms. For help in finding a CPA in your area, go to CPA Directory at http://www.cpadirectory.com/ or CPA Finder at http://www.cpafinder.com/.
4. **Tax attorney:** Tax attorneys specialize in understanding the ins and outs of tax law. Tyson says that you don't need a tax attorney unless you are super-rich and/or you are in major legal trouble when it comes to your taxes. Otherwise, they are too expensive. For help in finding a tax attorney, go to the American Bar Association Web site at http://www.abanet.org/legalservices/findlegalhelp/lawrefdirectory.html/.

Robert and Christy Heady offer the following advice about hiring and working with a tax professional:[23]

- **Shop around:** Interview at least five tax professionals face to face before you make a decision. Remember, you are going to be sharing intimate details about your financial life with this person. Make sure you will be comfortable working with them and that they have the education and experience your tax situation requires. Most important, be sure you understand their fees and charges. The Headys say that if you are planning to work with a CPA, ask for a letter of engagement spelling out the CPA's fees and services. Also ask the CPA how many returns he or she does each year and the percentage of extensions he or she files. Think twice about CPAs who handle more than 300 returns or files extensions for more than 20 percent of their clients. They may be overworked and not able to give your tax issues the quality of attention they deserve.

- **Be organized:** Don't just dump a box of receipts on your tax professional's desk and walk away. The best way to minimize fees and ensure that your tax return is prepared correctly, say the Headys, is to provide your tax preparer with accurate and organized records.

STASHING YOUR CASH: FINDING THE BANK THAT'S RIGHT FOR YOU

If you've taken our gurus' advice so far in this chapter, you've found ways to get more cash flowing into your coffers. Maybe you've gotten a raise or a better job with a bigger paycheck. Perhaps you finally have some investments that are producing a regular stream of cash. You may have taken your raise and investment income and bought a business of your own. Or maybe you just found some creative ways to cut your taxes. Congratulations—you're on your way to realizing your financial dreams.

But there is more you can do to boost your cash flow, build your net worth, and realize those financial dreams even faster. The next step is to tackle the spending side of your cash-flow statement. We'll tackle the issue of how to develop a spending plan in the next chapter. For now, there is one final matter to consider when it comes to making money. Where is a safe place to stash your cash?

If you are like most Americans, one of the first things you did when you started earning your own money was to open a checking account at a neighborhood bank. Your choice of bank was probably based on convenience and perhaps name recognition, but did you make the right choice? To answer that question and a number of others regarding your relationship with banks, we'll start with the most fundamental question—what is the purpose of a bank?

The Purpose of a Bank

The first thing to understand about banking, says Ric Edelman, is that it is not the bank's job to make money for you. Instead, their purpose is to "serve as short-term depositories of cash, as you move money from one place to another."[24] At most, banks should pay you enough interest on your money to keep you current with inflation. Fortunately, they do that very well and very safely thanks to the Federal Deposit Insurance Corporation (FDIC). Your deposits in a financial institution with FDIC coverage are insured up to $100,000 and may be insured for more than $100,000 if the deposits are maintained in different categories of legal ownership. (For a complete explanation of how FDIC works and definitions of the categories of legal ownership, see the document titled "Your Insured Deposit" available free from the FDIC at http://www.fdic.gov/deposit/deposits/index.html/.)

Types of Banks

As Jean Chatzky explains, you really have four options when it comes to banking—small banks, large banks, online banks, and credit unions. Here are her recommendations for when to use each.[25]

Small Banks

Chatzky says that small banks are a good option for you if you are a small-business owner and know that you are going to need loans on a regular basis. If the bank is small, you will have a better chance of getting to know the bank officers, and that will mostly likely make it easier for you to get the loans you need.

Large Banks

Chatzky says to consider a large bank if you are a heavy automatic teller machine (ATM) user because the bank will have ATMs in more locations and you will be able to avoid fees most banks now charge for using another bank's ATM.

Online Banks

Online banks usually charge lower fees than brick-and-mortar banks and offer better rates on money market accounts and CDs. They are a good option, says Chatzky, if you are prepared to make your deposits by mail or through direct deposit and accomplish your transactions without face-to-face assistance.

 Clark Howard warns that you should check with the FDIC at http://www. fdic.gove/ to make sure an online bank is insured. He reports terrible tales of people who deposited their money with what they thought were online banks only to find out that the so-called banks were nothing more than a sham.[26]

Credit Unions

Credit unions are nonprofit financial cooperatives that offer many of the same services as banks. Chatzky and most of our other gurus consider credit unions to be an excellent alternative for people who are looking for basic banking-type services at low cost. The major advantages and disadvantages of credit unions according to Stacie Zoe Berg have to do with rates, fees, and services.[27] When it comes to car loans, credit cards, CDs, money market accounts, and so on, credit unions offer better rates and fewer fees than most banks, particularly brick-and-mortar banks. On the other hand, banks usually offer more services than credit unions. For example, credit unions usually have fewer ATMs than banks and may not offer such services as cashier's and certified checks.

Whereas it was once difficult for many people to find a credit union to join, Jason Kelly points out that that is no longer the case. The best place to start looking for a credit union is with your employer because most large employers have an employee credit union. If that doesn't work, Kelly suggests that you check with the following to see if you can join a credit union through them:

- Trade organizations you belong to
- Your church
- Local civic organizations
- Your relatives (many credit unions offer membership to relatives of their members)[28]

If none of these work, Kelly recommends that you contact the Credit Union National Association at (800) 358-5710 for assistance. Also check the association's Credit Union Locator on line at http://www.cuna.org/data/consumer/culinks/cu_locator.html/.

Picking the Best Checking Account

Regardless of whether you bank with a large bank, small bank, online bank, or credit union, one of the key decisions you will have to make is what kind of checking account to open. Banks offer a bewildering variety of checking alternatives but, as Jane Bryant Quinn says, your choice comes down to a very simple test: "What is the lowest average balance you will leave on deposit every month?"[29] The reason this question is important is that most banks pay interest on your average daily checking account balance provided you maintain a minimum balance. Obviously, you are looking for an account that pays the highest interest rate on a minimum account balance you are likely to maintain, but as Quinn cautions, be careful to factor in monthly fees, check-writing fees, ATM fees, and so on when you are comparing offers from different banks. She warns: "Don't let your banker's hand be quicker than your eye. A checking account might deliberately carry a low monthly fee or no fee at all in order to make it look cheap to price-shoppers. But the bank might recoup by charging you extra for processing checks or using the ATM machines."[30] Therefore, says Quinn, be sure you ask and get complete answers about all of the relevant fees before you open the account.

Stacie Zoe Berg recommends gathering information about the following fees:[31]

- Monthly maintenance fees
- ATM fees, especially those assessed for using another bank's ATM
- Fees for transferring money between accounts such as checking to savings, savings to money market, and so on
- Check-processing fees
- Fees for allowing your account to drop below a minimum balance
- Cost of printing checks
- Cost of bouncing a check
- Cost for stopping a check
- Cost for getting a copy of a canceled check
- Overdraft charges
- Cost of cashier's checks
- Cost of debit card use

The gurus say that you can usually get checks cheaper if you order them from a supplier other than your bank. Brooke Stephens suggests the following sources:[32]

Current Checks, 800-204-2244, http://www.currentchecks.com/
Artistic Checks, 800-733-6313, http://www.artisticchecks.com/
Designer Checks, 800-239-9222, http://www.designerchecks.com/

Quinn cautions that you should watch out for a particularly onerous fee called the deposit item return (DIR) charge. In this case, the bank charges you a fee if you deposit an item, such as a check from a friend, and it bounces. You get hit with a charge even though you had no idea the check wasn't good. Quinn says you shouldn't accept such fees and that if you are charged them you should ask the bank to rescind the charge.[33]

Questions to Ask When Picking a Checking Account

Gurus Jane Bryant Quinn, Stacie Zoe Berg, and Jean Chatzky recommend that you ask your friendly banker these questions before opening a checking account, in addition to those you have already asked about fees:[34]

1. What is the minimum deposit to open the account?
2. Does the account pay interest? If so, how is the interest calculated? Does the bank pay interest truly from the day of deposit or only on the *collected balance* once the deposit has provisionally cleared?
3. What is the minimum balance you have to maintain to avoid paying a fee?
4. Do you get your canceled checks with your monthly statement?

5. Will the bank agree to eliminate at least some fees and charges if you purchase a CD from them or take out a loan? What breaks or tie-in deals do
they offer?

Using ATMs Wisely

When you open a bank account, you will almost certainly gain access to ATMs,
those wonderful devices that make your money available to you day and night, 365
days a year. However, the gurus warn that ATMs present two significant dangers to
your financial well-being. First, fast and easy access to your cash can mean that
you rapidly deplete the funds in your accounts. Worse, if you are like most people
and don't keep your ATM receipts, you may have no idea where your money went.
Second, as Jane Bryant Quinn notes, if you aren't cautious about how and when
you use your ATM card, you can become "a sitting duck for a cruising crook."[35]
Here is how to protect yourself from both dangers.

Avoid Fees

Jason Kelly says that the first thing you must do if you want to use your ATM
card intelligently is to avoid fees for using ATMs owned by banks other than yours.
In most cases, if you use another bank's ATM, you can be charged fees both by
your own bank AND by the other bank. To avoid the ATM fee trap, ask your bank
for a guide to local ATMs you can use without encountering a fee.[36]

Minimize Withdrawals

Kelly recommends reducing your use of ATMs for withdrawals. His experience
with clients indicates that people who use ATMs frequently wind up withdrawing
more cash. They take out $10 one day, $20 the next, then another $10, and so on.
Because they are only taking out small amounts at a time, it doesn't seem like a lot
of money; however, it adds up over time. To avoid these excessive withdrawals, determine how much cash you will need for a week and make only one withdrawal
for that week.

Stay ATM Safe

Quinn warns that you can be certain that ATM crime is growing, but you can be
equally certain that you won't hear much about it. Banks don't want you to be
scared away, and they don't want you to be encouraged to sue them for recovery of
any losses. The Electronic Funds Transfer Act (EFTA) gives you some protection
from ATM fraud (see our discussion on debit cards in Chapter 6) but only if you report the loss immediately. According to Quinn, it is not always clear what liability

the bank has if you are assaulted and robbed while using an ATM. Regardless, you should play it safe by avoiding making withdrawals at night, only using ATMs that are located in well-lit areas, and locking your doors when using a drive-up ATM.[37]

What to Do if You Have a Problem with a Bank

Edward Mrkvicka, author of *Your Bank Is Ripping You Off,* says that the best way to avoid problems with your bank, or at least get any problems corrected quickly, is to get to know people at your bank such as the head teller, bank manager, and loan officer.[38] Then you have to know and follow the chain of command to get a resolution to your problem. Start at the lowest level—usually a teller, loan clerk, or bookkeeper—then work your way up the chain.

Mrkvicka says that if you are tactful, assertive, and most important, persistent, there is a good chance you can eventually get your problem resolved. If, despite all of your efforts to reach a satisfactory resolution with your bank, you are still dissatisfied, Nancy Lloyd suggests sending a letter explaining the problem to one of the following organizations, depending on the type of financial institution you are dealing with, along with copies of any documentation you have of the problem and your attempts at a resolution:

> If your bank is state-chartered and a member of the Federal Reserve System: Board of Governors of the Federal Reserve System, 20th and C Streets NW, Washington DC 20551; (202) 452–3000. [http://www.federalreserve.gov/]
>
> If your bank is state-chartered but not a member of the Federal Reserve System: Federal Deposit Insurance Corporation, Office of Consumer Affairs, 550 17th Street NW, Washington, DC 20429; (800) 934–3342. [http://www.fdic.gov/]
>
> If your bank is a national bank (has "National" in the title or "NA" after its name): Comptroller of the Currency, Customer Assistance Group, 1301 McKinney Street, Suite 3710, Houston, TX 77010; (800) 613-6743. [http://www.occ.treas.gov/customer.htm]
>
> If your bank is a savings bank or a savings and loan (S&L) institution: Office of Thrift Supervision, Consumer Programs, 1700 G Street NW, Washington, DC 20552; (202) 906-6237 or (800) 842-6929. [http://www.ots.treas.gov/]
>
>   If your account is with a federally chartered credit union: National Credit Union Administration, Office of Public and Congressional Affairs, 1775 Duke Street, Alexandria, VA 22314-3428; (703) 518-6330. [http://www.ncua.gov/][39]

KEY POINTS

There are three types of income:
- Earned income—income that comes in the form of a paycheck
- Portfolio income—income from stocks, bonds, mutual funds, CDs, and so on
- Passive income—income that comes from things you own, such as real estate, patents, license agreements, and businesses

There are four legal ways to earn money:
- You can be someone's employee.
- You can be self-employed.
- You can own a business.
- You can be an investor.

Employees and the self-employed receive earned income. Business owners receive passive income. Investors receive portfolio income.

If you want to be rich, or for that matter even financially independent, you want as much passive and portfolio income as possible.

You become financially independent when you are receiving enough passive and/or portfolio income each month to cover your expenses.

It is not a bank's job to make you money. Banks are short-term depositories of cash.

Credit unions offer lower fees and high interest rates on CDs and money markets but provide less service than traditional banks.

Jacqueline Blix, coauthor of *Getting a Life*

Mark Bryan, coauthor of *Money Drunk, Money Sober*

Julia Cameron, coauthor of *Money Drunk, Money Sober*

Amy Dacyczyn, author of *The Complete Tightwad Gazette*

Joe Dominguez, coauthor of *Your Money or Your Life*

Ilyce Glink, author of *50 Simple Things You Can Do to Improve Your Personal Finances*

Andrew Hacker, author of *Money: Who Has How Much and Why*

David Heitmiller, coauthor of *Getting a Life*

Mary Hunt, author of *Mary Hunt's The Complete Cheapskate*

Deborah Knuckey, author of *The Ms. Spent Money Guide*

Deborah McNaughton, coauthor of *The Insider's Guide to Managing Your Credit*

Olivia Mellan, coauthor of *Overcoming Overspending*

Suze Orman, author of *Suze Orman's Financial Guidebook*

Vicki Robin, coauthor of *Your Money or Your Life*

4

Spending and Saving

You love to shop, right? Shopping's fun, exciting, and satisfying. But if you're like many people, you're probably overdoing it a bit. In this chapter, we take you through some exercises our gurus have developed to measure whether you are just spending or maybe overspending. If you or your spouse/partner are overspending, we'll show you some things you can do to get your spending under control. Then we will help you develop a spending plan—otherwise known as a budget—and discuss some ways you can save money relatively painlessly. But first, let's deal with that overspending issue.

ARE YOU OVERSPENDING?

Are you just spending or are you overspending? If you aren't sure, you may want to work through Exercise 4.1

If you answered "Yes" or "Yes, but I can explain" to 10 or more of these questions, our gurus say you *definitely are* an overspender. If you answered "Yes" or "Yes, but I can explain" to nine or more of these questions, they say you *probably are* an overspender. If you answered, "Yes" or "Yes, but I can explain" to eight or more of these questions, then you *may be* an overspender. If you answered "Yes" or "Yes, but I can explain" to seven or fewer or these questions, congratulations! You can go shopping.

It's Not My Fault . . . or How About This for an Excuse?

Okay, so you answered "Yes" or "Yes, but . . . " to a few more of those questions than you should have, but it's not your fault, right? At least that's what one of our gurus tells us. Deborah Knuckey, author of *The Ms. Spent Money Guide* says that if

EXERCISE 4.1. **Are You Overspending?**

Instructions: Answer each of the following questions with a No, Yes, or Yes, but I can explain. If you choose the latter, write your excuse in the space provided.

1. Do you buy things and hide them?
   NO [ ]   YES [ ]   YES, but I can explain. [ ]
   My excuse is:_____

2. When you shop, do you experience an emotional high and then crash?
   NO [ ]   YES [ ]   YES, but I can explain. [ ]
   My excuse is:_____

3. Do you worry more about having money to spend than how to make it?
   NO [ ]   YES [ ]   YES, but I can explain. [ ]
   My excuse is:_____

4. Do you play credit card roulette, filling up one card and then moving to the next?
   NO [ ]   YES [ ]   YES, but I can explain. [ ]
   My excuse is:_____

5. Do you impulsively buy things you don't need or can't afford?
   NO [ ]   YES [ ]   YES, but I can explain. [ ]
   My excuse is:_____

6. Do you rationalize useless purchases and extravagant gifts as "business"?
   NO [ ]   YES [ ]   YES, but I can explain. [ ]
   My excuse is:_____

7. Do you find it impossible to stay within your budget or shopping list when you shop?
   NO [ ]   YES [ ]   YES, but I can explain. [ ]
   My excuse is:_____

8. Do you continually drain your savings account or fail to have one?
   NO [ ]   YES [ ]   YES, but I can explain. [ ]
   My excuse is:_____

9. Do you joke about your overflow of gadgets or accessories?
   NO [ ]   YES [ ]   YES, but I can explain. [ ]
   My excuse is:_____

10. Do you spend money on the expectation that your income will rise?
    NO [ ]   YES [ ]   YES, but I can explain. [ ]
    My excuse is:_____

11. Do you take cash advances on credit cards to make payments on another credit card?
    NO [ ]   YES [ ]   YES, but I can explain. [ ]
    My excuse is:_____

12. Do you often fail to keep accurate records of your purchases?
    NO [ ]   YES [ ]   YES, but I can explain. [ ]
    My excuse is:_____

13. Have you applied for more than three credit cards in the past year?
    NO [ ]   YES [ ]   YES, but I can explain. [ ]
    My excuse is:_____

(continued)

EXERCISE 4.1. **(continued)**

14. Do you regularly pay for groceries with your credit card because you don't have enough cash to pay for them?
    NO [ ]   YES [ ]   YES, but I can explain. [ ]
    My excuse is:_____

15. Do you often hide credit card purchases from your family?
    NO [ ]   YES [ ]   YES, but I can explain. [ ]
    My excuse is:_____

16. Does carrying several credit cards make you feel richer?
    NO [ ]   YES [ ]   YES, but I can explain. [ ]
    My excuse is:_____

17. Do you collect cash from friends in restaurants, then pay the bill with your credit card?
    NO [ ]   YES [ ]   YES, but I can explain. [ ]
    My excuse is:_____

18. Do you regularly make only the minimum payment on your credit card bills?
    NO [ ]   YES [ ]   YES, but I can explain. [ ]
    My excuse is:_____

19. Would you have trouble imagining living your life without credit?
    NO [ ]   YES [ ]   YES, but I can explain. [ ]
    My excuse is:_____

20. Do you buy things to cheer yourself up or to reward yourself?
    NO [ ]   YES [ ]   YES, but I can explain. [ ]
    My excuse is:_____

21. Does more than one-third of your income go to pay bills (not including your mortgage or rent payments)?
    NO [ ]   YES [ ]   YES, but I can explain. [ ]
    My excuse is:_____

22. Do you juggle bill paying because you always seem to be living on the edge financially?
    NO [ ]   YES [ ]   YES, but I can explain. [ ]
    My excuse is:_____

23. Do you tend to keep buying more of your favorite things—clothes, compact discs, books, computer software, electronic gadgets—even if you don't have a specific need for them?
    NO [ ]   YES [ ]   YES, but I can explain. [ ]
    My excuse is:_____

24. If you have to say *no* to yourself, or put off buying something you really want, do you feel intensely deprived, angry, or upset?
    NO [ ]   YES [ ]   YES, but I can explain. [ ]
    My excuse is:_____

Sources: Based on the ideas of Mark Bryan and Julia Cameron, Money Drunk, Money Sober: 90 Days to Financial Freedom *(Los Angeles: Lowell House, 1992); Deborah McNaughton,* The Insider's Guide to Managing Your Credit *(Chicago: Dearborn Financial, 1998); and Olivia Mellan and Sherry Christie,* Overcoming Overspending: A Winning Plan for Spenders and Their Partners *(New York: Walker, 1995).*

FIGURE 4.1 **Your Score**

you are overspending, you may not be totally to blame. "The simple fact," writes Knuckey, "is that . . . the pressure to spend is everywhere; our whole economy revolves around it, and much of our culture does too. Also, we tend to live in the moment; it is easier to see the pleasure in a frozen yogurt on a hot day than to imagine a comfortable retirement on a day far away."[1] As Knuckey says, we all face a lot of external and internal pressure to spend, spend, spend. There are armies of psychologists, statisticians, copywriters, artists, and filmmakers who devote their lives to getting you into the store or on the Internet to buy.

Of course, whatever you buy, it is not going to last forever. Do you really think those Capri pants with the big flowers will still be in fashion five years from now? It's called "product life cycle," and marketers love it. What's hot this morning is old news by midafternoon. What are you going to do with all those compact discs now that you can download music to your MP3 player? You mean you don't have one of those yet? Well, just take out your credit card, write a check on your home equity line of credit, get an advance on your paycheck or tax refund, or borrow some money and buy one. You *want* it, right?

Want

Consider this definition of "want."

WANT = NEED

You ~~want~~ need what others have—the home, the car, the boat, the vacation to Europe. And, you ~~want~~ need it NOW! And according to the retailers, you can have it. No waiting. Pay nothing for 64 months.

We are all on one big "consumption escalator," says Knuckey. What did you do with that last 5 percent raise you got? Knuckey bets you spent it and 5 percent more—maybe 10 percent more.[2] But, you ~~wanted~~ needed that bigger house, a more powerful car, and new outfit. In some cases the extra spending may have been just a little "retail therapy"—she broke your heart, so you showed her by going shopping for something new.

Most of us have been there and done that. We ride the consumption escalator and have a grand old time until one day when we turn around and find that all of our money is gone. Where did it go?

What should you do if you (and/or your spouse/partner) are overspending? Gather your loved ones around you, says guru Olivia Mellan, because she has a plan—indeed several plans—for turning you and yours from mean and despicable overspenders into fine, upstanding tightwads.

Strategies for Dealing with Overspending

Here are some temptation-fighting strategies that Mellan says can help you deal with overspending:[3]

1. **Go for the goal:** Think about something important that you really want—for example, a home of your own or a college education for yourself or your kids. Take a picture of your goal or find a picture or drawing that illustrates your goal. Get a small notebook and carry it and the picture of your goal with you wherever you go. When you are tempted to spend money, take out your goal picture and look at it. Imagine what it is going to be like to read in that cozy den, cook in that gourmet kitchen, or luxuriate in that huge spa tub. Or imagine yourself watching your daughter as she gives the valedictory address at her graduation just before she launches her career as a world-famous heart surgeon. Take out your notebook and write down the item you have now decided not to buy and its price—a Pineapple Head Crunch Zone Tour compact disc, $29.95, or an Edith Designergirl purple-and-tangerine wrap skirt, $149.99. Close your notebook and walk away *sans* purchase and with a big smile on your face.

2. **Jam the trigger:** The idea here is that whenever you feel the urge to shop, you simply "jam the binge trigger" by doing something you really enjoy. Working with your spouse, partner, or friend, brainstorm some things you really like to do. For example, perhaps you really enjoy talking to a special friend, or maybe you like to read or take long walks or trips to a museum. When you find yourself getting the urge to spend, do something you enjoy instead.

3. **Bookend:** Have a buddy who has agreed to help you handle your compulsion to spend. Your buddy could be a friend, relative, or your spouse/partner. It could even be someone who is an overspender, too. When you find yourself getting the urge to jump in the car and head for the mall, call this person instead. Let your buddy help you get through your temptations.

4. **Stop, look, and listen:** The idea is that when you get the urge to spend you do the following:
   - ☐ **Stop** your immediate impulse (head to your favorite chair rather than the mall),
   - ☐ **Look** at what the impulse is telling you to do (Spend, buy something, do it now.), and
   - ☐ **Listen** to a different tape you play in your head ("I'll have just as good a time at the party no matter what I wear").

5. **Practice the nonhabitual:** Ultimately, says Mellan, if you are going to break the overspending habit, you have to replace it with some alternative non-overspending habits, and there is nothing like practice to get a new habit. These might include the following:
   - ☐ Put money in your wallet and don't spend it for a month.
   - ☐ Leave your credit cards at home for one week.
   - ☐ Wait 24 hours before buying anything over $10.
   - ☐ Comparison shop three locations before buying anything over $10.

6. **Find a better way to meet your needs:** Mellan says that if you are over-spending to enhance your self-esteem and make yourself feel better, then you need to find alternative ways to meet these needs. For example, instead of going shopping, take a course to learn something new and useful like car maintenance, cabinetmaking, or something just for fun. Join a club with people who share your special interest in jazz, Civil War history, or bike riding. You could also volunteer by becoming a Big Brother or Big Sister or helping Habitat for Humanity build a house.

7. **Avoid or minimize your exposure to slippery spaces:** Slippery spaces are those places and events that trigger your shopping urges. If malls are your downfall, try not to go to them. If you must go, make your trip short. Make a list of what you need and of the stores you need to visit; stick to your list, and find the shortest route into and out of the stores.

8. **Keep a journal to record your progress:** You're on the road to becoming a saver rather than a spender, but that doesn't mean that you can expect to get to your destination right away. The journey from overspender to tight-wad can be a long one. As time passes, you need a record to remind you of just how much you have accomplished. Keep one.

9. **Reward yourself:** When you reach milestones on your journey, such as not overspending for a week or month, Mellan says you should give yourself a reward. Have lunch with a friend, spouse, or partner and celebrate your suc-cess. Treat yourself to a movie or concert. Or, suggests Mellan, you might even go for a slow and deliberate shopping trip with a friend. She explains this way: "I believe that slow, deliberate spending can be a healing and strengthening experience."[4]

You now know whether you are a spender or overspender. If you are the latter, you know some tips, tricks, and techniques to get your spending under control. Now let's turn to our gurus' advice for how you can save money by developing a spending plan.

DEVELOPING A SPENDING PLAN

Earlier, we stated that there are two ways to get your cash flow and net worth in order. You can (1) increase you income and thus have more money to acquire assets or eliminate liabilities or (2) reduce your spending and use your savings to acquire assets and reduce liabilities. We discussed increasing your income in the last chapter, and we now turn to spending. According to our gurus, your first step in controlling your spending is to develop a spending plan.

Why You Need a Spending Plan (a.k.a. a Budget)

Notice that we have used the phrase "spending plan" instead of "budget." Can you guess why? Think about images the word *budget* conjures up.

> budget = straitjacket
> budget = deprivation
> budget = doing without
> budget = dieting
> budget = doing with less
> budget = being locked in (or locked up)
> budget = being controlled

A Spending Plan—Not a Budget

Most of our gurus avoid using the word "budget" and use "spending plan" instead. Here's why:

> spending plan = a plan
> spending plan = something you create
> spending plan = something you can control
> spending plan = something flexible

A spending plan doesn't dictate how much you should spend or what you should spend your money on. A spending plan puts you in control of your finances. It's not about deprivation; it's about making choices.

Constructing a Spending Plan

Most gurus offer advice on how to go about constructing a spending plan. We think Mary Hunt, author of *Mary Hunt's The Complete Cheapskate,* offers some of the best tips. She breaks the process down into the following eight steps:[5]

> **Step #1: Determine your average monthly income.** This should equal your pretax income; any deductions for taxes, insurance, investments, and so on will be treated as expenses in the spending plan.

EXHIBIT 4.1. **Monthly Spending Plan**

1 CATEGORY	2 PLANNED SPENDING	3 ACTUAL SPENDING	4 +/−	5 ESSENTIAL (E)/ OPTIONAL (O)
Housing				
Mortgage	$x,xxx			E
Payments				
Utilities	$x,xxx			E
Travel				
Beach	$x,xxx			O

Once you have filled in your planned expenses, Hunt says that you should then calculate your total planned spending and compare the total to your income. If the total of your planned spending is more than your monthly income, then go back over your optional expenses and see what you can reduce or eliminate. Trim your planned expenses down to, or preferably less than, your monthly income.

Step #2: Make a list of your expense categories. Refer to the cash-flow statement you prepared in Chapter 2. You listed your spending categories there.

Step #3: Draft your monthly spending plan. Hunt recommends developing a worksheet similar to the example in Exhibit 4.1. Hunt's worksheet consists of three columns, but we added two more—actual spending and +/−. Column one contains a list of spending categories. In column two you enter the amount you plan to spend next month for each category. Refer to your cash-flow statement as a guide to see what you have been spending. In column five, enter an "E" if you consider the expense is "essential" or an "O" if you consider it "optional." Your spending plan will look something like the one shown in Exhibit 4.1.

Step #4: Activate your monthly spending plan. Divide each month into four weeks. Treat days 1 through 7 as week one, regardless of what day of the week day 1 falls on. Treat days 8 through 14 as week two. Treat days 15 through 21 as week three. And treat days 22 through the end of the month as week four.

Step #5: Count and record. Track and record your expenses for each week just like you did in constructing your cash-flow statement.

Step #6: Face the month-end truth. At the end of the month, total your expenses for the four weeks. Enter the total in "Actual" column. Enter the difference in the "+/−" column.

Hunt declares that if you do these first six steps, she can predict what will happen during the first month:

1. You [will have] expenditures for which you had prepared no categories; and
2. You [will have spent] far more than you had planned.[6]

Don't despair. Although it might not seem like it, your spending plan is working. You are becoming aware of your true expenses. "Here's the beautiful thing about a Monthly Spending Plan," writes Hunt. "You are in charge! As a good manager, you need to start planning immediately for next month."[7] It's time for step 7.

> **Step #7: Rethink optionals.** If you are spending more than you planned in a category—or worse, more than your income—start looking at your optional expenses. Is there something you can cut? Maybe you could cancel cable television or mow the lawn yourself. (We will discuss several ways to cut expenses later in this chapter.)
>
> **Step #8: Prepare next month's spending plan.** Refer to this month's "actual" column. Enter a new "planned" figure making adjustments you decided upon in step 7, and repeat steps 4–8.

Suze Orman notes that because the unexpected can always be expected, you should try and allocate an extra $50 to $100 each month for miscellaneous unpredictable expenses, such as medical bills not covered by your insurance.[8]

BECOMING A TIGHTWAD

Amy Dacyczyn, author of *The Complete Tightwad Gazette,* declares that there are really only three ways to save money: (1) buy it cheaper, (2) make it last longer, or (3) use it less.[9] Dacyczyn may be right about that, but our gurus have found literally thousands of variations on these three ways, including the four general money-saving ideas we examine in the following sections.

Money Saving Idea #1: Repooling

In *The Courage to Be Rich,* Suze Orman notes that one of the chief reasons most people have a difficult time saving money is the way they think about their money.[10] Orman says most of us look at our money as a pool that gets drained each month as we pay our expenses and filled back up each month or every two weeks when we get our paycheck. Our money pool gets filled, drained, replenished, drained, refilled, and so on month after month. Many of our expenses such as child care costs, payments on installment loans, and so on occur every month, and we pay them almost by rote.

But, asks Orman, what happens when these expenses change? For example, if your preschooler starts school, you no longer have the day care expense. What do you do with the extra money? Orman bets that instead of saving the $200 per month you had been spending on day care, you dump it back into your money pool. You do the same when you pay off your auto loan or credit card debt, instead of saving all of the money that used to be flowing out for expenses you no longer have. Eventually, the money pool gets drained away on daily expenses, just like the rest of your money. No wonder you aren't saving anything.

Now, says Orman, suppose that instead of repooling that extra cash, you redirect it to savings or investments. Will you really miss the $200 you have been paying for the dining room set if it were redirected to a savings or investment account? Will you suffer if you keep living on your old paycheck and deposit your raise in a money market fund? Orman bets not, and in the meantime you are painlessly saving money and building your net worth.

If the idea of repooling all of the money from your raise or all of the savings from expenses you no longer have sounds too strict, why not repool just a portion of the savings?

Money Saving Idea #2: Trimming

An obvious way to save money is to do something drastic, such as selling your second car and making do with just one, refusing to eat out, or quitting a regular activity like golf and selling your equipment. The problem, says Orman, is that just like crash weight-loss diets, crash spending diets such as these rarely work. Instead of doing something drastic, suppose you just did a little trimming here and there. You might simply set a goal to cut $25 or $30 each month from some of your spending categories. Certain monthly expenses, like your mortgage, taxes, rent, and so on, are fixed, so look at expenses that you can control. For example, instead of having your hair colored and styled every four weeks, why not have it done only every six weeks? Instead of going out to eat and to the movies every Friday, how about staying home one Friday each month, popping some popcorn, and renting a movie? The nice thing about trimming, notes Orman, is that you can turn it into a game, finding how many ways you can trim expenses. Here are some examples of creative trimming Orman reports that her clients have accomplished:

- Cut back garbage pickup to every two weeks instead of every week. One family saved $200 per year this way.
- Do your own manicures. You could save $500 per year.
- Go through your compact discs and trade in the ones you no longer listen to. Savings: $600 per year for one client.[11]

Money Saving Idea #3: Sharing

When Orman's client started trading compact discs, he was not only finding a creative way to trim his spending, but he was engaged in another good money-saving practice called sharing. Joe Dominguez and Vicki Robin think that sharing is a great way to cut expenses without feeling the pain. After all, they note, you don't use *all* of your possessions *all* of the time, so why not let your friends use them on occasion in return for them allowing you to use some of their possessions? Think about what you could swap with someone and whom you could swap with.[12]

Money Saving Idea #4: Save the Change

In *50 Simple Things You Can Do to Improve Your Personal Finances,* Ilyce Glink recommends that every night before you go to sleep you go through your pockets or purse and empty them all change. Put that change in a container that you keep on your dresser or nightstand. You'll never miss the change, and you'll be surprised how quickly it adds up. Once a month, take whatever cash you have accumulated and deposit it in your bank account; then write a check for that amount to your money market or investment account.

To make this idea work even better, says Glink, add the bill ($1, $5, $10 and so on) with the lowest value in your pockets, wallet or purse to change you empty out each night. Then the next time you buy something, break the lowest-denomination bill you are carrying, and never pay with coins. If you really want to beef up your savings, put all of the change and the TWO lowest denomination bills into the container. Glink says she has saved as much as $100 per month easily and painlessly using this technique, and we've had similar luck.[13]

Now that you have four sure ways to get you on the painless road to saving, see Exhibit 4.2 for a final list of strategies to keep yourself on track.

GIVE ME THE SIMPLE LIFE

We hope you found at least some of the suggestions in the last section helpful. Maybe you found a painless way to save a dollar here and dollar there, or maybe even a hundred dollars here and there. If so, that's great, but some of our gurus have bigger things in mind than just having you squirrel away a little more cash; what they really want to do is change your lifestyle. They want you to simplify—get rid of the expensive clutter in your life—and become not only wise but healthy and wealthy.

We close this chapter with a look at some of their ideas about how you can simplify your life. First, we will look at what Joe Dominguez and Vicki Robin have to say about calculating your "fulfillment curve." Finally, we'll explore ideas from Jacqueline Blix, David Heitmiller, and Suze Orman on how to achieve simplicity through "unstuffing."

EXHIBIT 4.2. **Nine Sure Ways to Save Money**

Don't go shopping: About 70 percent of adults visit a mall each week, but only 25 percent are in pursuit of a specific item. In fact, the majority of grocery and nearly half of hardware purchases are spur-of-the-moment, impulse buys.

Live within your means: Wait until you have the money to pay in cash before you buy something.

Take care of what you have: Clean your tools; have the oil changed in your car; dust the coils on your refrigerator.

Wear it out: Use everything 20 percent longer than normal. Before throwing something away, see if there is another use for it. Save the screws and electrical cord from the broken toaster.

Do it yourself: Tune your own car; fix the plumbing leak yourself. Take an adult education class if you don't know how to do something.

Anticipate your needs: Watch for seasonal bargains on items you know you are going to need to buy in the near future.

Research value, quality, durability, and multiple use: Check *Consumer Reports* before you buy.

Get it for less: Order from mail-order discounters; shop discount stores; comparison shop by phone; ask for cash discounts; negotiate for a better deal.

Buy it used: Shop the Salvation Army and other thrift stores, flea markets, and garage sales.

Source: Joe Dominguez and Vicki Robin, Your Money or Your Life: Transforming Your Relationship with Money and Achieving Financial Independence *(New York: Penguin Books, 1999), pp. 171–181.*

Part of being an American is to feel that you deserve more than you have.

Andrew Hacker[14]

The Fulfillment Curve

In their book *Your Money or Your Life,* Joe Dominguez and Vicki Robin discuss what they call the "Fulfillment Curve,"[15] a graphic representation of the satisfaction (or fulfillment) you get from the dollars you are spending. The idea is that different levels of spending bring you different levels of satisfaction. At the "survival" level, you spend enough to acquire the basics of life: food, water, basic clothing, shelter, and so on. Spend a little more and you get some amenities (toys, a special piece of clothes, a rich dessert on occasion). Spend even more and you luxuriate. You buy not just a car but THE car. You take not just another vacation but the vacation of a lifetime.

EXHIBIT 4.3. **The Fulfillment Curve**

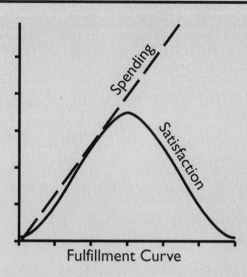

Fulfillment Curve

Source: Based on Joe Dominguez and Vicki Robin, Your Money or Your Life: Transforming Your Relationship with Money and Achieving Financial Independence (New York: Penguin Books, 1999), pp. 23–28.

Each increase in spending brings you more fulfillment, but only to a point, because, according to Dominguez and Robin, the Fulfillment Curve truly is a curve. Up to a point, each increase in spending brings you increased satisfaction. After that point, your satisfaction with extra spending levels off and eventually starts to decline (see Exhibit 4.3). Soon, you are spending more but actually feeling less satisfied. It's like eating a rich dissert—the first few mouthfuls are wonderful, but if you keep eating your body eventually says ENOUGH. Dominguez and Robin recommend using the Fulfillment Curve to measure whether you have reached or even passed ENOUGH. To prepare your Fulfillment Curve, you need two pieces of information. First, you need to know what you are spending. (Refer to your cash-flow analysis.) Second, you need a way of expressing your spending in terms of "life energy"—the hours you must work to earn one dollar to spend. The simplest way to do that is to divide your weekly income by the number of hours you work. For example:

$$\$500 \text{ per week} \div 40 \text{ hours} = \$12.50 \text{ per hour}$$

You can then calculate what anything costs you in life energy by dividing the cost of the item by your hourly earnings.

$$\text{Cost of new dress} = \$50 \div \$12.50 \text{ per hour} = 4 \text{ hours}$$

In other words, to buy the dress, you must give up four hours of your life.

Furthermore, to calculate the life energy the dress costs you with even greater accuracy, say Dominguez and Robin, you need to be a little more precise regarding the hours you work. In reality, even people who work precisely 40 hours on the job each week spend more than 40 hours earning their paycheck. In addition to the actual time on the job, most people have to spend some time commuting to and from work; they have to get dressed for work; they have to "decompress" after work; they take to their sick bed so many hours each year because the stress made them physically ill; and so on. That 40-hour-per-week job often translates to 70 or 80 hours per week of expenditure, meaning that your hourly earnings are actually much less than you think and the "life energy" cost of things you buy is a lot more.

$$\$500 \text{ per week} \div 80 \text{ hours} = \$6.25 \text{ per hour}$$

so

$$\$50 \text{ dress} \div \$6.25 = 8 \text{ hours}$$

The dress really costs you eight hours of your life, not four.

EXHIBIT 4.4. Life Energy Expenditures

Category	Monthly Expenses	Life Energy in Hours @ $6.25 per hour	Fulfillment	Alignment	After Cross Over
Housing	$695	111 hours	0	0	0
Transportation	$370	59 hours	−	−	−
Food	$325	52 hours	+	0	0
Clothing	$130	20 hours	−	−	−
Entertainment	$110	17 hours	+	0	0

Key:

Fulfillment = Did I get fulfillment from this spending?

Alignment = Is this level of expenditure in line with the way I want to spend my Life Energy?

After Cross Over = Would I increase, decrease, or maintain this level of spending if I didn't have to work for a living?

+ = Increase

− = Decrease

0 = Leave as is

Source: Based on Figure 4.3 in Joe Dominguez and Vicki Robin, Your Money or Your Life: Transforming Your Relationship with Money and Achieving Financial Independence (New York: Penguin, 1992), pp. 128–132.

FIGURE 4.2

Now that you know your real hourly rate of pay, you can calculate the life energy you are expending each month for what you buy. Go back to your spending analysis (Exhibit 4.1), where you arrived at the total amounts you were spending in each expense category each month. Divide the amounts by your real hourly rate of pay to get the life energy in hours that each type of expense is costing you. Now make a table that looks like the one in Exhibit 4.4.

Review each category in Exhibit 4.4 and ask yourself the following questions:

1. Did I get fulfillment from this spending? Enter a "+" if you receive so much fulfillment from this spending that you would like to spend more on this category. Enter a "−" if you don't receive enough fulfillment to justify this much spending. Enter a "0" if the level of spending generates about the right amount of fulfillment.
2. Is this spending in alignment with the way you want to spend your life energy? Enter a "+," "−," or "0" as you did for question 1.
3. How would you change this level of spending if you had reached the crossover point, where you had enough income from your assets that you no longer needed to work for a living? Again, enter a "+,""−," or "0" depending on how you would change your spending.

Dominguez and Robin predict the following: "Asking yourself, month in, month out, whether you actually got fulfillment in proportion to life energy spent in each category awakens that natural sense of knowing when enough is enough."[16]

When you come to realize that you are spending far too much of your life energy on things that give you less satisfaction, our gurus bet that you will be willing to start getting rid of a lot of doodads and start simplifying your life. That's where "unstuffing" comes into play.

Unstuffing

Unstuffing is a term Jacqueline Blix and David Heitmiller, coauthors of *Getting a Life,* use to refer to a new way of thinking about the material world and a new way of behaving when it comes to spending money and acquiring possessions. First, they say, you use some type of analysis, like the fulfillment chart, to "unstuff" your mind of the notion that the quality and quantity of your possessions define who you are. Then you literally "unstuff" your material world by disposing of all those things that you have collected throughout your life that you suddenly realize you don't need, don't want, don't value, and can't use. But, Blix and Heitmiller warn, the process of physical unstuffing is easier and less traumatic if taken in phases, as they learned from their own experience:

> We started by walking through each room of our house with a notebook in hand and evaluating how we used (or even *if* we used) the spaces and the stuff in them. On our first walk-through we noted things we definitely wanted to keep, things that were superfluous to our happiness, and some things that we were not sure about yet. Using our "walk-through" lists, we gathered the unwanted stuff together and, over the next two years, "unstuffed" ourselves by giving things to friends and relatives, donating unwanted items to charity, and holding garage sales. . . . Our charitable contributions were tax deductible, and to our surprise, we banked several hundred dollars from the garage sales and never missed the stuff we sold.[17]

When you get your head unstuffed and your house uncluttered, our gurus predict that you will feel a whole lot better. Orman guarantees that when you have less, you'll really have more: "More space, more awareness, more honesty, more possibility, more hope for tomorrow, and ultimately, more money."[18]

When you are fully unstuffed, you'll finally understand what Henry David Thoreau meant when he wrote, "A man is rich in proportion to the things he can afford to let alone."[19] You'll also be ready to tackle the next big money management issues, like how to buy insurance, cars, and houses. We'll deal with those issues next. For now, let's review our key tightwad ideas.

🔑 KEY POINTS

🔑 You may be an overspender if you do any of the following:
- Buy things and hide them
- Shop impulsively
- Joke about your overflow of gadgets and accessories
- Hide credit card purchases from your family

- Make only the minimum payment on your credit cards
- Juggle bill paying
- Feel deprived if you have to deny yourself a purchase

Just about everyone is on a big "consumption escalator." As soon as we make more money, we increase our spending.

To fight the temptation to spend, try the following:
- Decide on an important goal to work toward, such as buying a home or sending your kids to college
- Find something else pleasurable to do when you feel the urge to spend
- Get a "buddy" to work with you to get through a spending crisis
- Avoid places and situations where you are tempted to overspend
- Reward yourself for your success

The advantage of a spending plan over a budget is that it is a plan—something you create, something you control, and something that is flexible.

An easy way to save is simply to cut discretionary spending by a small amount each month.

A creative way to save is to swap items with your friends and neighbors.

You can save as much as $100 per month simply by saving the coins in your pocket at the end of each day.

The key to simplifying your life is "unstuffing"—getting rid of all the material things you no longer want, need, or use but that you have to maintain, protect, and store.

Robert Allen, author of *Multiple Streams of Income*

Stacie Zoe Berg, author of *The Unofficial Guide to Managing Your Personal Finances*

Ric Edelman, author of *New Rules of Money*

Debra Englander, author of *How to Be Your Own Financial Planner*

Christy Heady, coauthor of *The Complete Idiot's Guide to Managing Your Money*

Robert Heady, coauthor *of The Complete Idiot's Guide to Managing Your Money*

Clark Howard, author of *Get Clark Smart*

Mary Hunt, author of *Mary Hunt's Debt-Proof Living*

Mary Ivins, author of *Financial Security for Women*

Jason Kelly, author of *The Neatest Little Guide to Personal Finance*

Mark Levine, coauthor of *Die Broke*

Nancy Lloyd, author of *Simple Money Solutions*

Ted Miller, author of *Kiplinger's Practical Guide to Your Money*

Stephen Nelson, author of *The Millionaire Kit*

Suze Orman, author of *The 9 Steps to Financial Freedom*

Stephen Pollan, coauthor of *Die Broke*

Jane Bryant Quinn, author of *Making the Most of Your Money*

Dave Ramsey, author of *Financial Peace*

Charles Schwab, author of *You're Fifty—Now What?*

Don Silver, author of *The Generation Y Money Book*

Brooke Stephens, author of *Wealth Happens One Day at a Time*

Eric Tyson, author of *Personal Finance for Dummies*

5

All about Insurance

Robert Allen, author of *Multiple Streams of Income,* says that whenever he is on an airplane and wants to sit alone, he simply turns to the person sitting next him and introduces himself as a "born-again insurance agent."[1] Allen declares that his tactic invariably works and he never sees his seatmate again until the bags arrive. It's not surprising. Most of us find the topic of insurance either excessively boring, depressingly uncomfortable, or both.

Having the right kind and amount of insurance is critical to your family's and your financial well-being. As Jason Kelly explains, "There's little point of spending less than you earn and investing the difference if you allow the years of hard work to be wiped out by a single accident. . . . You buy insurance to protect your money. That's it. You spend a small amount of money on insurance to prevent spending a big amount on catastrophes."[2]

Let's repeat that bit of wisdom.

You buy insurance to protect your money

Health insurance doesn't protect your health; it protects your money should you have an expensive illness. You don't buy auto insurance to protect your car; you buy auto insurance to protect your money should you have a wreck and your car needs expensive repairs. Life insurance doesn't protect your life; it protects your money and the financial future of your loved ones after you die.

Kelly says that if you will just keep this one reality in mind, then you will avoid many of the mistakes people make in purchasing insurance. In this chapter, we share our gurus recommendations for how you can provide the most protection at the least possible cost for the following six types of insurance:

- Life insurance
- Disability insurance

- Health insurance
- Long-term care insurance
- Homeowner's/renter's insurance
- Auto insurance

We'll start with some general tips from our gurus that apply to most forms of insurance.

USEFUL, UNIVERSAL, INSURANCE RULES OF THUMB

 Here are some general insurance tips and useful rules of thumb offered by our gurus that apply to all types of insurance. Think of them as the universal insurance "dos and don'ts."

#1: Buy Insurance to Protect Yourself against General Risks, Not Specific Events

 As Stephen Nelson, author of *The Millionaire Kit,* points out, "By insuring against general risks—like loss of life, ability to earn an income, and lost property—you don't have to think up all the different ways you can lose your life, your income-earning ability, or some piece of property."[3] In addition, our gurus say, insurance that protects you from a specific type of loss, such as a cancer policy as opposed to general medical insurance, is enormously expensive when you consider the benefits you derive from what you pay in premiums. Following this rule, here are some of the kinds of insurance that our gurus consider bad ideas and say you should NOT buy.

 Extended warranty and repair plans: As little as 7 percent of purchases are ever repaired under extended warranties.
Home warranty plans: There are so many restrictions on the types of problems for which most home warranty plans will pay, particularly major problems, that they are of little value.

 Mortgage insurance: First, mortgage insurance is just term life insurance, but the premium is 300 to 400 percent more than you would pay for regular term life insurance. Second, as you pay off the mortgage, the amount of the benefit goes down even though the premiums stay the same. Finally, if you do die, the benefit is paid to the mortgage company and not to your surviving spouse.
Dental insurance: The coverage is usually not worth the cost.

Credit life and credit disability insurance: The potential benefits of these policies are so small that they are some of the most expensive insurance policies you can purchase. Choose general life insurance and disability insurance instead.

Daily hospitalization insurance: The amount you are likely to get in benefits is miniscule compared with what you will pay in premiums.

Cancer and/or ICU insurance: Again, you need comprehensive major medical insurance, not some policy that only covers one type of illness or hospitalization.

Wedding insurance: Your homeowner's insurance and the liability insurance held by the owners of the reception site should be adequate to cover you if a guest gets injured.

Tuition insurance: Even if your child is injured or becomes ill, the college or university will usually work with you either to refund at least a part of the tuition or to arrange to have your child complete his or her coursework or exams at some later date at no additional cost.

Flight insurance: The odds of dying in an airplane crash are very small, and you should have general life insurance to protect your loved ones in case of your death for any reason.

#2: Take as High a Deductible as You Can Afford

When purchasing most forms of insurance, you will have an option to choose your deductible, which is the amount you must pay before your insurance kicks in. Beware, however, because as Jason Kelly points out, there is a relationship between the deductible you choose and the premium you pay for the insurance.

If you choose a lower deductible, then you must pay more in premiums. Conversely, if you choose a higher deductible, then your premium will be less. As he says, it's like a see-saw—when the deductible goes up, the premium goes down; when the deductible goes down, the premium goes up. Eric Tyson says that as you

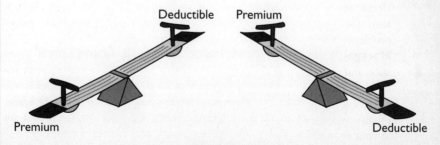

FIGURE 5.1

make a determination about your deductible, you should keep something in mind—on average, insurance companies pay out only 60 cents on every dollar collected.[4] Our gurus recommend that you think like the insurance companies and ask yourself what the real odds are that you will get sick, have an accident, or lose your possessions in a fire or to a thief. If you do, how much of the loss could you cover yourself without creating a significant financial hardship? Think about the see-saw relationship between premium and deductible, and find the highest level of deductible with which you feel comfortable.

#3: Always Check Out the Financial Strength of the Insurance Company BEFORE You Buy a Policy

In *Making the Most of Your Money,* Jane Bryant Quinn writes, "Buying life insurance is an act of faith."[5] Insurance company failures are rare, but they do happen. Twenty companies became insolvent in 1998 and another 35 in 1999.[6] To find out how a company stands, you have to check its ratings by contacting one or more of the following rating organizations:

- **A.M. Best:** (800) 424-Best; http://www3.ambest.com/
- **Standard & Poor's:** (212) 208-1527; http://www.standardandpoors.com/RatingsActions/
- **Moody's:** (212) 553-0377; http://www.moodys.com/
- **Weiss Ratings, Inc.:** (800) 289-9222; http://www.weissratings.com/

Another source of information on insurance company ratings recommended by our gurus is the annual ratings report of The Insurance Forum. Look for their *Special Ratings Issue* in your local library, or order it from their Web site at http://www.theinsuranceforum.com/ratings.html/.

Be aware that these rating companies use different ratings systems. For example, an "A" rating doesn't mean the same thing from one company to another. Generally, our gurus say, look for an "A" or better rating from Best, an "AA or Aaa" or better rating from Standard & Poor's and Moody's, and a "B" or better rating from Weiss.

#4: Get Quotes from at least Three Different Companies

The price of identical insurance can vary as much as 300 percent from company to company. All of our gurus recommend that you shop carefully when you are thinking about buying any type of insurance, and don't assume that your insurance broker or agent is going to give you the best advice.

You may also want to check quotes on the Internet, including the following insurance quote services:

- **Insurance Quote Services:** http://www.iquote.com/
- **Master Quote of America:** http://www.masterquote.com/
- **QuickQuote:** http://www.quickquote.com/
- **Quotesmith:** http://www.quotesmith.com/
- **Term-quote:** http://www.termquote.com/

In addition, you can get general information and insurance buying tips at the following sites:

- http://www.insure.com/
- http://www.quicken.com/ (click on the "Insurance Quotes" tab)
- http://moneycentral.msn.com/ (click on the "Planning" tab and then "Insurance")
- http://insurance.yahoo.com/

#5: Make Sure You Are Comparing Apples to Apples

Our gurus warn that you need to be extremely careful when comparing policies. According to Charles Schwab, you should pay particular attention to deductibles, premiums, and copayments (that part of each claim that you pay). He adds that "this is very definitely a time to read the fine print."[7]

LIFE INSURANCE

Life insurance is designed to protect your money—or more precisely, your dependents' financial well-being—when you die. Stephen Nelson, author of *The Millionaire Kit,* says the best way to think of life insurance is as "earnings replacement" insurance.[8]

Do You Need Life Insurance?

See Exercise 5.1 for a simple test to determine if you are a candidate for life insurance.

How Much Life Insurance Do You Need?

Exhibit 5.1 summarizes some guru guidance on deciding how much life insurance you will need to replace 100, 75, or 60 percent of your after-tax income.

EXERCISE 5.1. **Your Life Insurance Needs**

Instructions: Answer the following question as truthfully as possible:

Does anyone depend upon your income for their financial well-being?

YES [ ]   NO [ ]

If you answered YES, then read the rest of this section because you probably need at least some amount of life insurance. If you answered NO, then go to the next section of this chapter. You may not need life insurance now, but your answer to the needs test may change in the future.

The first thing you will notice in Exhibit 5.1 is the tremendous range of our gurus' estimates. Depending on whose formula you use, you need as little as $94,500 and as much as $700,000 of life insurance if you make $35,000 per year. Given such a range, you probably would like to have a more precise way of estimating your actual needs. Charles Schwab suggests that you first make a rough estimate and then refine your estimate by adding additional expenses and/or adjustments you think are necessary.[9]

You may also want to reference the following Internet sites:

- Insure.com Life Insurance Needs Estimator Tool at http://www.insure.com/life/lifeneedsestimator/
- MSN MoneyCentral Life Insurance Needs Estimator at http://money central.msn.com/investor/calcs/n_life/main.asp

Key Life Insurance Savings Tips

Although insurance companies use a number of different names to refer to their life insurance policies, there are really only two major types—term and cash value.

 Term insurance is pure insurance. You buy a policy for a given premium, and if you die within the time period covered by the policy, the insurance company pays your beneficiary the amount specified in your policy. Cash value life insurance provides you with insurance protection and adds a savings/investment component. Most of our gurus recommend term insurance for the following reasons:

- Cash value policies are much more expensive than term policies for the same amount of insurance.
- The "savings" you can earn under cash value policies are usually considerably less than you could earn from other investments.
- The argument some agents make that you should buy a cash value policy when you are young because you won't be able to buy a term policy when you get older is bogus.

EXHIBIT 5.1 **Estimated Amount of Life Insurance Needed to Replace Annual After-Tax Income**

Guru	Formula	Income	Replace 100%	Replace 75%	Replace 60%
Eric Tyson					
Replace 30 years income	Income × 20*	$35,000	$700,000	$525,000	$420,000
Replace 20 years income	Income × 15	$35,000	$525,000	$393,750	$315,000
Replace 10 years income	Income × 8.5	$35,000	$297,500	$223,125	$178,500
Replace 5 years income	Income × 4.5	$35,000	$157,500	$118,125	$ 94,500
Clark Howard	Income × 10	$35,000	$350,000	$262,500	$210,000
Debra Englander					
No children	Income* × 5	$35,000	$175,000	$131,250	$105,000
One child	Income × 6	$35,000	$210,000	$157,000	$126,000
Two children	Income × 7	$35,000	$245,000	$183,750	$147,000
Suzie Orman	$100,000 per $500 of monthly income needed. (Monthly income needed/ $500) × $100,000	$ 3,000 per month	$600,000	$450,000	$360,000

*If you have a two-income family, use the highest income.

Sources: Adapted from Debra Wishik Englander, How to Be Your Own Financial Planner: Your Step-by-Step Guide to a Worry-Free Future (Roseville, CA: Prima, 1995), p. 110; Clark Howard, Get Clark Smart: The Ultimate Guide for the Savvy Consumer (Atlanta, GA: Longstreet Press, 2000), p. 143; Suze Orman, The 9 Steps to Financial Freedom: Practical and Spiritual Steps So You Can Stop Worrying (New York: Three Rivers Press, 2000), p. 71; and Eric Tyson, Personal Finance for Dummies (Foster City, CA: IDG Books Worldwide), p. 345.

DISABILITY INSURANCE

Like life insurance, disability insurance is another form of earnings replacement insurance. This type protects your income against an illness or injury that prevents you from working for a short period of time or even for the rest of your life.

Do You Need Disability Insurance?

Jane Bryant Quinn says that if you are single and aren't wealthy, then you need disability insurance because you have no one to support you if you can't work. If you are married, she says, you should ask yourself the following questions: "If you had no paycheck, could your spouse's salary support the family, including the extra costs of your disability (special home care, perhaps)? Are you certain your spouse could keep working rather than tending to you? Alternatively, could you live on your savings for many years?"[10] If you answered yes to all of these questions, Quinn says that you do not need disability insurance; otherwise, it is a must for you.

The gurus argue that almost everyone who earns an income needs some level of disability insurance. In fact, they consider disability insurance to be one of the most important forms of insurance you can have for one simple reason: You are much more likely to suffer a financial loss during your lifetime because of a disability than for almost any other reason. (See Exhibit 5.2.)

EXHIBIT 5.2. **Probability of Financial Loss by Cause**	
CAUSE OF FINANCIAL LOSS	PROBABILITY OF OCCURRING BEFORE THE AGE OF 65
Automobile accident	1 in 70
Home fire	1 in 88
Catastrophic illness	1 in 105
Disability	1 in 8

Source: Mary F. Ivins, Financial Security for Women: Using Your Head and Heart to Achieve It (Chicago: Symmetry, 1999), p. 123.

Despite these statistics, people are less likely to carry disability insurance than any other kind of coverage. According to Ric Edelman, only 15 percent of Americans have any disability insurance beyond worker's compensation and Social Security.[11] Unfortunately, according to our gurus, worker's compensation and Social Security fall far short of what you need. For one thing, worker's compensation covers you only if you are injured at work, varies greatly in quality from state to state, and usually has a low cap on what it will pay. In addition, if you are self-employed, you don't have worker's compensation unless you have bought your own.

Social Security provides you with some general disability coverage, but the benefits are limited and very difficult to get; as Quinn puts it, to qualify "you have to be so pulverized, physically or mentally, that you cannot work in any substantial job."[12]

Tips for Getting the Best Deal on Disability Insurance

Given the fact that disability insurance is both important and expensive, it pays to shop around. Here are some tips from our gurus on what to look for:

- **Coverage:** Look for policies that will provide you with 60 to 70 percent of your pay if you are disabled.
- **Definition of "disability":** Purchase a policy that deems you disabled if you cannot perform the duties of your own occupation, not the more restrictive definition used by Social Security, which pays only if you cannot perform almost any type of work.
- **Residual benefits:** If you are partially disabled—that is, you have to reduce your normal hours of work per week—a policy with residual benefits pays you a pro rata share of your benefits based on how much you are able to earn.
- **"Noncancellable" versus "guaranteed-renewable":** "Noncancellable" means your policy can't be canceled and your premiums can't be raised as long as you make the premium payments. "Guaranteed renewable" means that your policy can't be canceled, but your premiums may go up if the insurance company decides to raise them. Ideally, you want noncancellable coverage, but our gurus warn, you may not be able to find it.
- **How long benefits will be paid:** You want benefits to be paid as long as you are disabled, or at least to the age at which you normally would retire. If you are young, retirement for you might be age 67 or even 70, and your policy should reflect those additional working years.[13]
- **Elimination period:** The elimination period is the length of time you must be disabled before the insurance company starts paying; it can range from 60 to 180 days. The gurus recommend that you go for the longest period you feel you can comfortably handle from your own funds. Don't forget to take into consideration sick pay or short-term disability benefits from your employer when making this determination.
- **Waiver of premium:** "Waiver of premium" means that you don't have to pay the policy premium while you are disabled. Naturally, you want this provision.
- **Return of premium:** The gurus recommend avoiding this provision, which refunds part of your premiums if you don't have a claim or only a small claim for 5 to 10 years. Your premiums will be as much as 50 percent higher, and it is not worth the gamble.

- **Cost-of-living inflation protection:** This provision, which is recommended by the gurus, increases your coverage every year by some set percentage to keep up with the consumer price index.
- **Option to purchase additional insurance:** This provision allows you to purchase additional insurance coverage at a future date regardless of your health or other factors. It is a good idea if you expect your income to rise substantially over time, but avoid policies that make automatic adjustments.[14]

HEALTH INSURANCE

Most people get health insurance through their employer and are basically restricted to whatever options their employer offers. If you aren't fortunate enough to get health insurance coverage through your employer or your spouse's employer, you may be able to get some individual coverage if you are young and healthy and/or you can join a professional association that offers a group plan. If you lose your group coverage because you are laid off or otherwise lose your job, you can continue that coverage for up to a maximum of 36 months under a federal law called COBRA (Consolidated Omnibus Budget Reconciliation Act), although your premiums will increase dramatically. (See the Web site http://cms.hhs.gov/hipaa/hipaa1/default.asp for more information.) If you're an individual or employee of a small company, you may be able to get some benefit by establishing a Medical Savings Account. Otherwise, you may just have to go without health insurance and face the terrible personal and financial consequences of being uninsured.

What to Look For in a Health Care Plan

Chances are that you will have to choose between a health maintenance organization (HMO) or a preferred provider organization (PPO) for your medical care. Basically, HMOs differ from PPOs in the degree of restrictions they place on your choice of doctors and medical treatment facilities. HMOs offer a lower premium and lower out-of-pocket costs but generally restrict you to doctors and facilities that are within their network. PPOs allow you to go to doctors or facilities out of their network, but when you do so, your out-of-pocket cost can be considerably higher.

Here are some of the things that Jane Bryant Quinn says you should consider when evaluating a health care plan, regardless of whether it is an HMO or PPO.[15]

1. **The premium:** What you pay for your policy each month.
2. **The deductible:** The amount you must pay in a single year before the insurance plan begins to pay.

3. **The copayment, or "coinsurance":** The amount you pay for each medical service.

4. **The annual cap:** The maximum amount you must pay out of pocket in a year for covered medical bills.

5. **The lifetime cap:** How much the plan will pay in all. Quinn says this should be at least $1 million.

6. **The annual limits:** Any limits to how much the plan will pay for certain services in one year, such as a dollar cap on dental bills or chiropractor services.

7. **The services not covered:** Things you have to pay for yourself.

8. **The cost of choice:** The difference you have to pay in copayments if you go outside the network of doctors and treatment facilities.

9. **The gender costs:** Watch out for plans that charge women higher rates than men on the presumption that women under 45 or 50 will have more medical claims than men.

Quinn adds that a good policy should cover the following at a minimum:

1. **The cost of basic hospital services,** including a semiprivate room, board, emergency room, nurses, intensive care, medicines, ambulance services, X-rays, and lab tests.

2. **The cost of surgery,** including the surgeons, assistants, anesthesiologists, and outpatient surgery that are "usual and customary."

3. **The cost of outpatient care,** including good home health support.

4. **Good coverage for children,** including stepchildren and foster children. Although most policies cover children to age 19, or to 21 or 25 if they are full-time students, mentally or physically disabled children should be covered permanently.

5. **Care for an infant from birth.**

6. **Most doctor bills.**

7. **Part of the bill for convalescing in a nursing home.**

8. **Part of the cost of prescription drugs.**

9. **Part of the treatment for mental or emotional problems, as well as drug and alcohol abuse.**

10. **Most of the cost of incidental expenses,** such as physical therapy, oxygen, and medical devices.

11. **Part of the cost of oral surgery,** such as impacted teeth.[16]

Lowering the Cost of Prescription Drugs

In 2001, Americans spent an estimated $100 billion on prescription drugs. That's more than $50 billion above such expenditures in 1990. The increase is a result of both the availability of a greater variety of drugs and the increase in drug prices over the last decade at a rate twice that of inflation.[17] If you are lucky, you participate in a health plan that covers a large part of your prescription drug costs. Of course, if you have no insurance, you have to pay for the drugs yourself. The same is true if you are a senior on Medicare because, as of 2002, it did not cover prescription drugs.

Here are some recommendations from Nancy Lloyd on how to cut your prescription costs if you don't have prescription coverage:

- Purchase less-expensive generic medications rather than brand names.
- Get price quotes from at least three pharmacies.
- Order several months' supply of a drug you take regularly if you can get a discount and your insurance company will allow you to do so.
- Count your pills when you get them. You may have been shortchanged.
- Ask for a partial fill of prescriptions you have not taken before to determine whether they work for you and you can take them without reaction.[18]

Finally, Clark Howard recommends that you consider having your prescriptions filled in Canada, where you will pay 30 to 70 percent less than in the United States. If you live too far from Canada to just drive across the border, Howard suggests you check out the discounts at http://www.canada.meds.com, where you can order your medicine by mail.

LONG-TERM CARE INSURANCE

Long-term care insurance covers you if you have to enter a nursing home at some time during your life. The probability of that happening, say our gurus, is fairly high. Suze Orman places the odds at one in three, and if you are over the age of 65, one in two.[19] You'll recall that our gurus said that the chances of becoming disabled are one in eight, so if Orman is right, you have a much better chance of needing long-term care insurance than disability insurance.

Today, the average person enters a nursing facility at the age of 84, stays there two years and nine months (eight years if they have Alzheimer's), and spends between $5,000 and $10,000 per month or between $165,000 and $330,000 for the entire stay. The gurus estimate that 30 years from now, the cost of a nursing home stay will exceed $12,000 per month, or nearly $400,000 for the average two-year and nine-month stay.

Getting the Best Deal on Long-Term Care Insurance

Long-term care insurance is relatively new and extremely complicated. Those two realities make it difficult for consumers to know whether they are getting a good deal. To help, the gurus provide the following rules of thumb:

- Optimal age to purchase = 59 or 60
- Amount of premium = not more than 5 percent of your income
- Daily benefit = $130 or average for your local area
- Inflation protection = 5 percent compounded inflation
- Benefit period = four years minimum, lifetime coverage preferred
- Elimination period (number of days in a care facility before policy begins paying) = zero days or the minimum you can afford
- Home care = home care rider ideally at 100 percent of facility rate
- Definition of facility = wide range of facilities covered from skilled nursing care to assisted living
- Gatekeepers (condition you must be in to be eligible) = policy covers medical necessity, activities of daily living, and cognitive impairment:

  ☐ Medical necessity: Your doctor, not the insurance company, determines that you need long-term care for you based on your medical condition.

  ☐ Activities of daily living (ADLs): You qualify for benefits if you are no longer able to perform two or more of the following normal daily activities: (1) be ambulatory; (2) bathe yourself; (3) feed yourself; (4) clothe yourself; (5) get in and out of chairs, your bed, and so on without assistance; (6) be continent; or (7) use the toilet.

  ☐ Cognitive impairment: You have Alzheimer's disease or simply can no longer think clearly enough to care for yourself.

- Hospital stay as a condition of benefits = no hospital stay required
- Preexisting conditions = none or only six months
- Waiver of premiums = waive premiums while in long-term care
- Restoration of benefits = restoration of benefits after 180 days
- Guaranteed renewable = seek guaranteed renewal

Choosing a Long-Term Care Insurance Company

When you purchase long-term care insurance, you are purchasing an insurance that you may not, and you hope you will not, have occasion to use for 20 years or more. You want to make sure that the company with which you are doing business is honest, reliable, and financially strong and will be around 20 years from now to pay your benefits if you need them. For that reason, our gurus say you should be extremely cautious when choosing a long-term care insurance provider. Be sure to check out the company carefully, as we suggested earlier in our general insurance rules of thumb.

Here are some questions Suze Orman says you should ask any long-term care insurance provider you are considering, along with what she considers to be the only acceptable answers you should hear:

- **How long have you been selling LTC insurance?** The only acceptable answer is: Ten years, minimum. . . .
- **How much LTC insurance do you currently have in force?** The only acceptable answer is hundreds of millions of dollars, with that much money in LTC care, they are already making a handsome profit—and not thinking of getting out of the business. . . .
- **How many times have you had a rate increase for those who already own a policy?** The only acceptable answer is two times or fewer. . . .
- **In how many states are you currently selling LTC insurance?** The only acceptable answer is: Every state.[20]

Orman adds that you should make sure that the company has a high rating by at least two of the ratings firms we discussed previously under the general insurance rules of thumb.

Sources of Additional Information on Long-Term Care Insurance

Here are some organizations and Internet sites that our gurus recommend for additional information on long-term care insurance:

- MAGA, Ltd.: http://www.magaltc.com/
- Long-Term Quote: (800) 587-3279; http://www.longtermquote.com/
- LTCare: (877) 582-2732 www.ltcarequote.com/
- http://www.aarp.org/
- http://www.angelfire.com
- http://www.alfa.org
- http://www.benefitslink.com
- http://www.ccal.org
- http://www.elderweb.com
- http://www.hcfa.gov/medicaid/ltc1.htm
- http://www.ncal.org
- http://www.nursinghomereports.com

HOMEOWNER'S AND RENTER'S INSURANCE

Stephen Pollan and Mark Levine explain that homeowner's insurance is actually a bundle of three types of insurance: (1) insurance to protect you from financial losses resulting from damage to you home's structure, (2) insurance to reimburse you in the case of loss or damage to your personal property, and (3) personal liability insurance.[21] Similarly, renter's insurance is a combination of personal property and personal liability insurance.

All of our gurus recommend that you carry homeowner's insurance if you own your home and renter's insurance if you rent. In fact, if you have a mortgage on your home, the mortgage company most likely will require you to carry a minimum amount of homeowner's insurance. Suze Orman says that the problem most people have with homeowner's or renter's insurance is not that they don't have any—the problem is that they don't have enough or they pay too much for the coverage that they do have.

Types of Homeowner's/Renter's Coverage

Homeowner's/renter's insurance comes in several standard flavors, each carrying an "HO" designation. Here's a description from Suze Orman:

HO-1: This is a basic policy that protects your home from 14 named perils: fire, lightning, external explosion, windstorms, hail, volcanic eruption, riot, civil commotion, vehicles, aircraft, smoke, vandalism and malicious mischief, glass breakage, and theft. [Because these catastrophes are rare,] many states are phasing out this kind of coverage.

HO-2: This is a broad policy that covers you against all the named perils included in HO-1 plus falling objects; the weight of ice, snow, or sleet; the collapse of buildings; accidental discharge or overflow of water or steam, or the explosion of steam or hot water systems; frozen plumbing, heating units, air-conditioning systems, and domestic appliances; and power surges. People who have mobile homes are normally eligible for a variation of this type of policy.

HO-3: This is a special policy that protects your home against all perils except for those that are explicitly excluded by the policy. Usually, the excluded perils are earthquakes, floods, termites, landslides, war, tidal waves, and nuclear accidents. This is the most common homeowner's policy.

HO-4: This is renter's insurance. It normally protects the possessions of tenants in a house or apartment against the same perils specified in HO-3. It also provides some liability coverage but does not cover the actual dwelling, which it is the landlord's responsibility to insure.

HO-6: This is a policy for co-op and condominium owners. Like HO-4, it provides coverage for liability and personal property. If you have made improvements to your particular unit (such as a deck or built-in kitchen cabinets), you need to cover them under this policy type, rather than the policy that the co op or condo association has for the actual dwelling.

HO-8: This is a type of policy that covers perils like those listed in HO-1, but is meant for people who own older homes. It insures the house only for repair costs or its actual cash value as opposed to its replacement cost in cases when rebuilding the home with the materials and details of the original would be prohibitively expensive. Basically, this policy will pay to restore the damaged property but not at the level of quality or authenticity of the original. This policy is rarely offered anymore.[22]

How Much Coverage Do You Need?

Our gurus say that the only right way to calculate how much insurance you need is to find out what the current construction cost per square foot is in your local area and multiply that number by the size of your home in square feet.

Insured amount =
construction cost per square foot × square feet of floor space

Don't depend on the insurance agent to give you this number. Nancy Lloyd recommends that you call some construction companies in your area and get estimates of construction costs per square foot yourself.[23] Also, the gurus advise that you redo this calculation at least every five years using updated construction cost data.

Here is a composite of additional tips for making sure that you purchase the right type and amount of insurance from Jane Bryant Quinn, Nancy Lloyd, Stephen Pollan, Eric Tyson, Suze Orman, and Clark Howard:[24]

- **Purchase guaranteed replacement coverage if you can afford it.** Guaranteed replacement "promises that, if your house is destroyed, the insurer will repair or replace it in virtually every detail, even if the cost exceeds the policy's face value."[25]
- **Never insure for less than 80 percent of the replacement costs.**
- **Get replacement cost coverage on your personal belongings.**
- **Raise the limit or get scheduled coverage for valuables.** Most policies have a fixed limit on what they will pay for items like jewelry, computers, and rare coins. To insure such items you can do one of the following:
  1. Pay extra to raise the limits on certain categories of items.
  2. Have individual items appraised and get what is known as scheduled coverage—a specified amount minus any deductibles.

- **Avoid off-premise protection (protection if an item is lost or stolen while you are away from home) if you have to pay extra for it.**
- **Consider umbrella liability coverage,** which will provide you some level of protection should you be sued by someone who gets hurt on your property or suffers a loss due to your negligence.
- **Consider whether you need earthquake or flood insurance.** If you think you don't need this coverage, think about the following:
  - ☐ One of the strongest earthquakes in the last century happened in the Midwest.
  - ☐ Government assistance to disaster victims is most likely to come in the form of low-interest loans and not as direct grant. The loans must be paid back.
  - ☐ Twenty to 25 percent of flood insurance claims come from low- to moderate-risk areas.
  - ☐ Most floods are too small and localized to qualify for Federal Emergency Management Agency (FEMA) assistance.

Saving Money on Homeowner's and Renter's Insurance

The general guru wisdom concerning insurance applies in spades when it comes to homeowner's and renter's insurance. They recommend the following:

- Take the highest deductible you can afford.
- Always check out the financial strength of the insurance company you are considering.
- Get quotes from at least three companies.

Beyond these general tips, here are some money-saving ideas from five gurus, including Nancy Lloyd, Brooke Stephens, Mark Levine, Stephen Pollan, Jason Kelly, and Jane Bryant Quinn.[26]

- Read the policy carefully.
- Ask for discounts.
  - ☐ **Safety discounts** for fire extinguishers, deadbolts, smoke alarms, burglar alarms, and so on
  - ☐ **Lifestyle discounts** for not smoking, working at home, being retired, and so on
  - ☐ **Senior citizen discounts**

□ **Age of house discounts** for homes built within the last seven years

□ **Rebuild or remodel discounts** for bringing an older house up to code[27]

- Buy multiple policies from one company.
- Pay annually.
- Look for group coverage.

AUTO INSURANCE

Clark Howard remarks that the most important thing you should know about auto insurance is that you should carry it.[28] Unfortunately, he notes, an estimated one-third of the people operating cars in America today don't have such insurance even though they are required to do so in most states. These people are not only breaking the law, but they are putting themselves and everyone who drives or rides in a car at financial risk. If you are going to own and operate a car, buy the coverage, even though it is expensive.

When you go to buy auto insurance, many of your basic choices will already have been made for you. As Pollan and Levine note, most states have some minimum requirements for coverage, and if you lease or buy a car, the leasing company or lender will have its own minimum requirements. In fact, if you get a car loan and refuse to buy the minimum auto insurance the lender mandates, the lender can actually buy the insurance itself and tack the cost onto what you owe. Howard says such "force-place" insurance can be five to six times as expensive as insurance you might buy on your own and is a real moneymaker for lenders. As Pollan and Levine put it, when it comes to auto insurance, "there's not much room to maneuver."[29] That said, in this section we will review the basics of auto insurance and what it normally covers.

Fault versus No-Fault Insurance

The second thing you need to know about auto insurance (other than the fact that you need it) is whether you live in a "fault" or "no-fault" state. It makes a major difference in what happens should you have an accident. If you live in a fault state and you are involved in an accident, the person or the insurance company of the person who caused the accident (is at fault) pays for economic damages (medical bills, lost wages, and so on) and noneconomic damages (pain and suffering) he or she caused the other person.

If you live in a no-fault state and are involved in an accident, your insurance company pays for any damages you suffer (medical bills, lost wages, and so on). You, or your estate, are prohibited from suing the person who caused the accident for so-called noneconomic damages (pain and suffering) unless your injuries (1) are serious as defined by state law, (2) result in your death, and/or (3) your medical bills reach a certain dollar amount.

The Basic Elements of an Auto Insurance Policy

Auto insurance, like homeowner's insurance, is actually a bundle of different types of protections. The most common are liability insurance, medical and/or personal injury protection, collision coverage, and comprehensive coverage.

These are general descriptions of typical coverage and may not reflect coverage in your individual policy or coverage required in your state. Read your insurance policy or call your agent to get specifics about coverage in your state.

Liability Insurance

If you look at your auto insurance policy or read a description of your state's mandatory requirements for coverage, you are likely to see something that looks like a very strange date.

100/300/50

Automobile liability insurance protects you if you have an accident and are sued by an injured party. The 100/300/50 refers to the cap or limit on the amount your insurance company will pay.

100 refers to the maximum amount in thousands of dollars your insurance company will pay for bodily injury per *person*. In this case, the limit per person is $100,000.

300 refers to the maximum amount in thousands of dollars your insurance company will pay for bodily injury per *accident*. In this case, the limit is $300,000 for any single accident.

50 refers to the maximum amount in thousands of dollars your insurance company will pay for property damage. In this case, the limit is $50,000.

How Much Liability Insurance Do You Need?

Your state most likely will specify a minimum amount of coverage that you must carry. For example, as of 2002 the state of Georgia required 25/50/25, which is significantly lower than the 100/300/50 given in the previous example. Again, our gurus recommend 100/300/50, and some recommend even more.

Medical and Personal Injury Protection

Medical protection covers the medical bills, up to the limit specified, for anyone riding in your car at the time of an accident, without regard to who is at fault. It also covers you and members of your family should you be injured as a pedestrian. Clark Howard says that if you have adequate health insurance, you don't need this type of coverage because it duplicates your medical insurance,[30] and most of our other gurus agree.

Personal injury protection (PIP) covers your medical bills, lost wages, funeral expenses, and in some cases, other expenses such as hiring someone to care for your children while you are in the hospital if you have an accident. If you are in a no-fault state, you probably will be required to carry at least a minimum level of PIP even though, like medical payments coverage, it duplicates medical, life, and disability insurance you may already have. Our gurus say you should check to see if PIP duplicates your other insurance; if so, buy the minimum you are legally required to carry.

Collision and Comprehensive

Collision coverage pays for repairing damage to your car that results from a collision with another car or object. **Comprehensive coverage** covers noncollision damage to your car or losses due to theft, vandalism, broken windshields, hail, floods, hurricanes, and a wide assortment of other misfortunes that life may visit upon you and your poor vehicle. Your insurance company's responsibility for payments under collision and comprehensive is limited to the amount of your coverage minus a deductible. If the cost of repairing your car exceeds 75 to 80 percent of its retail value, then your insurance company may decide to "total" your car and pay you for its market value.

Collision coverage and comprehensive coverage are optional, although if you lease your car or have an auto loan, the leasing company or lender may require you to carry a minimum amount of coverage. You may want to consider going without collision and/or comprehensive coverage if you have the option and your car is old.

 Here is Howard's rule of thumb for collision and comprehensive coverage: If the cost of annual premiums for collision and comprehensive coverage exceed 10 percent of the value of your car, don't carry the coverage.[31]

Saving Money on Auto Insurance

The gurus offer a range of ideas concerning how you can reduce the cost of your auto insurance. Here are some of the most popular.[32]

- **Ask for a safe driver discount:** You may be entitled to a discount if you have a clean driving record.
- **Ask for an age/marital discount:** Single women and married men can usually get a discount at age 25; single men at age 30. Also, married women may be able to get a discount regardless of their age.
- **Ask for a good student discount:** If you are in college, you may be able to get a discount if you have a high grade point average and/or are on the dean's list. Teen drivers may also be able to get discounts for being a good student.
- **Ask for a safety equipment discount:** You may be eligible for a discount if your car has air bags, antilock brakes, theft alarm, and/or other safety and security equipment.
- **Insure with one company:** If you have several vehicles, you may be able to save some money by insuring them all with the same company.
- **Avoid making a lot of small claims:** Clark Howard notes that most insurance companies will not only raise your rates but may cancel your policy if you make a lot of claims.[33] Therefore, if a claim isn't much more than your deductible, pay the difference yourself.
- **Shop around:** Howard says you should definitely shop around when buying auto insurance; the difference in price between two companies for the same level of coverage on the same driver can be enormous.
- **Buy through a warehouse club:** Our gurus recommend that if you are a member of a warehouse club such as Sam's Club or Costco, you should check to see if they offer auto insurance.
- **Pay your premium annually rather than monthly or semiannually:** Paying less often usually correlates to paying less money.
- **Drive a cheaper and less "faddish" car:** Check with your agent about rates on different makes and models. For a full list of the top 10 most and least expensive cars to insure, go to http://www.insure.com/auto/mostexpensive.html and http://www.insure.com/auto/leastexpensive.html.
- **Keep your mileage low:** The insurance companies look at it this way. The fewer miles you drive, the less chance you have of getting into an accident.
- **Don't let your teen drive:** This may not be possible, so let your teen drive, but do the following:
  - ☐ Send your teen to driver's education.
  - ☐ Make a deal that to be allowed to drive, your teen needs to make good grades to qualify for a good student discount.
  - ☐ Have your teen drive the oldest and least-expensive car, as long as it is safe.

☐ Don't buy your teen his or her own car, and especially not a make and model that appears on the "10 most expensive to insure" list.

☐ If your teen is not going to drive the car to school every day, see if your insurance company will let you list him or her as an "occasional" driver.

KEY POINTS

☛ Buy insurance to protect your money against general risks, not specific events.

☛ Take as high a deductible as you can afford.

☛ Always check the financial strength of an insurance company BEFORE you take out a policy.

☛ Get quotes from at least three different insurance companies.

☛ Life insurance is "earnings-replacement insurance." You need it only if someone is dependent upon your income.

☛ Term life insurance is usually the best deal for most people who need life insurance.

☛ You need disability insurance if you have no one to support you in the event that you can't work.

☛ Your chances of becoming disabled for 90 days or more sometime before the age of 65 are at least one in eight.

☛ Worker's compensation and Social Security are not enough to cover the needs of most people should they become disabled.

☛ The following are the key things to consider in selecting a health plan:
- The amount of the premiums
- The amount of the deductible
- The lifetime cap
- The annual limits
- The services NOT covered
- The cost of choice of doctors and/or treatment facilities
- The gender costs

☛ If you are in a managed care plan such as an HMO, make sure that the doctor you are seeing and/or the hospital or treatment facility you are going to is in your plan; otherwise, you may be subject to a large bill.

☛ Take steps to reduce the cost of prescription drugs.

- The chances of your needing long-term care are one in three, and one in two if you are over age 65.

- Medicare and Medicaid do not provide adequate long-term care insurance coverage for most people.

- You should spend no more than 5 percent of your income on long-term care insurance.

- The only right way to determine how much homeowner's insurance coverage you need is to multiply the square footage of your house by the construction cost per square foot in your area.

- Consider umbrella liability coverage and whether you need earthquake or flood insurance.

- Read your policy carefully for factual errors that might increase the premium.

- Purchase your home, auto, life, and liability coverage from the same company to get a discount.

- Pay annually and look for group coverage.

- Make a complete inventory of your possessions and/or take a video of your house and belongings.

- The most important thing you should know about auto insurance is that you should carry it.

- Auto insurance is a bundle of four different types of protections: liability insurance, medical and/or personal injury protection, collision coverage, and comprehensive coverage.

- Gurus generally recommend that you carry 100/300/50 liability coverage.

Nancy Castleman, coauthor *Slash Your Debt*

Amy Dacyczyn, author of *The Complete Tightwad Gazette*

Gerri Detweiler, coauthor of *Slash Your Debt*

Marc Eisenson, coauthor of *Slash Your Debt*

Ron Gallen, author of *The Money Trap*

Neale S. Godfrey, author of *Making Change*

Bob Hammond, author of *Life after Debt*

Clark Howard, author of *Get Clark Smart*

Mary Hunt, author of *Mary Hunt's Debt-Proof Living*

Azriela Jaffe, coauthor of *The Complete Idiot's Guide to Beating Debt*

Mike Kidwell, coauthor of *Get Out of Debt*

Deborah Knuckey, author of *The Ms. Spent Money Guide*

Nancy Lloyd, author of *Simple Money Solutions*

Mark Miller, author of *The Complete Idiot's Guide to Being a Cheapskate*

Edward Mrkvicka, author of *Your Bank Is Ripping You Off*

Stephen Nelson, author of *The Millionaire Kit*

Suze Orman, author of *The 9 Steps to Financial Freedom*

Greg Pahl, author of *The Unofficial Guide to Beating Debt*

Jonathan Pond, author of *Your Money Matters*

Jane Bryant Quinn, author of *Making the Most of Your Money*

Dave Ramsey, author of *Financial Peace*

Steve Rhode, coauthor of *Get Out of Debt*

Steven Strauss, coauthor of *The Complete Idiot's Guide to Beating Debt*

Howard Strong, author of *What Every Credit Card User Needs to Know*

Eric Tyson, author of *Personal Finance for Dummies*

6

Debt and Credit

Deborah Knuckey considers "debt" to be one of those four-letter words your mother never warned you about.[1] Debt was once treated as a social secret that you didn't discuss even with your closest friends. You could even be imprisoned for being a debtor. Now we are all debtors, and people can get credit before they are old enough to drive.

DEALING WITH DEBT

In this section, we examine what our gurus have to say about the subject of debt. First, let's deal with the general issue of the merits of debt. Is all debt bad?

Good Debt and Bad Debt

The gurus admit that some types of debt are bad, but they consider other types good, or at least acceptable. Here is how you can tell the difference, according to

Good Debt	Bad Debt
■ Allows you to achieve a worthwhile goal you might not otherwise be able to achieve, such as starting a business or or going to college	■ Is debt incurred for things you don't really need and/or that you will quickly consume, such as clothes, meals, vacations, and so on
■ Enriches your life	■ Causes stress
■ Is manageable	■ Seems impossible to pay back
■ Is not a burden to you	■ Causes fights between you and those you love
	■ Makes you feel guilty

Steven Strauss and Azriela Jaffe, coauthors of *The Complete Idiot's Guide to Beating Debt*.[2]

Eric Tyson defines bad debt as debt incurred for consumption—going into debt to buy something that will quickly be used up, such as a vacation or food—or for something that will go down in value, such as a car or clothes. On the other hand, he defines good debt as debt incurred in order to make an investment—borrowing money to attend college or to start a business.[3]

The Signs of Too Much Debt

How do you know if you have taken on too much debt, particularly too much bad debt? Our gurus answer this question in two different ways. First, they ask you to calculate your current outstanding debt as a percentage of your income and/or assets and compare your answer to some rule-of-thumb limits. Second, they ask a series of questions about your behavior when it comes to debt. The pattern of your answers may reveal problems. Let's look at each of these methods.

EXHIBIT 6.1 **Your Current Ratio**

A more accurate way to assess your level of indebtedness, according to Greg Pahl, is to calculate your current ratio:

$$\text{assets} \div \text{liabilities} = \text{current ratio}$$

For example, if your assets are valued at \$60,000 and your liabilities total \$35,000, then the calculation of your current ratio would look like this:

$$\$60,000 \div \$35,000 = 0.58 \text{ (or 58 percent)}$$

(See Chapter 2 of the present work for information on how to determine your assets and liabilities.)

Pahl interprets the results of these calculations as follows:

30 percent or less	You're in good shape.
30 to 50 percent	You're okay, but you should be starting to pay off some of your debt to reduce your ratio if it is starting to approach 50 percent.
50 to 100 percent	You are carrying too much debt and definitely should start reducing it.
Over 100 percent	You are in serious trouble.

Source: Greg Pahl, The Unofficial Guide to Beating Debt *(Foster City, CA: IDG Books Worldwide, 2000), pp. 172–175.*

Pahl notes that an alternative method for determining if you have too much debt is to calculate the current ratio that compares your debt to your assets. See Exhibit 6.1.

Percentage-of-Income Method

One way to determine if you are carrying too much debt, say our gurus, is to calculate what percentage your current debt is of your current net income.

(monthly debt payments ÷ net monthly income) × 100 = debt as percent of income

For example, assume that you have monthly debt payments of $400 and your net monthly income is $1,600. The calculation would look like this:

($400 ÷ $1,600) × 100 = 25 percent of income

Here is how Greg Pahl, author of *The Unofficial Guide to Beating Debt,* evaluates the results for this calculation.[4]

Less than 10 percent:	You're in good shape.
10 to 20 percent:	Still okay, but be careful about taking on any more debt.

Pahl says if you are single, middle-aged, and have a good income, 20 percent is probably okay. If you are married and in a two-income family, then 20 percent is okay unless you have children (your debt shouldn't exceed 15 percent of your combined income). If you are retired and on a fixed income, Pahl recommends that you keep your debt to 10 percent or less of your net income.

20 to 35 percent	No serious danger but you should be trying to get your debt down to 20 percent or less.
35 to 50 percent	You definitely need to reduce your indebtedness, particularly if your future employment is uncertain or you are about to have some major new expenses such as college tuition or the birth of a child.
Over 50 percent	You definitely have a problem with debt.

Behavior Method

Another way to determine if you have a problem with debt is to examine your behavior. Many of our gurus provide quizzes or self-tests to determine if you are in trouble with debt or are about to find yourself in trouble with debt. Exercise 6.1 is an example of such a quiz that Pahl loosely based on a list originally published by the Money Management Institute.

EXERCISE 6.1. **The Debt Test**

Instructions: Answer YES or NO to the following questions.

- Are you spending increasing amounts of your income to pay your bills?
- Do you put off paying your bills because you don't have enough money to cover them? Are you at or over the limit on your credit accounts?
- Have you been turned down for credit purchases because you're over the limit?
- Are you taking 60 or 90 days to pay your bills when you used to pay them in 30?
- Are you frequently making only minimum payments on your bills?
- Are you chronically late in paying your bills, including your mortgage or rent?
- Are you routinely paying late penalties on your bills?
- Are you constantly juggling your bills every month?
- Are you paying your bills with money that was supposed to go for something else?
- Are you using your credit cards to pay for normal living expenses?
- Are you paying half of your bills one month and half the next?
- Are your current savings low or nonexistent?
- If you lost your job, would you be in immediate financial difficulty?
- Are you paying off one loan with another one?
- Have any of your credit cards been canceled by the issuer because you have been consistently late or over your limit?
- Have you had to cancel your auto, medical, or life insurance because you can't afford the premiums?
- Are you getting letters, phone calls, or collection notices from your creditors regarding late payments or unpaid bills?
- Are you working overtime or moonlighting in order to pay your bills?
- Have your utilities been shut off, or have you received shut-off notices?
- Are you repeatedly overdrawn at the bank?
- Are you living beyond your means?
- Are you frequently writing bad checks?
- Do you worry a lot about money?
- Do you and your spouse argue about money problems?
- Are you afraid that someone might find out how far in debt you are?

Source: Greg Pahl, The Unofficial Guide to Beating Debt (Foster City, CA: IDG Books Worldwide, 2000), pp. 167–169.

You can score your answers to the questions in Exercise 6.1 as follows:

- **NO to all of the questions:** You are probably in good shape.
- **YES to one or a few of the questions:** You may or may not have a debt problem depending on your particular circumstances. For example, Pahl says that "if you've just gone through a divorce or had to pay for expensive medical bills, the fact that you are temporarily behind may not be too serious in the long run. But, if you are drawing down your savings to make minimum monthly payments on all of your credit card bills, then the alarm bells should be ringing loud and clear."[5]
- **YES to many or most of these questions:** You definitely have a problem with debt and should get help.

Rapid Debt Reduction

Let's assume that you answered YES to more of the questions in the debt quiz than you would have liked and that your debt-to-income percentage places you in the debt danger zone. What can you do about it? Almost all of our gurus advocate some version of the following rapid debt reduction plan.

Step #1: No More Debt

You must make a strong personal commitment not to take on any more debt. You *must not* take out a loan to buy a new car. You *must not* borrow against your home equity to remodel your kitchen. Most important, you *must stop* using credit cards except in an absolute emergency, and preferably not even then.

STOP BORROWING AND PAY CASH!

Step #2: List All of Your Debts in Order by Interest Rate

Next, you want to build a table showing all of your current outstanding debts with the balance you owe on them, the interest rate you are being charged, the number of months left to pay, and the monthly payment you are making. For the monthly payment for credit cards, use the minimum monthly payment for the current month. Your table will look something like the one shown in Exhibit 6.2.

To calculate the number of months it will take to pay off your credit card debt, go to the following Web page at bankrate.com: http://www.bankrate.com/brm/calc/MinPayment.asp?nav=cc&page=calc_home/.

EXHIBIT 6.2. Sample Debt Table

	Dept. Store	MasterCard	Visa	Student Loan	Auto	Home Mortgage	Total
Balance	$2,500	$3,500	$5,000	$6,000	$20,000	$200,000	$237,000.00
Interest Rate	14.00%	10.75%	10.74%	8.25%	7.40%	6.00%	
Months to Pay	24	178	200	120	36	360	
Monthly Payment	$120.00	$87.50	$125.00	$50.00	$621.21	$1,199.10	$2,202.81

Step #3: Add an Extra Payment to the Debt with the Highest Interest Rate

Decide how much you can afford to add to the minimum amounts you have been paying on your debt. See Chapter 4 for help in finding the extra money. Let's say you can add $100 per month. Add $100 to your payment on the debt carrying the *highest* interest rate. In our example, you would pay $220 toward the department store debt versus the current $120 because the department store is charging the highest interest rate.

By paying an extra $100 per month, you will pay off the department store loan in about half the time you would have otherwise. Once that debt is paid off, you have $220 to add to your payment on the debt with the *next highest* interest rate. In the sample, you would begin paying $370 toward the MasterCard payment rather than $87.50 ($87.50 + $220). When you pay off the MasterCard debt, you then have $370 to add to your payment on the debt with the *next highest* interest rate— in this case the Visa debt. Continue this process with the Visa debt, the student loan, and so on. Notice that the total amount you are paying each month remains the same. Also, notice in Exhibit 6.3 that each time you pay off a debt you have a *higher* amount to use to pay off the next debt, so it gets paid off faster.

Our gurus swear that this rapid debt pay-off plan works. However, some disagree on which debts you should pay off first. In our example, we instructed you to arrange your debts in order by interest rate and to pay off your debts with the highest interest rate first. That's what Bob Hammond, Suze Orman, and a number of other gurus recommend.[6] The obvious reason these gurus suggest you focus on the highest interest debt first is that you are paying the most for that debt. However, several other gurus, including Dave Ramsey, Mark Miller, and Mary Hunt, think that you should pay off debts with the *lowest balance* or *shortest pay-off time* first.[7] They reason that by doing so, you will be eliminating debts faster, get a heightened sense of accomplishment, and thus be more motivated to stick with the pay-off plan.

PROS AND CONS OF HOME EQUITY LOANS

As we noted, almost all of our gurus swear by some form of the rapid debt reduction method. But even that method takes time, and perhaps rapid debt reduction isn't rapid enough for you. You want to get out of debt now! Well, don't worry. Look in any paper, go online, or turn on your TV set, and you will be bombarded with offers from friendly people just waiting to help you get out of debt.

All you have to do is put up your home as collateral. Mortgage lenders love these loans because they are big money makers that carry little risk. They call them HELs for home equity loans. Amy Dacyczyn, author of *The Complete Tightwad Gazette,* says she thinks the lenders' acronym is missing an "L."[8] Indeed, almost all of our gurus dislike HEL[L]s because they consider them just too risky for most people. Mary Hunt calls home equity loans "semi-stupid debt." They start out sounding intelligent. They end up making you feel stupid.[9]

EXHIBIT 6.3 **Rapid Debt Reduction**

	Dept. Store	Master Card	Visa	Student Loan	Auto	Mortgage	Home Total
Balance	$2,500	$3,500	$5,000	$6,000	$20,000	$200,000	$237,000.00
Interest Rate	14.00%	10.75%	10.74%	8.25%	7.40%	6.00%	
Months to Pay	24	178	200	120	36	360	
Monthly Payment	$120.00	$87.50	$125.00	$50.00	$621.21	$1,199.10	$2,202.81
Month							
1	$220.00	$ 87.50	$125.00	$ 50.00	$621.21	$1,199.10	$2,302.81
2	$220.00	$ 87.50	$125.00	$ 50.00	$621.21	$1,199.10	$2,302.81
3	$220.00	$ 87.50	$125.00	$ 50.00	$621.21	$1,199.10	$2,302.81
4	$220.00	$ 87.50	$125.00	$ 50.00	$621.21	$1,199.10	$2,302.81
5	$220.00	$ 87.50	$125.00	$ 50.00	$621.21	$1,199.10	$2,302.81
6	$220.00	$ 87.50	$125.00	$ 50.00	$621.21	$1,199.10	$2,302.81
7	$220.00	$ 87.50	$125.00	$ 50.00	$621.21	$1,199.10	$2,302.81
8	$220.00	$ 87.50	$125.00	$ 50.00	$621.21	$1,199.10	$2,302.81
9	$220.00	$ 87.50	$125.00	$ 50.00	$621.21	$1,199.10	$2,302.81
10	$220.00	$ 87.50	$125.00	$ 50.00	$621.21	$1,199.10	$2,302.81
11	$220.00	$ 87.50	$125.00	$ 50.00	$621.21	$1,199.10	$2,302.81
12	$ 80.00	$227.50	$125.00	$ 50.00	$621.21	$1,199.10	$2,302.81
13	0	$307.50	$125.00	$ 50.00	$621.21	$1,199.10	$2,302.81
14	0	$307.50	$125.00	$ 50.00	$621.21	$1,199.10	$2,302.81
15	0	$307.50	$125.00	$ 50.00	$621.21	$1,199.10	$2,302.81

(continued)

EXHIBIT 6.3 (continued)

16	0	$307.50	$125.00	$ 50.00	$621.21	$1,199.10	$2,302.81
17	0	$307.50	$125.00	$ 50.00	$621.21	$1,199.10	$2,302.81
18	0	$307.50	$125.00	$ 50.00	$621.21	$1,199.10	$2,302.81
19	0	$307.50	$125.00	$ 50.00	$621.21	$1,199.10	$2,302.81
20	0	$307.50	$125.00	$ 50.00	$621.21	$1,199.10	$2,302.81
21	0	$307.50	$125.00	$ 50.00	$621.21	$1,199.10	$2,302.81
22	0	0	$432.50	$ 50.00	$621.21	$1,199.10	$2,302.81
23	0	0	$432.50	$ 50.00	$621.21	$1,199.10	$2,302.81
24	0	0	$432.50	$ 50.00	$621.21	$1,199.10	$2,302.81
25	0	0	$432.50	$ 50.00	$621.21	$1,199.10	$2,302.81
26	0	0	$432.50	$ 50.00	$621.21	$1,199.10	$2,302.81
27	0	0	$432.50	$ 50.00	$621.21	$1,199.10	$2,302.81
28	0	0	$432.50	$ 50.00	$621.21	$1,199.10	$2,302.81
29	0	0	$432.50	$ 50.00	$621.21	$1,199.10	$2,302.81
30	0	0	$432.50	$ 50.00	$621.21	$1,199.10	$2,302.81
31	0	0	0	$482.50	$621.21	$1,199.10	$2,302.81
32	0	0	0	$482.50	$621.21	$1,199.10	$2,302.81
41	0	0	0	0	0	$1,199.10	$2,302.81

Home equity loans come in two varieties. They can be straight fixed-rate loans. You put up the equity in your house (value of your house minus what you owe), and the lender gives you cash to use to pay off debt, remodel your home, buy a car, and so on. You get the cash in a lump sum and promise to pay it back at a fixed interest rate typically over 5 to 15 years.

The second variety of home equity loan is the home equity line of credit (HELOC). HELOCs are adjustable-rate loans (see our discussion of such loans in Chapter 7), meaning that the amount of the interest rate you pay varies over the life of the loan. They work much like credit cards. You have a limit on what you can withdraw over the life of the loan, but you don't have to take the whole amount all at once. You access your HELOC by writing a check or using a special credit or debit card.

The Advantages of Home Equity Loans

The following are the advantages of home equity loans as touted by lenders and accepted by our gurus.

HEL[L] Advantage #1: You swap high-interest debt for low-interest debt

Interest rates for home equity loans are usually higher than interest rates for first mortgages, but they are usually significantly cheaper than credit card interest rates.

HEL[L] Advantage #2: You may get a tax deduction for the interest you pay

The interest you pay on credit cards isn't deductible, but the interest you pay on a home equity loan *may be*. (Ask your accountant.)

HEL[L] Advantage #3: You painlessly and instantly get out of debt

Unlike the rapid pay-off plan we discussed earlier, you don't have to work months or years to pay off the debt you have accumulated.

The Disadvantages of Home Equity Loans

Our gurus say that HEL[L]s are fraught with disadvantages that make them highly risky for most people.

HEL[L] Disadvantage #1: Most people with home equity loans stretch out their payments over a long period

As Stephen Nelson, author of *The Millionaire Kit,* notes, one of the reasons you get a lower interest rate for a home equity loan than for other loans is that the home equity loan is secured by collateral (your home) that can be expected to last a long time; therefore, the lender feels safe in letting you pay back the loan over an extended period.[10] Most people with home equity loans take out a loan for 5, 10, or 15 years and take that long to pay off the money they borrowed for the clothes they are wearing, the vacation they took last year, or the car they bought two years ago. They get nice low payments and an easy payment schedule.

It sounds great except for one problem. As Nelson cautions, it violates a cardinal rule of borrowing money:

Always pay for an item before it wears out.

HEL[L] Disadvantage #2: The HEL[L] tax deduction may be of little or no value to you

Gerri Detweiler, Marc Eisenson, and Nancy Castleman say that the home equity tax deduction may or may not be of any benefit to you.[11] First, they note, if you don't itemize deductions, the ability to deduct HEL[L] interest has no value to you, and the standard deduction is now so high that most people don't have enough deductions to itemize. Second, even if you itemize, you may not be able to deduct the full amount of interest you pay on your home equity loan because of Internal Revenue Service limits. (See the document "IRS Rules on the tax deduction for home equity loan interest" at http://www.irs.gov/formspubs/page/O,,id=12832,00.html/ for an explanation.)

HEL[L] Disadvantage #3: Many people just go on borrowing

A major disadvantage of home equity loans for many people is that they don't solve the problem of overspending. Ron Gallen, author of *The Money Trap,* notes that although many people use home equity loans to pay off credit card debt and then swear they will never get back in trouble with debt again, studies show that only 30 percent of home equity borrowers are still free of credit card debt 11 months after they take out their HEL[L]; 70 percent are right back at it.[12]

> Pond's Law of Home Equity Credit Lines
> Heretofore unrecognized opportunities to spend large sums of money will become immediately apparent after you open a home equity credit line.
>
> *Jonathan Pond[13]*

HEL[L] Disadvantage #4: You could lose your home

When you take out a home equity loan, you bet your house on your ability to pay the loan back plus interest and any fees the lender might charge. Miss a payment and you will be threatened with foreclosure. Miss too many payments and you will *lose your home*.

> If you use your home as a short-term piggy bank, you damage your future.
>
> *Clark Howard[14]*

SELECTING THE BEST CREDIT CARD FOR YOU

Jonathan Pond calls them "public enemy number one."[15] Clark Howard says that if you've caught the debt disease and are considering a risky home equity loan as a cure, they are most likely what caused your illness. Of course, we are talking about . . .

FIGURE 6.1

You probably have several credit cards in your purse or wallet. If you are like most Americans, you owe the financial institutions that supplied you with these cards more than $7,000, and you pay them $1,000 or more in interest and fees each year. Some of you owe a lot more—as Clark Howard reports, some Americans have credit card balances that exceed $20,000.[16] In fact, he says, some people owe more on their credit cards than they make in an entire year, and the abuse of credit cards is a major cause of personal bankruptcy. To make matters worse, most people know very little about those little pieces of plastic they use almost every day. How much do you know? Take the credit card quiz (see Exercise 6.2).

EXERCISE 6.2. **Credit Card Savvy**

Instructions: Answer the following True or False.

1. The interest rate on a fixed-rate credit card can never change.
2. You are not liable for charges on your credit card if it is stolen or used without your authorization.
3. Accepting all of the preapproved credit cards you are offered helps your credit rating.
4. If you are only one day late with your payment, your credit card issuer may assess a large late payment fee, raise your interest rate, and/or cancel your card.
5. If you accept a "preapproved" credit card offer with a high credit limit and a low interest rate, you may get a card with a low credit limit and a high interest rate.
6. If you take a cash advance on a credit card that charges 13 percent interest for purchases, you may be charged 40 percent or more in interest and fees.
7. Paying for merchandise with a credit card "convenience check" (which bills the check amount to your credit card) is the same as paying with a credit card.
8. If you accept your card issuer's offer to "skip a payment," you won't owe finance charges for the month you skip.
9. If you carry a balance on your card, you will pay less in finance charges if you make your payments early in the month.
10. If your credit card is tied to your home's equity and you miss payments, the bank can foreclose on your home.

Sources: Questions 1–3 were adapted from Neale S. Godfrey, Making Change: A Woman's Guide to Designing Her Financial Future (New York: Simon & Schuster, 1997), pp. 102–103; questions 4–10 were adapted from Nancy Lloyd, Simple Money Solutions: 10 Ways You Can Stop Feeling Overwhelmed by Money and Start Making It Work for You (New York: Times Business, 2000), pp. 46–49.

The Credit Card Quiz

Here are the answers to the questions in Exercise 6.2:

1. *False.* Your card issuer can change the interest rate with as little as 15 days' notice.
2. *False.* You are liable for $50 unless the card is a debit card; then you can be liable for the full amount.
3. *False.* Having a lot of cards, even if you never use some of them, hurts your credit rating because lenders look at your total available credit and not just the credit you actually use. If you have a lot of cards, you will appear to be overextended even if many of those cards have low or no balances on them.
4. *True.* Any of these are possible. The only way to know is to read the fine print on the insert that comes with your bill. Also, be aware that the card issuer can change the fees, terms, and conditions with as little as 15 days' notice.

5. *True*. Lloyd points out that many of the unsolicited offers you may get for low-interest/high-balance cards are bait-and-switch come-ons. Lloyd says that if you apply for one of these preapproved cards and don't get what you were promised, cut up the card and call the card issuer to close the account.[17]

6. *True*. You typically pay a higher interest rate for a cash advance than you do for purchases you make directly with the card. You also may be assessed a fee for the cash advance, and you will be charged interest from the date of the advance even if your account is paid in full. Our gurus warn that cash advances are almost always a bad idea.

7. *False*. Convenience checks are a big convenience to the card issuer because they make more money from them. If you use a convenience check, you may be charged a substantial fee for the privilege of using the check, pay a higher interest rate than you would if you simply charged your purchase, and lose your rights to other benefits, such as extended warranties, protection against defective merchandise, and so on, that are automatic when you use your card.

8. *False*. You will still pay a finance charge. Also, Lloyd says these skip-a-payment offers are most often sent to customers who pay their balances in full every month. It's the card issuer's way of tricking you into carrying a balance in order to hit you with a finance charge.

9. *True*. If the finance charge on your card is calculated using the average-daily-balance method, then you save money by making your payment early in the month, thereby reducing your average daily balance.

10. *True*. That's just another danger of home equity lines of credit.

So, how did you do? The gurus predict that you got many of these answers wrong. Most of us know very little about the fees, terms, conditions, restrictions, and so on that are written in legalese and appear in small print on the little flimsy inserts credit card issuers send us. Read on for the truth about credit cards.

Selecting a Credit Card That's Right for You

Here are the things our gurus say you need to know in order to compare credit card offers and select the card that is right for you.

Much of the information that you need to answer these questions must be provided to you by law and can be found in what is called the Schumer Box, which you can usually find on the back of the credit card application and/or your monthly statement.

Is There an Annual Fee?

When we checked the Web site Bankrate.com in the fall of 2002, card issuers were offering cards with an annual fee ranging from $0 to as much as $98. Other things being equal, our gurus say you obviously want a card with no annual fee.

Are There Other Fees?

The answer to the question of whether there are other fees is always YES. The following are some of the possibilities in addition to annual fees:

- Account closing fee
- Balance transfer fee
- Cash advance fee
- Declined check fee
- Fees for paying all your charges each month
- Copying fee
- Finance fee
- Inactivity fee
- Late payment fee
- Maintenance fee
- Overlimit fee
- Research fee
- Stop-payment fee

What Is the Grace Period?

The grace period is that amount of time you have between the time you purchase an item on the credit card and the time the card issuer starts charging you interest. When we checked in the fall of 2002, most card issuers were allowing a 25-day grace period; however, some offered only 20 days, and a few offered no days at all (i.e., you pay interest from the date of purchase). Our gurus say you want the longest grace period you can find.

What Are the Fees and Interest Rate for Cash Advances?

In addition to charging you a fee for cash advances (perhaps as a percentage of the amount of the cash advance), many card issuers charge a higher interest rate on cash advances than they do for purchases made directly on the card. Howard Strong says you should also inquire about how a cash advance effects your grace period. Typically, you have no grace period for a cash advance, but Strong cautions that some card issuers go further than that[18]—they eliminate your grace period entirely for all your charges during any month in which you have a cash advance. You want a low or no fee for cash advances, the same or a low-interest rate on cash advances as on direct charges, and you don't want to lose your grace period.

Are You Penalized for NOT Carrying a Balance?

All card issuers want you to carry a balance. When you don't carry a balance, credit card companies make less money and may punish you by charging you a fee. Don't do business with such companies.

How Is the Outstanding Balance Calculated?

This may be the most important question of all because its answer makes a major difference in how much the credit card costs you. Credit card companies use at least six different ways to calculate outstanding balance, and the method they choose makes a significant difference in the finance charge you pay. The six most common methods are the following:

Average daily balance method including new purchases. The balance is the sum of the outstanding balances for every day in the billing cycle (including new purchases and deducting payments and credits) divided by the number of days in the billing cycle.

Average daily balance method excluding new purchases. The balance is the sum of the outstanding balances for every day in the billing cycle (excluding new purchases and deducting payments and credits) divided by the number of days in the billing cycle.

Two-cycle average daily balance method including new purchases. The balance is the sum of the average daily balances for two consecutive billing cycles. One daily balance, that for the current billing cycle, is calculated by summing the outstanding balances for every day in the billing cycle (including new purchases and deducting payments and credits) and dividing that total by the number of days in the billing cycle. The other daily balance is that from the preceding billing cycle.

Two-cycle average daily balance method excluding new purchases. The balance is the sum of the average daily balances for two consecutive billing cycles. One daily balance, that for the current billing cycle, is calculated by summing the outstanding balances for every day in the billing cycle (excluding new purchases and deducting payments and credits) and dividing that total by the number of days in the billing cycle. The other daily balance is that from the preceding billing cycle.

Adjusted balance method. The balance is the outstanding balance at the beginning of the billing cycle minus payments and credits made during the billing cycle.

Previous balance method. The balance is the outstanding balance at the beginning of the billing cycle.[19]

Try to avoid any card issuers who use either of the two-cycle average-daily-balance methods because these methods generally produce the highest finance charges. Look instead for companies that use the average-daily-balance method, excluding new purchases, or the average-daily-balance method, including new purchases. Also, the adjusted balance and previous balance methods might generate lower finance charges depending on the kind of balance you carry and when in the month you make purchases and payments.

What Is the Interest Rate You Charge for Direct Purchases, Cash Advances, and Convenience Checks? Are These Rates Fixed or Variable?

Once you know the method a card issuer uses to calculate your outstanding balance, you then need to know the interest rate you will be charged on that balance. This is normally expressed as the periodic rate, which is the annual percentage rate (APR) divided by 12. Thus, an APR of 12 percent has a periodic rate of 1 percent (12 percent $\div 12 = 1$).

Chances are that the card provider will charge different rates for cash advances and convenience checks than for direct purchases, so check these rates closely if you think you will ever take cash advances or use the checks the card provider will undoubtedly be sending you.

Also ask if the rates you are being quoted are fixed or variable. If the rates are variable, you will want to find out how often the rate is subject to change and the index to which it is tied.

Finally, ask if the card company charges any penalty rates. For example, some companies significantly increase the interest they charge if you are late in making your payments twice in any six-month period.

The Financial Death Card?

Our gurus warn you to be very careful how you use all types of credit cards, but there is one type of card they say you should approach with extreme caution. Howard Strong dislikes this particular type of card so much, he calls them "Financial Death Cards."[20] Strong is referring to what the industry calls debit cards, and there is a strong possibility that you have one in your wallet whether you know it or not. Banks and merchants have been pushing these cards for very good reasons. First, says Mary Hunt, it costs banks five times more to process a check than to handle your debit card transaction.[21] Second, Hunt explains that merchants are very willing to pay the banks' fees when you use your debit card because they know something you probably don't realize—most studies indicate that shoppers will spend more with a debit or credit card than they will paying with a check or cash.

Types of Debit Cards

There are two types of debit cards:

- **Online debit cards:** Also called ATM cards, these cards let you withdraw funds from an ATM. When you use your card, the funds are immediately withdrawn from your account.
- **Offline debit cards:** These look like credit cards, even carrying the Visa® or MasterCard® logo, but they function like ATM cards. You can use an offline debit card to withdraw funds from an ATM machine, but you can also use it like a credit card to buy merchandise or services from many merchants. Unlike a credit card, however, funds are usually withdrawn directly from your bank account, within two to three days of your purchase.

Some of our gurus dislike both types of debit cards. Most are extremely cautious about the second. In this section, we will talk primarily about the offline debit card because it raises the most concerns from our gurus.

The Advantages and Disadvantages of Debit Cards

Exhibit 6.4 is a compilation of the pros and cons of offline debit cards according to several of our gurus.

Caution!!! The Major Disadvantage of a Debit Card

There is one other major disadvantage to a debit card that all gurus point out. Here is how Howard Strong explains it:

> If your Financial Death Card [i.e., debit card] is stolen or lost, the thief can take all the money you have in the bank. Unless you act right away, there may be no way of getting it back from the bank, even if the bank knew that a thief and not you was getting money. . . .
>
> With a Financial Death Card, a crook can take all the money in your bank accounts and then get into your over-draft and other line-of-credit accounts. The thief can use his access to those accounts to drive you thousands and thousands of dollars in debt. Again, some protections do exist, but the burden is on you to act quickly.[22]

You might ask how these terrible things could happen. After all, your bank assured you that you were protected. Well, they are possible because of a difference in your legal rights when you use a credit card versus a debit card. Here is a description of those rights as provided by the Federal Trade Commission. Read it carefully:

EXHIBIT 6.4. **Pros and Cons of Debit Cards**

PROS

CONS

PROS

- Debit cards are easier to obtain than credit cards.
- You don't need to carry as much cash or write checks.
- You don't need to carry traveler's checks when you travel.
- Merchants will accept your debit card when they wouldn't accept your personal check.
- Debit cards provide an alternative form of plastic if you are swearing off credit cards.
- You don't run the risk of running up balances and having to pay interest like you would with a credit card.
- You can't spend any more money than you have in the bank.

CONS

- You lose any float or grace period that you might have had if you used a credit card or wrote a check.
- Using a debit card does not help you improve your credit rating like a credit card does.
- You may be charged a fee per transaction that you wouldn't be charged if you wrote a check or used a credit card.
- You could find yourself having to pay hefty fees and high interest rates if you accept the overdraft protection that many banks offer with these cards. Overdraft protection gives you a draw against a line of credit. If you happen to overdraw your account, the bank uses the line of credit to cover your overdraft. The problem, says Mary Hunt, is that they transfer funds in increments of, for example, $100. Thus, you "borrow" $100 even if your overdraft is only $1. You are hit with interest charges on the entire $100, not just the $1 you needed.
- If the wrong amount is deducted from your account, even because of some innocent error, you will have to fight with the bank to get the money put back in your account. If you bounce a check because of the error, the bank may take no responsibility.
- If you use a debit card to rent a car, pay for or reserve a hotel room, and/or buy gas, the company you are doing business with may put a hold on your account for hundreds of dollars until your account is settled, which could take a week or more.
- Typically, when you use a credit card and are dissatisfied with the product or services you purchased, you can dispute the charge, and the card issuer will reverse the charge and work with you and the merchant to get the matter resolved. You may have no such purchase protection if you use a debit card.

Sources: Adapted from Clark Howard, Get Clark Smart: The Ultimate Guide for the Savvy Consumer (Atlanta, GA: Longstreet Press, 2000), pp. 68–69; Mary Hunt, Mary Hunt's Debt-Proof Living (Nashville, TN: Broadman & Holman, 1999), pp. 216–217; Edward F. Mrkvicka, Your Bank Is Ripping You Off, (New York: St. Martin's Griffin, 1999), p. 175; Greg Pahl, The Unofficial Guide to Beating Debt (Foster City, CA: IDG Books Worldwide, 2000), p. 51; Jane Bryant Quinn, Making the Most of Your Money (New York: Simon & Schuster, 1997), pp. 225–226; and Steve Rhode and Mike Kidwell, Get Out of Debt: Smart Solutions to Your Money Problems (Rockville, MD: Debt Counselors of America, 1999), p. 71.

Credit Card Loss or Fraudulent Charges: Your maximum liability under federal law for unauthorized use of your credit card is $50. If you report the loss before your credit cards are used, the FCBA [Fair Credit Billing Act] says the card issuer cannot hold you responsible for any unauthorized charges. If a thief uses your cards before you report them missing, the most you will owe for unauthorized charges is $50 per card. Also, if the loss involves your credit card number, but not the card itself, you have no liability for unauthorized use.

ATM or Debit Card Loss or Fraudulent Transfers: Your liability under federal law for unauthorized use of your ATM or debit card depends on how quickly you report the loss. If you report an ATM or debit card missing before it's used without your permission, the EFTA [Electronic Funds Transfer Act] says the card issuer cannot hold you responsible for any unauthorized transfers. If unauthorized use occurs before you report it, your liability under federal law depends on how quickly you report the loss.

For example, if you report the loss within two business days after you realize your card is missing, you will not be responsible for more than $50 for unauthorized use. However, if you don't report the loss within two business days after you discover the loss, you could lose up to $500 because of an unauthorized transfer. You also risk unlimited loss if you fail to report an unauthorized transfer within 60 days after your bank statement containing unauthorized use is mailed to you. That means you could lose all the money in your bank account and the unused portion of your line of credit established for overdrafts. However, for unauthorized transfers involving only your debit card number (not the loss of the card), you are liable only for transfers that occur after 60 days following the mailing of your bank statement containing the unauthorized use and before you report the loss.[23] (Emphasis ours.)

Using Your Debit Card Wisely

If you find that you have no options or if you just like the convenience of a debit card, here are some useful suggestions from Steve Rhode and Mike Kidwell, coauthors of *Get Out of Debt,* on avoiding unpleasant and costly surprises:

1. Budget diligently and know how much money you have in your account. Write all withdrawals into your check register. Reconcile all ATM receipts with bank statements as soon as possible.
2. Memorize your PIN [personal identification number] and don't carry your PIN in your wallet, purse, or keep your PIN near your card. Never use your address, birthday, phone number or social security number as your PIN.

3. Hold onto your receipts from your debit card transactions. A thief may get your name and debit card number from a receipt and order goods by mail or over the telephone.
4. Check your debit card account statements to make sure there are no mistakes. If you lose your card or it is stolen, call your card issuer immediately and follow up the call with a confirmation letter.
5. Avoid using your debit card for specific types of purchases [such as travel] because the money is taken out of your checking account [almost] immediately [and may be hard to recover if your plans change].
6. Think twice before linking your savings account to a checking account with debit card access [because a thief could access and drain both accounts].[24]

Strong goes further with this final suggestion. He recommends that if you are going to have a debit card, you should have it at a bank where you have no other accounts and no loans. Plus, he says, you should keep only a few hundred dollars at most in that account. In Strong's opinion, that's the only way you can fully protect yourself and make sure that a thief can't someday take all of your money.

USING CREDIT CARDS WISELY

Picking the right credit card is important and can save you a great deal of money. However, say our gurus, there is no point picking the right card if you use it foolishly. In fact, most people who end up in financial difficulty get there because of the way they use their credit cards, not because of the cards they pick to use. Here are some tips from Mary Hunt on how to use credit cards wisely.[25]

- **Use only one or two cards:** Hunt recommends that you use only one card and cancel all of the others. Other gurus say it is okay to carry two cards, but not more than that.
- **Understand the terms and conditions:** As Hunt puts it, "Never forget that what the big print giveth the small print taketh away,"[26] so read the big print, small print, and all of the print. Also, examine your statement very carefully each month not only to check the accuracy of your charges but to see if any provisions have been changed. "Scrutinize every square millimeter [of the statement] and question any charge or entry you do not understand."[27]
- **Take control of your credit limit:** Keep your credit limit to no more than $500 to $1,500 per card. At a maximum, you shouldn't accept a credit limit for more than you think you could reasonably repay in one month.
- **Leave home without it:** If you don't have the credit or debit card with you, you won't be able to run up charges.

- **Don't pay late:** If your payment is late getting to the card issuer, you will most likely be hit with late-payment fees in addition to extra interest payments. You are responsible for getting the payment to them on time, and because you are sending the check through the mail to a processing center, many things can delay its arrival. So allow plenty of time for your payment to get there.
- **Pay early:** Although it may cut into your float, paying early in the month can work to your advantage if you carry a balance. First, if you pay early, you're not going to get hit with a late payment fee. More important, if your outstanding balance is calculated using the average daily balance method, you will save considerable money on interest because you reduce your balance for more days during the billing cycle.
- **Don't fall from grace:** Pay attention to the grace period you are allowed, and time your purchases and payments accordingly. Steve Rhode and Mike Kidwell say this is particularly important if you are making a major purchase because your savings on the float can mount up.[28] You can also take advantage of the grace period to extend your protections under the Fair Credit Billing Act (FCBA). The FCBA allows you to withhold payment for damaged or poor-quality goods and services purchased on a credit card, provided the amount in question is over $50 and the purchase occurred in your home state or within 100 miles of your billing address.

For a good summary of other rights and protections you have under federal law, see the Federal Reserve Board's *Consumer Handbook to Credit Protection Laws.* It is available at no cost at http://www.federalreserve.gov/pubs/consumerhdbk/.

EXHIBIT 6.5. Government Agencies to Contact about Credit Card Problems

---

If you have questions about your rights with respect to credit and/or debit cards or problem with a card issuer, you can contact the following agencies:

- Board of Governors of the Federal Reserve System: Regulates state-chartered banks that are members of the Federal Reserve System, bank holding companies, and branches of foreign banks. Contact at:
  Division of Consumer and Community Affairs, Stop 801
  20th and C Streets, NW
  Washington DC 20551
  202-452-3693
  www.federalreserve.gov/
- Federal Deposit Insurance Corporation: Regulates state-chartered banks that are not members of the Federal Reserve System. Contact at:
  Division of Compliance and Consumer Affairs

(continued)

EXHIBIT 6.5. **(continued)**

---

550 17th Street, NW
Washington DC 20429
877-ASK-FDIC (275-3342)
www.fdic.gov/
- National Credit Union Administration: Regulates federally chartered credit unions.
  Contact at:
  Office of Public and Congressional Affairs
  1775 Duke Street
  Alexandria, VA 22314-3428
  703-518-6330
  www.ncua.gov/
- Office of the Comptroller of the Currency: Regulates banks with "national" in the name
  or "N.A." after the name. Contact at:
  Office of the Ombudsman
  Customer Assistance Group
  1301 McKinney Street, Suite 3710
  Houston, TX 77010
  808-613-6743
  www.occ.treas.gov/
- Office of Thrift Supervision: Regulates federal savings and loan associations and federal
  savings banks. Contact at:
  Consumer Programs
  1700 G Street, NW
  Washington DC 20552
  800-842-6929
  www.ots.treas.gov/
- Federal Trade Commission: Regulates other credit card and debit card issuers. Contact at:
  Consumer Response Center
  600 Pennsylvania Avenue, NW
  Washington DC 20580
  877-FTC-HELP (382-4357)
  www.ftc.gov

For specific questions about your rights or to lodge a complaint concerning a credit card issuer, see the agencies listed in Exhibit 6.5.

- **Death to cash advances:** Cash advances bring you high interest rates, fees, and loss of your grace period. Hunt's advice is simple: "Don't even think about cash advances on a credit card."[29] Most of our gurus say the same thing about those convenience checks credit card companies send you—tear them up.

- **Watch the mail:** Your grace period may be changed or may disappear entirely. Your account could be sold to another company or your interest rate changed. That letter in the mail that looks like another piece of junk mail might just be your credit card company's notification of changes it has made in the terms of your account.

- **Know where you are:** Treat every credit card purchase like a check. Keep a record of every charge you make in a notebook, and reconcile the charges on your monthly statement with the charges your recorded in your notebook. This is the only way you can really be sure fraudulent or incorrect charges aren't appearing on your statement.

- **Become a deadbeat, and soon:** Credit card companies call card users who pay their balances off in full each month "deadbeats," and those who carry a balance each month "revolvers." Whereas the credit card companies love their revolvers, the gurus want you to become a deadbeat as fast as you can. Here's how: Get a card with no annual fee and a 25-day grace period. Then:

Pay your balance in full each month!

On that sage advice, we will conclude this discussion of credit cards and recap our key points.

KEY POINTS

- All debt isn't bad. Good debt allows you to achieve a worthwhile goal.

- Bad debt is debt that is incurred to buy things that are quickly consumed or lose their value.

- You have taken on too much debt if your monthly debt payments are more than 35 percent of your net family income or your total liabilities are more than 50 percent of your total assets.

- The best way to get out of debt is to use the rapid debt reduction plan, whereby you stop borrowing and begin paying off debts one at a time, starting with the debt carrying the highest interest rate.

- A fixed interest rate on a credit card can be changed by the card issuer with 15 days' notice.

- If your credit card is stolen or used without your authorization, you are liable for the first $50 of fraudulent charges. If the card is a debit card, you may be liable for the full amount.

- Having a lot of credit cards hurts your credit rating regardless of the size of the card balances or the frequency of their use.

- Understand fully the terms and conditions of any credit cards you use.

- Take control of your credit limit. Don't accept a credit limit for more than you think you could reasonably pay off in one month.

- Pay early to avoid late payment fees and to reduce your outstanding balance.

- Pay close attention to the grace period, and time your purchases and payments accordingly.

- Never take a cash advance on your card or use the convenience checks provided by your card issuer. In addition, be wary of skip-a-payment offers.

- Watch the mail closely for notices of changes in the terms of your account.

- Keep a careful record of every charge you make, and check your monthly statement to reconcile all of your charges.

- Become a deadbeat as soon as you can by paying off your balance each month.

Murray Baker, author of *The Debt-Free Graduate*

Nancy Castleman, coauthor of *Invest in Yourself*

Jean Chatzky, author of *Talking Money*

Jonathan Clements, author of *25 Myths You've Got to Avoid If You Want to Manage Your Money Right*

William Danko, coauthor of *The Millionaire Next Door*

Gerri Detweiler, coauthor of *Invest in Yourself*

Ric Edelman, author of *The Truth about Money*

Marc Eisenson, coauthor of *Invest in Yourself*

Bob Hammond, author of *Life after Debt*

Christy Heady, coauthor of *The Complete Idiot's Guide to Managing Your Money*

Robert Heady, coauthor *of The Complete Idiot's Guide to Managing Your Money*

Clark Howard, author of *Get Clark Smart*

Mary Hunt, author of *Mary Hunt's Debt-Proof Living*

Azriela Jaffe, coauthor of *The Complete Idiot's Guide to Beating Debt*

Jason Kelly, author of *The Neatest Little Guide to Personal Finance*

Dwight Lee, coauthor of *Getting Rich in America*

Nancy Lloyd, author of *Simple Money Solutions*

Richard McKenzie, coauthor of *Getting Rich in America*

Edward Mrkvicka, author of *Your Bank is Ripping You Off*

Suze Orman, author of *The 9 Steps to Financial Freedom*

Jane Bryant Quinn, author of *Making the Most of Your Money*

Thomas Stanley, coauthor of *The Millionaire Next Door*

Steven Strauss, coauthor of *The Complete Idiot's Guide to Beating Debt*

David Teitelbaum, author of *The Procrastinator's Guide to Financial Security*

Eric Tyson, author of *Personal Finance for Dummies*

7

Borrowing for
Big-Ticket Items

In the last chapter, we discussed the types of credit that cover items like clothing, household appliances, vacations, Christmas shopping, and other day-to-day purchases we may choose to finance through bank and/or store credit cards. Although the total balances on these credit accounts can grow to disturbingly high amounts, they are usually an accumulation of relatively small purchases—$200 for school clothes, plus $150 for an anniversary dinner, plus $1,200 for airline tickets to Orlando, and so on. In this chapter, we want to look at three specific types of credit or borrowing associated with big-ticket items—auto loans, student loans, and mortgages—beginning with auto loans.

AUTO LOANS

Here are some guru tips for getting the best deal on an auto loan.

- **Avoid dealer financing:** Yes, we know the dealer seems to make it so easy and cheap to finance the car through the dealership, but our gurus say don't do it. Clark Howard maintains "it's critical to finance the purchase of a car in advance at a credit union, an online lender, or a bank—not at the dealership."[1]

When you allow the dealer to arrange financing, all kinds of terrible things can happen. If you drive your new car home and give the dealer your trade-in, you're in trouble if, as happens more and more, the financing later collapses.

Here's what happens when the dealer calls you a few weeks later with the sad news that your loan didn't go through. Because the loan and purchase are done separately, you may not be able to undo the sale. Even if you can, your old car may be long gone. So you either have to come up with a lot more money for a down payment, or pay an exorbitant rate of interest, so that a lender will accept the loan. You can try to get the dealer to undo the sale and give you the value of your used car in cash. But depending on the laws in each state, you may have to fight to reverse the deal.[2]

In addition, warns Howard, you can end up paying a much higher rate for an auto loan at a dealership than you might have to pay if you got the loan elsewhere.

Dealers will sell a loan to a customer at whatever rate they can get the customer to pay. A disgruntled finance manager told me the dealership may get the loan at 8 percent and mark it up to 14 percent or 18 percent if they can get the customer to pay that much. The spreads are scary. The finance manager gets the car buyer to pay a higher rate by pointing out blemishes on their credit report, scaring them into thinking they might not be approved. When they're done psyching the customer out, the customer is ecstatic to get the loan at the high rate.[3]

Our gurus are equally skeptical of "manufacturer financing" that promises such seemingly impossible interest rates of 2 percent, 1 percent, or even 0 percent. Check them out, but don't be surprised if you find one or more of the following:

1. They are only available to people with perfect or near-perfect credit ratings (as interpreted by the dealer).
2. They only apply to the less-desirable models.
3. The dealer makes up the difference by charging you more for the car.
4. The "low-interest/no-interest" loan you are offered isn't a simple-interest loan.[4] (See our discussion of such loans later in this section.)

■ **Get your loan from a credit union, bank, or thrift institution:** Credit unions usually offer the cheapest rates. If you are not a member of a credit union, your next best bet is a bank or thrift institution. Eisenson, Detweiler, and Castleman recommend that when negotiating for a loan with one of these institutions, you should ask if they will give you a discount on the loan rate if you allow them to deduct the payments automatically from your account. These gurus say that you may be able to get anywhere from 0.5 percent to as much as 1.5 percent trimmed off the loan rate if you agree to automatic deduction.[5]

■ **Get a simple-interest loan:** You will come out ahead with a simple-interest loan, the kind most frequently offered by credit unions and banks. With a simple-interest loan, the interest you owe each month during the term of the loan is based on your outstanding balance. If you pay extra toward the principal and/or pay your loan off early and your loan has no prepayment penalty, you save money because you don't pay as much interest as you would have had you kept the loan for the entire term. For example, if you have a 36-month loan and pay it off in 24 months, you won't pay as much interest as if you had kept the car and the loan for the entire 36 months.

 The gurus recommend that you avoid what are called "precomputed" loans. These loans obligate you to pay interest for the full period of the loan regardless of when you pay off the loan. Therefore, if you have a 36-month loan and pay it off in 24 months, you still owe the remaining 12 months of interest.

- **Avoid the Rule of 78s:** The Rule of 78s method of calculation, also known as the "sum of digits" method, requires you to pay more interest during the early months of your loan than during later months. For example, if you had a 12-month loan, you would owe 12/78ths of the interest in the first month, 11/78ths in the second month, 10/78ths in the third, and so on. Most of the interest on this type of loan is paid in the first few months of the loan.

 In 1992 Congress outlawed the use of Rule of 78s formulas for auto-type loans, but only for loans of 61 months or longer. Many states have outlawed the use of the formula altogether. In addition, as of 2001 at least one bill had been introduced in Congress to ban the use of the Rule of 78s in all credit transactions. Still, say our gurus, you should be on guard for this consumer-unfriendly way of calculating interest. They warn you to be especially careful to watch for the Rule of 78s if you are considering an auto loan through a "buy here, pay here" auto dealer or subprime lender that specializes in loans to borrowers with no or poor credit. See http://www.bankrate.com/nsc/news/auto/20010827a.asp for more information on the Rule of 78s and what to watch for in loan documents.

- **Don't just focus on the amount of your monthly payment, or you might end up going "upside-down":** If you are like most people, the first thing you think about when buying a car is how much your monthly payment will be. Auto dealers and lenders know this, so as cars have become more expensive, they have found a nifty little way to reduce the size of your monthly payment. They just stretch them out over a longer period of time. The dealer just recalculates your payments using 60 months rather than 36, and suddenly, as if by magic, that dream SUV fits in your budget. It sounds good, but our gurus warn that taking out a long-term auto loan can get you into a lot of financial trouble. It's called going "upside-down" in the loan. Here is how Clark Howard explains going upside-down, along with his argument for never taking out an auto loan for more than 42 months:

The sixty-month loan is a poor financial choice because in that period, the value of the car declines much faster than the loan balance. So, for much of those five years, you're "upside-down" in the loan—you owe more than the vehicle is worth.

Being "upside-down" can be a major problem. Let's say you decide after a couple of years that you can't stand your car. Selling it won't generate nearly enough money to pay off the loan. Unless you can come up with several thousand dollars to pay off the balance of the loan, you're stuck in the vehicle. If the vehicle is totaled in an accident, you could end up owing the lender thousands of dollars. You have to cover the gap between the amount the insurance company pays and what you owe.[6]

Howard says that if you keep your auto loan to 42 months or less, then the amount you owe on your loan is much more likely to track the value of your vehicle, at least after the first year of ownership. In short, you are not as likely to find yourself upside-down should you decide to trade the car or sell it before you have paid off the loan.

- **Make as big a down payment as you can afford:** Most lenders will require you to make a down payment of 10 to 20 percent when you take out an auto loan; however, you may be able to find a lender that will require much less— maybe even zero percent. Robert and Christy Heady advise against taking that deal. Instead, they say, you should make the largest down payment you can afford. The Headys explain that the higher your down payment, the lower your interest rate is likely to be, and in the long term, it is the interest you pay that really costs you.[7]

- **Be wary of variable-rate auto loans:** The interest rate on most auto loans stays the same during the entire period of the loan. However, you may find some lenders offering variable-rate loans that allow the interest rate to go up or down over the course of the loan according to some measure of overall interest rates. Jane Bryant Quinn says that variable-rate loans can be a good deal, but only if you can get them for one percentage point or less than the *cheapest* fixed rate you can find.[8] When you accept a variable rate, you are putting yourself at some risk because the interest rate could go up. Consequently, says Quinn, you deserve to get some discount on the going rate for your willingness to take such a risk. Other gurus, such as Robert and Christy Heady, maintain that variable-rate loans aren't worth the risk even if you do get a discount.[9]

Variable-rate loans don't necessarily mean that your monthly payment will go up or down as the prime rate changes. What may happen instead is that your payment stays the same but the length of your loan (number of payments you must make) goes up when rates go up and shortens when rates go down.

- **Take advantage of rebates:** Manufacturers sometimes offer you a choice of either low-interest financing or a rebate. For example, they may offer either a 3 percent loan or $1,000 rebate. Which should you take? Our gurus say it depends on the length of the loan you are planning to take out and the interest rate you can get elsewhere, such as at your local bank. You need to calculate your overall cost for both options and decide which is best for you.

First, calculate your cost if you choose the rebate by following these steps:

1. Deduct the amount of the rebate from the cost of the car (but only the cost that you would finance).
2. Determine what interest rate you can get from a credit union or bank.
3. Calculate the total amount you will pay over the life of the loan, including principal and interest, for the amount determined in step 1.

Now calculate your cost if you take the manufacturer's offer of a lower-cost loan by doing the following:

Calculate the total you will pay over the life of the loan, including principal and interest, by multiplying the total amount you will finance by the manufacturer's offered interest rate.

Now compare the two. Which is best for you?

- **Shop around:** Our gurus definitely recommend that you shop around when looking for an auto loan. Check rates at your local credit union, banks, and thrift institutions, and go online to sites such as Bankrate.com (http://www.bankrate.com/) to get quotes.

Shopping around can make a big difference. In October 2002, auto loan rates for a 36-month new-car loan in Atlanta, Georgia, according to Bankrate.com, ranged from 4.75 percent with no fees to as high as 9.35 percent with $150 in fees. That's quite a spread.

- **Hock your house?** We include this piece of advice with a great deal of reluctance and only because some gurus mention it. The idea is that instead of taking out an auto loan to buy your new car, you tap into the equity in your house with a home equity loan or line of credit. You get the advantage of a cheaper rate, and if you itemize deductions, you can deduct the interest on your income tax.

Many gurus warn, and we concur, that it is extremely foolhardy to put your home at risk to buy a depreciating asset like a car. Worse, when you start using home equity loans to buy things, you can find yourself slipping into real financial trouble, as Jane Bryant Quinn explains:

> Your banker—no slouch when it comes to collecting interest payments—
> may let you stretch the [home equity] loan over 10 or 15 years. But what if
> you want a new car 3 years from now? No problem. You just borrow
> against your home equity again. And borrow again, 3 years after that. At that
> point, you'd be paying for your present car plus two old cars you no longer
> drive. That's a never-ending spiral down.[10]

Quinn says that the only way to avoid getting into this trap is to find out
what you would have been paying for a three- or four-year auto loan and
pay down your home equity loan at that rate.

   Note: For some additional advice on buying and leasing cars, visit our
Web site at http://www.jboyett.com/auto.

STUDENT LOANS

Dwight Lee and Richard McKenzie, coauthors of *Getting Rich in America,* note
that the way people pay for college has changed dramatically over the last 30
years. In the late 1960s, more than one-third of college students paid for their education themselves and only 15 percent took out student loans. By the late 1990s,
the payment methods had almost reversed—nearly one-third of students used
loans and only 10 percent used their own money.[11] If you are going to college or
have a child getting ready to go, an important financing option to consider is taking out a student loan.

   Although most people today fund at least part of their college education with
student loans, a number of our gurus think borrowing to go to college is a bad
idea. For example, Mary Hunt says that "putting the cost of college on credit to
be paid for over the next twenty-five to thirty years . . . borders on the unthink-
able."[12] Ric Edelman adds that student loans are a bad idea that most people live
to regret, and Jason Kelly ranks them last among four college financing options,
behind work-study programs, grants and scholarships, and investments.[13] What
worries these gurus is that college students take out these loans with little if any
thought as to how or whether they will be able to pay them off after they graduate. Most just assume that somehow they will have the necessary funds, and it is
only after they graduate that they realize they are tens of thousands of dollars in
debt with monthly payments that they have to struggle to meet. What is worse,
says Mary Hunt, is that many students use the loans to finance not just tuition and
books but computers, cars, and even ordinary living expenses.[14] Still, our gurus
recognize that loans are a reality for most students, and given that reality, their
basic advice is to borrow only for true educational expenses and even then, only
the minimum you absolutely have to borrow.

You can consult the following sources for additional information about student loans and financial aid:

- *The Student Guide: Financial Aid from the U.S. Department of Education,* available at http://www.ed.gov/prog_info/FSA/ Student-Guide/2002–3/index.html/.
- Free Application for Federal Student Aid (FAFSA). A complete explanation of the federal student aid program including eligibility requirements and an online application is available at http://www.fafsa.ed.gov/index.htm/.
- For information on student loans available directly from the U.S. government, see http://www.ed.gov/DirectLoan/.
- General information and advice for parents and students on student financial aid from the National Association of Student Financial Aid Administrators are available under the "Parents and Students" tab at http://www.nasfaa. org/Home.asp/.
- Students and parents should also contact the student's high school guidance office and the college financial aid office of the college the student will be attending.

As Murray Baker, author of *The Debt-Free Graduate,* says, "[T]he main thing to remember about student loans is that they should supplement, not replace, funding from other sources: jobs, savings, income from other investments, scholarships, grants, and, of course, the Bank of Mom and Dad."[15]

MORTGAGES

Unless you are very rich, chances are pretty good that you are going to have to borrow most of the money you need to buy your dream home. In other words, you will need to get a mortgage. Let's look at some of the issues the gurus address when it comes to this type of borrowing.

How Big a Mortgage Can You Obtain?

The gurus approach the question of how much money mortgage companies will lend you in three ways: (1) the multiple-of-income method, (2) the percent-of-income method, and (3) the formula method. We will examine each of these in this section.

Multiple-of-Income Method

The easiest way to determine the *maximum* amount you can afford to spend for a home is simply to multiply your gross family income by two. In other words, if your gross family income (income before taxes) is $100,000, then you wouldn't want to spend more than $200,000 for your house, including your down payment.

> If you're not yet wealthy but want to be someday, never purchase a home that requires a mortgage that is more than twice your household's total annual realized [taxable] income.
>
> *Thomas Stanley and William Danko*[16]

Of course, some people will find this method too restrictive, especially if the house they really want costs more than two times their income. Eric Tyson says you may be able to get a loan for more than two times your income if mortgage interest rates are low. For instance, if rates are high (10 percent), then two to two-and-half times your income might be the limit you can borrow. As interest rates decline, the multiple increases, so at a low rate of 5 percent or less, you might be able to borrow as much as four to four-and-a-half times your income.[17] See Exhibit 7.1.]

Percent-of-Income Method

Another popular way to determine how much you can borrow for a home is to look at your housing and debt expenses as a percentage of your income. These so-called lending limits are usually stated as "28/36," as Jane Bryant Quinn explains:

- No more than **28 percent** of your gross monthly income [should be] spent on housing expenses—mortgage payment, insurance, and taxes. On FHA loans, [your] expenses can rise to **29 percent**. "Income" is the regular income you've had for at least a year. If part of it comes in bonuses, commissions, overtime pay, alimony, or child support, lenders will want proof that this money will keep coming (most likely, a portion of this income won't be counted at all). If you're self-employed, they'll look at your net income after expenses. Lenders vary in how they qualify people applying for adjustable-rate loans. [See our later discussion of adjustable rate mortgages.] . . . Some let you meet the 28 percent test based on the loan's first-year discount interest rate; some use the probable second-year rate or the first-year rate plus the annual cap (usually 2 percent).
- Total debt payments (monthly mortgage and consumer debt) not exceeding **36 percent** of your gross monthly income. Count as consumer debt any bills with at least 10 monthly payments left. You might be restricted to 33 percent of income if you're putting less than 10 percent down.[18]

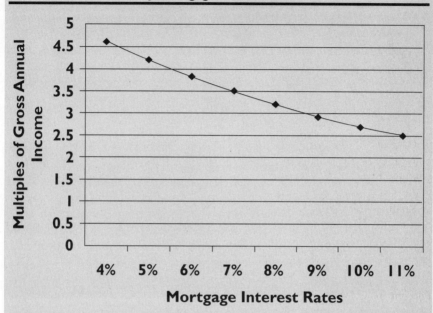

EXHIBIT 7.1. **Multiples of Gross Annual Income by Mortgage Interest Rate**

Source: Adapted from Eric Tyson, Personal Finance for Dummies (Foster City, CA: IDG Books Worldwide, 1997), p. 285.

Ric Edelman cautions that the 28/36 lending limit may be too high and that if you base your mortgage amount on that limit, you may be saddling yourself with too much debt. Edelman explains it this way:

The problem is that the two lending limits weren't always 28/36. The limits used to be 22/28. In other words, the monthly mortgage payment for a home owner was once limited to 22% of income, while today's buyers can have mortgage payments equal to 28% of income. Thus, you now can obligate a much higher percentage of your total income to your mortgage than before. This is a dangerous trend, especially considering that taxes also take a higher percentage of your income than ever before. Therefore, if you follow today's lending limits, at best you will be house-rich and cash-poor, and at worst, you will lose your home, destroying your credit record—and maybe your marriage—in the process.

Indeed, there's a lot more to owning a home than a mortgage payment—like insurance, utilities, maintenance, repairs, improvements, and decorating. If you stretch to buy as expensive a house as possible, you won't be able to afford anything else.

You need to set aside money for these expenses, and that means you should not buy as expensive a home as you think you can afford. And that, in turn, means foregoing the current lending limits and sticking with the old limits.[19]

Edelman says he once had a client who fell in love with a house on a five-acre lot. The man was able just to meet the 28/36 lending limits but got into financial difficulties later on. He hadn't factored in the expenses of maintaining five acres of property, such as the $3,600 per year it cost to have the grass mowed.[20]

Formula Method

Suze Orman says she dislikes both the percent-of-income and multiple-of-income methods of calculating your lending limit for the simple reason that they are both based on your gross income. Orman believes that relying on gross income as an indicator of the size of mortgage you can handle is a real mistake because it 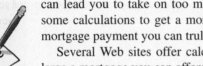 can lead you to take on too much debt.[21] She says you should do some calculations to get a more accurate estimate of the monthly mortgage payment you can truly afford (see Exercise 7.1).[22]

Several Web sites offer calculators to help you determine how large a mortgage you can afford. See the following, for example:

- http://www.bankrate.com/brm/rate/calc_home.asp
- http://www.kiplinger.com/spending/home/buying/buying2.html
- http://www.bloomberg.com/money/loan/mtge_calc.html

Also see links to other calculators from Suze Orman's Web site, http://www.suzeorman.com/resources/homeownership.asp?section=calculators.

Finding a Mortgage Company

When it comes to mortgages, says Jane Bryant Quinn, "it's nuts not to shop,"[23] and she's right. When we checked rates for a 15-year conventional mortgage in Georgia in the fall of 2002, we found quotes that differed by more than three-quarters of a percentage point. What impact does that have? Quinn calculates that each percentage point saved on a 15-year, $100,000 loan is worth over $18,000 over the life of the loan, or more than $100 per month.[24]

Here are some of Quinn's suggestions for how you can find the cheapest rates.

1. Check your local newspapers for lists of lenders and their currently offered rates.
2. Ask your real estate agent for a recommendation. However, Quinn cautions that you shouldn't automatically take your agent's recommendation because the agent may earn a fee from the lender for the referral.

EXERCISE 7.1. **Estimating Maximum Monthly Mortgage Payment**

Monthly income: _____

(Get this from the cash-flow statement you created in Chapter 2, "Getting Your Finances in Order.")

Monthly expenses: _____

(from your cash-flow statement)

Current rent/housing expenses: _____

(from your cash-flow statement)

Adjusted monthly expenses: _____

(monthly expenses − current rent/housing expenses)

Adjusted monthly expenses as percent of income: _____%

(adjusted monthly expenses ÷ monthly income ×100)

 Orman says that if your adjusted monthly expenses are more than 30 percent of your income, you should stop here. You can't afford to buy a house until you eliminate some debt. See Chapter 6 for information on how to manage your debt better.

Housing expense limit: _____

(monthly income − adjusted monthly expenses)

Maximum mortgage: _____

(housing expense limit × 0.70.)

Orman recommends that you reserve 25 to 30 percent of your housing expense limit to cover other housing expenses you will have, such as property taxes, homeowner's insurance, maintenance, private mortgage insurance (PMI), and other miscellaneous expenses. She says this is the true maximum amount you can afford for monthly mortgage payments.

3. Call a mortgage broker. As Eric Tyson explains, "[I]nsurance agents peddle insurance, real estate agents sell real estate, and mortgage brokers deal in mortgages. They buy mortgages wholesale from lenders and then mark them up to retail to you. The difference, or *spread,* is their income."[25] Tyson says you can expect the broker to charge 0.5 to 1 percent of the loan amount as a commission, but you should ask for a discount because these commissions are negotiable. The advantage of talking to a broker, says Tyson, is that you can get some sense of what the mortgage market is like. Good brokers will know where the best deals can be found and can be of real help if you are too busy to do the mortgage shopping yourself. But be aware that all brokers aren't the same. Quinn suggests looking for a broker who has been in the business for at least five years and who does business with a large number of lenders.[26]

4. Shop the Web. If you are online, this is probably the easiest way to search for a good deal on a mortgage. Here are some sites to check:

    ☐ http://www.eloan.com/
    ☐ http://www.hsh.com/
    ☐ http://www.iown.com/
    ☐ http://www.mortgage.com/C3/_Start.bus
    ☐ http://quickenloans.quicken.com/

Key Mortgage Decisions

Regardless of whether you find your lender through the Web, your agent, or a broker, you will have to answer a number of questions. Here are three of the most important:

1. Do you want a fixed- or adjustable-rate loan?
2. Do you want a 30-year loan or something shorter?
3. Are you willing to pay points to get a reduced rate?

Here are our gurus' recommendations concerning each of these issues.

Do You Want a Fixed- or Adjustable-Rate Loan?

The two most common types of mortgages that lenders offer are fixed and adjustable rate. As the name implies, the interest rate you pay on a fixed-rate loan is fixed or constant, and therefore the amount of your monthly payment stays the same for the life of the loan. With an adjustable-rate loan, your interest rate and monthly payment can change. Which type of loan is best? Quinn says it depends on your situation.

When a Fixed-Rate Loan Is Best

The chief advantage of a fixed-rate loan, says Quinn, is that it is safe and predictable. Your monthly payments will stay the same for the life of the loan, and if interest rates go up, you could find yourself with a real bargain. Even if interest rates go down, you aren't stuck because you can simply refinance at a lower rate. Quinn recommends considering a fixed-rate loan if the following apply to you:

1. The size of the payment doesn't stop you from getting the house you want.
2. You want to lock in your mortgage payments because you can't count on earning a higher income in the years ahead.
3. You couldn't afford your house if your mortgage payments rose.
4. The thought of rising mortgage payments scares you stiff.
5. You think current mortgage rates are unusually low.
6. You're near retirement, at which point your income will drop.[27]

When an Adjustable-Rate Mortgage Is Best

The chief advantage of adjustable-rate mortgages (ARMs) is that they are usually two to three percentage points cheaper than fixed-rate loans, so you can borrow more money and buy more house with an adjustable-rate loan. Quinn says you should consider an adjustable-rate loan if the following applies to you:

1. You need the lower monthly payment in the first year to buy the house you want.
2. You can handle higher payments when they come.
3. You won't panic when payments rise because you have faith that they'll fall again.
4. You expect to own the house for only four or five years.
5. You have plenty of money or plenty of confidence that your income will rise.
6. You're thinking about resale. ARMs can generally be assumed by the buyer, which eliminates his or her closing costs.[28]

Questions to Ask If You Are Considering an Adjustable-Rate Loan

Because adjustable-rate loans are more complicated than fixed-rate loans, our gurus warn that it is particularly important for you to understand exactly how any ARM you are considering will work. Here are some questions the gurus say you should ask your lender.[29]

1. **How often does the interest rate change—annually, every three years, every five years?** Quinn says if you plan to keep the mortgage for a long period of time, frequent interest-rate changes might work to your advantage because the rates can be expected to go up and down. On the other hand, if you plan to keep the mortgage for only a few years, Quinn recommends that you go with an ARM that locks in your rate for several years.

2. **What is the interest rate linked to?** Most ARM interest rates are tied to one of the following:

- U.S. Treasury securities
- The Federal Cost of Funds index
- The 11th District Cost of Funds Index (COFI)
- The London Interbank Offer Rate (LIBOR)

Your major concern, according to Suze Orman, is the volatility of the index. She notes that some indexes, such as COFI, are much more volatile than others, like the six-month Treasury bill index. Look for an ARM that is tied to a stable (non-volatile) index when interest rates are low because you want to be able to hold on to that low rate as long as possible. On the other hand, you should look for a faster-moving (more volatile) index when interest rates are high to take advantage of quicker responses to a decline in rates.[30]

3. **What is the spread between the stated mortgage-interest rate and the underlying index?** The spread is the difference between the interest rate you pay and the interest rate of the underlying index. Quinn says you should expect the spread to be anywhere from one to three percentage points. For example, if the index rate is 4 percent and you pay 6 percent, the spread is two percentage points. Obviously, the less the spread, the better for you.

4. **Is there a teaser rate?** Lenders occasionally offer very low interest rates for the first year or so of a loan to get your business. These teaser rates typically run one to three percentage points under the regular rate. Although they save you money for a short time, teasers eventually go away, and your remaining interest rate and mortgage payments go up. The gurus say you should make sure you understand exactly how long the teaser rate will be in effect and what will happen to your mortgage payments when it expires.

5. **What are the annual cap, lifetime ceiling cap, and minimum interest rate?** Caps and minimum interest rates limit the amount your interest rate and payment can vary over the life of the loan. The annual cap limits the amount your interest rate can increase in any one year. The lifetime ceiling cap specifies the maximum interest rate you can be required to pay over the life of the loan, and the minimum interest rate specifies the least you will have to pay. Here is a description of how these caps and minimum interest rate would work if you had a three-year ARM that started at 7 percent with a 2 percent annual cap and 15 percent lifetime ceiling cap:

> During the first three years of your loan, your interest rate will be fixed at 7 percent [three-year ARM]. In the fourth year, no matter what interest rates are, the most you will have to pay is 9 percent (7 percent plus the 2 percent annual cap); and the least you will pay is 5 percent (because your rate can't drop below that figure). In the following years, the worst that could happen would be that the bank would raise your interest rate by another 2 percent a year, say, from 9 to 11 percent and then from 11 to 13, until the interest rate on your loan reaches 15 percent. Even if interest rates go to 18 or 20 percent, your interest rate will remain at 15 percent.[31]

When you are comparing ARMs, Quinn advises that you choose the one with the lower caps to avoid wide swings in rates and payments.

6. **Is there any risk of negative amortization?** Negative amortization occurs when your monthly payments become so low that you aren't paying enough to

cover the total amount of interest you owe the lender. When that happens, the lender adds the difference to your principal. Pretty soon you would end up owing more than the original mortgage, and you would see your mortgage go up over time rather than going down. Our gurus say you should avoid any ARM that can result in negative amortization.

7. **Is there a prepayment penalty?** Loans with a prepayment penalty require a charge (perhaps 2 to 3 percent of the loan amount) if you pay the loan off early. Because you never know when you might want to refinance your mortgage to take advantage of better interest rates, the gurus recommend avoiding any ARM with a prepayment penalty.

8. **How can I check my rate?** Quinn says that if she had a dollar for every mistake lenders made in recalculating ARM payments when rates changed, then she would be a millionaire. Edward Mrkvicka, author of *Your Bank Is Ripping You Off,* says that independent surveys indicate that interest rates and mortgage payments on as many as 80 percent of ARMs are calculated incorrectly.[32] A lot can go wrong either by accident or intentionally. For example, says Quinn, "the bank may pick the wrong index, loan balance, or adjustment date; it might round the rate up when it should have been rounded down; a new loan servicer might get your loan terms wrong; principal prepayments might not have been credited properly."[33]

With so much room for mistakes, our gurus strongly recommend that you check the rate yourself if you have an ARM. Fortunately, you can get help at http://www.hsh.com/pamphlets/ack.html.

Do You Want a 30-Year or Shorter Mortgage?

Mortgages come in different lengths, but the most popular are the 30-year and 15-year mortgages. The chief advantage of a shorter-term mortgage is that it costs you less in interest payments over the life of the loan. The chief disadvantage of the shorter mortgage is that your monthly payments will be higher, even if you get a reduced interest rate for borrowing the money for fewer years.

The gurus generally agree with the recommendations of Marc Eisenson, Gerri Detweiler, and Nancy Castleman, who say that "unless you are absolutely certain that you'll be able to meet the higher payment every month, take a 30-year loan—and pay it off as if it were a 15-year loan."[34] For example, you have the option of taking out a $100,000 mortgage at 8 percent for 30 or 15 years. The 30-year mortgage has a monthly payment of $734, whereas the 15-year mortgage has a monthly payment of $956. If you take out the 30-year mortgage but pay $956 instead of $734 each month, you are paying $222 extra each month toward your principal. You will pay off the 30-year loan in 15 years and save $92,000 in interest. It's like having a 15-year loan but with a big advantage—you aren't obligated to pay the higher amount. If you're running short of cash one month, you can just send in the $734!

Not all gurus are excited about you paying off your mortgage early or even taking a 15-year mortgage. They think you will come out much better if you just get a 30-year mortgage, make the regular payments, and invest the difference. David Teitelbaum makes the case for investing by comparing fictitious baby boomers *A, B,* and *C,* all of whom purchase a home at the age of 40. All three have $1,000 per month to pay on their mortgages or to invest. *A* takes out a 30-year fixed mortgage at $700 per month and invests $300 each month. *B* takes out the same 30-year loan but adds $75 per month to his mortgage payment in order to pay off the mortgage in 22 years instead of 30. He invests $275 per month for 22 years while he is paying off his mortgage and then from age 62 on invests $1,000 per month. Finally, *C* gets a 15-year fixed rate loan at $928 per month. He invests $72 per month while he is paying off the loan and then invests $1,000 per month from age 57 on. Who do you think comes out ahead, *A, B,* or *C?* Surprisingly, says Teitelbaum, the answer is *A,* and here is why:

> [A] . . . has invested $108,000 in stocks, which have grown to $795,300. B has invested more money, $155,400, but has only $718,900. Meanwhile, C has invested the most money, $193,000, but has only $616,200. So even though A paid out $47,100 more in interest, he or she has had the greatest appreciation in net worth.
>
> This result may not make intuitive sense, but it works because of the power of compound interest. The extra money A invested early on outweighs the increased investments by B and C later on. After fifteen years, the value of A's investments is $137,500, whereas C's is $33,000. Even though C can invest $1,000 a year for fifteen years while A is investing $300, the value of C's investment cannot catch up.[35]

Of course, as Teitelbaum admits, this only works if you actually invest the money and, as Jonathan Clements adds, if you make more on your investments than you would save from paying the mortgage off early.[36]

For more about the power of compounding, see Chapter 9, "Investing for Retirement."

Are You Willing to Pay Points to Get a Reduced Rate?

A point is equal to 1 percent of the loan amount and is, in effect, interest paid in advance. You may have the option of paying a point or points to get a lower interest rate. Here are the pros and cons of points, according to Nancy Lloyd:

On the plus side:

- You only pay the points once (when you take out the mortgage), but you get a lower interest rate for the entire life of the loan.
- You may get to write off the points on your taxes in the year you buy the house. The alternative is to amortize the amount, deducting a fraction (1/30 of each point paid on a 30 year loan) each year, over the life of the loan.

On the minus side:

- For each point you pay, you may buy the interest rate down only 1/8 percent, so it would take you about eight years to recoup that one point (1 percent) interest you paid ahead (when you took out the mortgage). Homeowners, on average, keep a mortgage less than eight years, so unless you expect to own the house longer, you might be ahead by paying the 1/8 percent higher interest while you hold the mortgage, instead of paying the points.
- Paying a point or more up front, in order to buy down (lower) your mortgage interest rate, may not be the best use of this money For instance, if your mortgage is for a little over 80 percent of the appraised value, and your lender is requiring that you buy PMI (private mortgage insurance), why not use the money earmarked for buy down points to increase your down payment to 20 percent instead? You can then avoid paying the PMI now and for the life of the loan.[37]

What If Your Mortgage Application Is Rejected?

Suppose you find a house you love, apply for a loan, and are rejected. What can you do? First, says Bob Hammond, go talk to the lender personally. Lenders have to tell you in writing why you are being turned down for a loan, but Hammond says you shouldn't accept the written notification as the lender's final word. By speaking to someone personally, you may be able to get more specific information concerning why you were rejected, and you may even be able to get the lender to reconsider. Here are some things Hammond says you can do to improve your chances of getting the lender to reconsider, depending on the reason you were rejected.[38]

IF YOU WERE REJECTED BECAUSE . . .	**. . . THEN DO THE FOLLOWING**
The appraisal of the property was too low.	■ Renegotiate with the seller to get a lower purchase price. ■ Get the seller to agree to make repairs or improvements to increase the appraisal or to set aside funds in an escrow account to make repairs after the sale.
Your credit rating is poor.	■ Get a free copy of your credit report from each credit reporting agency. ■ Repay your debts to get current and reapply.
You have insufficient savings for the down payment.	■ Get the seller to agree to finance a second mortgage in order to reduce the amount of down payment you need. ■ See if you can qualify for a lease-purchase mortgage loan through a nonprofit group. The nonprofit group buys the house and leases it back to you at a rental fee that covers both the monthly mortgage payment and an extra amount that accumulates toward a down payment. You have an option to buy the property when you have funds to cover the down payment.
You have insufficient income.	■ If your current rent payment is equal to or more than the mortgage payment and you have been paying your rent consistently and on time, point that out to the lender. ■ If you are due a raise that will increase your income to the level where you can meet the lender's qualifying formula, ask the lender if a letter to that effect from your employer would help.
You have too much debt.	■ If you are close to qualifying and have an excellent credit history, make this known to the lender. ■ Choose a less-expensive house. ■ Pay down your debt and try again.

If none of these works and you are a low-to-moderate-income buyer, Hammond suggests checking to see if you qualify for a nonprofit or government alternative financing program such as these:

- Community Home Buyer's Program
- Housing Finance Agency Programs
- Subsidized Second Mortgage
- Lease-Purchase Mortgage Loans
- Community Home Improvement Mortgage Loan
- Community Land Trust Mortgage Loan

For more information concerning home-buying programs by state, go to http://www.hud.gov/buying/localbuying.cfm/.

Finally, if you suspect that you have been discriminated against, file a complaint with the lender's regulatory agency and/or the U.S. Department of Housing and Urban Development (HUD). For more information on your rights and how to file a complaint, go to http://www.hud.gov/offices/fheo/FHLaws/index.cfm/.

When Should You Refinance?

If you keep your mortgage long enough, you are almost certain to consider getting a new one. Maybe you have an ARM and it's just gone up, or maybe the thought that it might go up soon is making you nervous. Perhaps you have seen newspaper headlines announcing that mortgage interest rates have hit an all-time low. Whatever your reason, how do you know if refinancing makes sense?

As Jean Chatzky notes, the old rule of thumb for refinancing was the rule of twos:[39]

Refinance if . . .

- Your current mortgage is at least *two* years old,
- Your new mortgage will cut your interest rate by at least *two* points, and
- You plan to live in the house for at least *two* more years.

Today's gurus say that things have gotten more complicated and that the old rule of twos may not always be right. Here are some additional things to consider, courtesy of Steven Strauss and Azriela Jaffe:[40]

- **What is the true cost of refinancing?** The old rule of twos assumed that you needed a two percentage point difference and two additional years in the house to make up for the costs of the refinancing transaction itself. Today, you have more loan options, and the cost of refinancing has come down dramatically. The only way to know if refinancing makes sense for you, say

Strauss and Jaffe, is to ask the mortgage lender or broker to give you a breakdown of all of the costs associated with the refinancing and perform some calculations to see just how much you will really save. If you need help with the refinancing calculations, go online to http://www.kiplinger.com/ for some automated help.

- **How comfortable are you with possible payment changes over the life of the loan?** The bottom line, say Strauss and Jaffe, is that if you aren't sure you are going to be saving money, there is no point in refinancing.

- **Why are you refinancing?** If it is because you want to save money on your home purchase, then our gurus say to go ahead and consider refinancing. If, on the other hand, you are refinancing because you need—or want—cash to pay off credit card debt, then most of our gurus say you should give the matter more thought. The danger is that you will take out the cash and either not pay off the debt or pay it off and then just run up a lot of new debt. As we said in Chapter 6, you'll just put your house at risk and have no financial gain to show for it.

As we said at the beginning of this chapter, auto loans, home loans, and student loans are the big-ticket items for most people. How well you do in handling borrowing to fund these common expenses will make a significant difference in how much you have left over for meeting the important goal of investing. We cover that topic in the final two chapters of this book. But first, let's review the key points we covered in this chapter.

KEY POINTS

- Avoid dealer financing when buying an automobile. Get your auto loan from a credit union, bank, or thrift institution.

- Be wary of low-interest or "zero"-interest manufacturer financing.

- Get a simple interest loan, and avoid precomputed loans, the Rule of 78s, and going "upside-down" on your auto loan.

- Be wary of variable-rate auto loans.

- Take advantage of any manufacturer rebates.

- Student loans should be kept as low as possible and used to cover costs directly related to education.

- How much house you can afford depends on the cash you have available for a down payment and the size of mortgage you are able to obtain.

- Mortgage companies will generally lend you from two to four times your gross family income depending on interest rates.

☞ When it comes to mortgages, it is extremely important to shop for the cheapest rates; rates on the same type of mortgage can vary greatly between lenders.

☞ The two basic types of mortgages that most lenders offer are "fixed-rate" loans and "adjustable-rate" loans. Adjustable-rate loans are more complicated than fixed-rate loans.

☞ Many gurus recommend that you take a 30-year mortgage but add to your monthly payment to pay the loan off in 15 years.

☞ Some gurus argue that you should take a 30-year mortgage and invest any extra cash rather than using it to pay off your mortgage sooner. They believe that you can earn more from your investments than you will save in interest from paying off your mortgage early.

☞ The old rule of thumb for refinancing was to do so only if your loan was at least two years old, your new mortgage would cut your interest rate by two points, and you planned to keep the mortgage for at least two additional years.

Robert Allen, author of *Multiple Streams of Income*

Gary Belsky, coauthor of *Why Smart People Make Big Money Mistakes and How to Correct Them*

David Caruso, coauthor of *Let's Talk Money*

Jean Chatzky, author of *Talking Money*

Jonathan Clements, author of *25 Myths You've Got to Avoid If You Want to Manage Your Money Right*

Ric Edelman, author of *New Rules of Money*

David Gardner, coauthor of *The Motley Fool Investment Guide*

Tom Gardner, coauthor of *The Motley Fool Investment Guide*

Thomas Gilovich, coauthor of *Why Smart People Make Big Money Mistakes and How to Correct Them*

Christy Heady, coauthor of *The Complete Idiot's Guide to Managing Your Money*

Robert Heady, coauthor of *The Complete Idiot's Guide to Managing Your Money*

Bambi Holzer, author of *Retire Rich*

Dee Lee, coauthor of *Let's Talk Money*

Arthur Levitt, coauthor of *Take on the Street*

Marshall Loeb, author of *Marshall Loeb's Lifetime Financial Strategies*

Peter Lynch, coauthor of *Learn to Earn*

Olivia Mellan, coauthor of *Money Shy to Money Sure*

Mark Miller, author of *The Complete Idiot's Guide to Being a Cheapskate*

Ted Miller, author of *Kiplinger's Practical Guide to Your Money*

Suze Orman, author of *The 9 Steps to Financial Freedom*

James O'Shaughnessy, author of *How to Retire Rich*

Jane Bryant Quinn, author of *Making the Most of Your Money*

Terry Savage, author of *The Savage Truth on Money*

Charles Schwab, author of *Charles Schwab's Guide to Financial Independence*

Robert Sheard, author of *The Unemotional Investor*

Julie Stav, author of *Fund Your Future*

David Teitelbaum, author of *The Procrastinator's Guide to Financial Security*

Eric Tyson, author of *Personal Finance for Dummies*

8

Investment Basics

L et's say you have tried out the techniques, followed the tips, and adhered to the advice our gurus offer for making and saving money. As a result, you finally have a few extra dollars to invest. Congratulations. Now the issue is where to invest those dollars. There is no shortage of investment options available to you. As of 2002, more than 7,000 companies were trading on the New York Stock Exchange and NASDAQ alone, and there were more than 12,000 mutual funds. There are also thousands of bond issuers and countless choices of CDs, savings accounts, and money market funds. In this chapter, we look at basic investment options and outline our gurus' rules of thumb for deciding which type of investment is the right one under different circumstances. We'll start with a brief overview of your major options.

THE MAJOR TYPES OF INVESTMENTS

There are really five major types of investment vehicles: stocks, bonds, real estate, cash equivalents, and investments our gurus say most people should avoid.

Stocks

As Robert and Christy Heady note, "[T]he word *stock* is a shortened form of the phrase *common stock*. Common stock is a security that represents ownership in a company."[1] When you buy stock, you are buying *equity* in a company; in other words, you are becoming a part owner of the company. Because the value of stocks can fluctuate more than other types of investments, our gurus say you should consider them only when you are prepared to invest for the long term, meaning a minimum of five to seven years.[2]

Stocks come in a variety of forms, depending on the size of the company and the characteristics of the company's stock.

Size of Company: Large-Cap, Mid-Cap, Small-Cap, and Micro-Cap

One way to distinguish between types of stock is according to the size of the company in terms of its market capitalization or market value. Our gurus generally talk about four levels of market capitalization—large-cap, mid-cap, small-cap, and micro-cap. Although people disagree as to how big a company has to be to be classified as large-cap, mid-cap, and so on, here are some rules of thumb that Motley Fool's David and Tom Gardner say would be an acceptable guideline as of the year 2000.[3]

- **Large-cap:** Companies with a market capitalization over $5 billion. These are America's biggest companies, such as Procter & Gamble, GE, Coca Cola, and so on.
- **Mid-cap:** Companies with a market capitalization between $1 billion and $5 billion.
- **Small-cap:** Companies with a market capitalization between $250 million and $1 billion.
- **Micro-cap:** Companies with a market capitalization below $250 million.

The size of the company matters because, as a general rule of thumb, the stock of small companies tends to fluctuate more and therefore is riskier than the stock of large, established companies.

Characteristics of the Company's Stock: Growth, Income, or Value

There are two ways to make money investing in stocks. First, you can buy stock in a company that generates profits that are distributed to its shareholders in the form of *dividends*. Second, you can make money from the profit or *capital gains* you make when you sell a stock that goes up in value. Here are some basic characteristics of stocks:

- **Growth stocks** tend to pay small dividends, so you receive little in the way of steady income. The goal of owning them is to make a profit from what you hope will be a large capital gain when you sell the stock sometime in the future.
- **Income stocks** pay higher dividends but may not generate as great a capital gain as growth stock.
- **Value stocks** get their name from the fact that they are considered to be undervalued by the stock market.

Bonds

As we said, when you buy stocks, you obtain equity or ownership in a company. When you buy bonds, you are lending a company or a government agency money in return for a promise that you will be paid back the principal plus interest at some point in the future. As Jane Bryant Quinn says, "when you 'buy' a bond, . . . you are accepting an IOU."[4] Basically, bonds can be distinguished by the issuer (who is borrowing the money), the default risk (how likely it is that the borrower will pay back the principal and interest on time), and maturity (for how long you are lending the money).

Issuer

There are four basic types of bond issuers:

- **The U.S. government** issues U.S. government bonds or treasuries.
- **U.S. government agencies** such as the Government National Mortgage Association (Ginnie Mae), Federal Home Loan Mortgage Corporation (Freddie Mac), and Federal National Mortgage Association (Fannie Mae) issue or guarantee pools of bonds backed by mortgage loans called mortgage-backed bonds or mortgage-backed securities.
- **State and local governments and local government agencies** issue municipal bonds, or munis.
- **Corporations** issue corporate bonds.

Default Risk

U.S. government–and U.S. government agency–backed bonds are considered the most risk free, followed by munis, and finally by those issued by corporations. Corporate bonds come in two default flavors:

1. **Investment-grade bonds:** Those rated "BBB" or "Baa" or better by the bond raters Standard & Poors and Moody's, respectively
2. **Junk bonds:** Those rated "BB" or "Ba" or worse

Our gurus do not recommend anything less than investment-grade bonds for most investors. Junk bonds are just too risky. Some gurus such as Marshall Loeb say that most investors (that means you) should stay away from any bonds rated less than AAA or AA.[5]

Maturity

Bonds come in a wide range of maturities, from 90-day treasury bills to 30-year or longer corporate bonds. Generally, longer-term bonds pay higher interest rates, but they are also riskier if you don't hold them to maturity, as Suze Orman explains:

> Imagine, for example, that you bought $10,000 worth of a ten year bond that pays a 6 percent [interest rate.] . . . Now, suddenly, the Fed raises interest rates to 8 percent. Understandably, you might want to sell your bond and buy one with the higher interest rate. Trouble is, who in their right mind would want to buy your bond at the price you paid for it . . . or $10,000?—when the [interest rate] . . . is only 6 percent? No one, since any one who wants a bond can go out and buy a new one and get an 8 percent [interest rate.] . . . So, in order to sell your bond, you would have to lower the price. Think about it. If the selling price for your bond were lowered to about $8,000 and the person who bought your bond would be getting $600 a year (6 percent of the $ 10,000 face value of the bond), then, at the $8,000 price, the bond's yield would rise to 7.5 percent. Someone might think about buying it at that price—especially because, when the bond matures, it will pay him or her the face value, or $10,000. So not only would the buyer be getting a good current yield, but his yield to maturity would be so good that it would make this bond competitive with the new bonds paying higher interest rates.[6]

Stocks and bonds are the most common investments most gurus recommend for long-term growth. They have their own advantages and disadvantages. In the next chapter, we will discuss our gurus' recommendations for creating a mixed portfolio of stocks and bonds that is right for you. For now, we'll examine a third type of investment that some gurus recommend highly and others think is highly risky—real estate.

Real Estate

Our gurus are divided on the issue of real estate as an investment. Some, like Ric Edelman, consider real estate "a very risky investment, and one to engage in only after you already own cash, bonds, and stocks (or mutual funds of bonds and stocks), and even then only if you have the financial (and emotional) resources to withstand a worst-case scenario."[7] Other gurus such as Robert Allen, author of *Multiple Streams of Income,* argue that real estate is "the greatest source of wealth."[8] Whether "very risky" or the "greatest source of wealth," practically all of the gurus would agree with Jane Bryant Quinn's observation that "to make money in real estate today you need a system"[9] such as the one offered by Allen.

Allen's system consists of three critical activities—finding, funding, and farming.

Critical Activity #1: Finding

The bedrock principle underlying successful real estate investing, according to Allen, is this: "While the vast majority of sellers are inflexible in their prices and terms, a small percentage of sellers are highly motivated to sell."[10]

Allen calls these highly motivated sellers "Don't-Wanters." He says that when you are reading property descriptions such as in newspaper ads or real estate listings, look for words/phrases such as the following:

- "Owner transferred"
- "Low down" or "No down"
- "Out-of-state owner"
- "Take over payments"
- "Desperate"
- And so on

Any of these words or phrases may signal a Don't-Wanter Condition and a hot lead on a bargain property. To narrow your search further, Allen recommends that you evaluate each hot lead on the basis of five conditions and score the property as follows on a scale of 1 to 3.

1. **Seller's motivation:** Score one point if the seller won't budge on the price, two points if the seller might consider a small discount, and three points if the seller is pressed for cash and willing to negotiate.

2. **Location:** Score zero points if the property is located in a declining and/or high-crime area, two points if it is in a clean but older neighborhood, and three points if the property is in a highly desirable neighborhood such as one with good amenities and access to transportation.

3. **Financing:** Score one point if you have to pay more than 15 percent down and/or you will have a negative cash flow for more than two years or a balloon payment within three years. Score two points if the down payment is less than 15 percent and/or there is no balloon payment for at least five years. Score three points if there is no negative cash flow for the first year and/or you have to put less than 5 percent down.

4. **Price:** Score one point if the price is 10 percent or more above the reasonable market price and consider only if you can get excellent financing. Score two points if the price is within 5 percent of the market price. Score three points if the price is 10 percent or more below the market price.

Jonathan Pond says that a good way to evaluate the price you have to pay for a piece of property is to use the "rent multiplier." To get the rent multiplier, divide the selling price by the gross annual rental you expect. For example, if the selling price is $150,000 and the gross annual rental is $15,000, then the rent multiplier is 10. According to Pond, properties with rent multipliers of seven or more are not usually good investment properties. Many real estate professionals won't consider properties with a multiplier higher than five or six.

5. **Property condition:** Score one point if you will have to spend 10 percent or more of the purchase price to get the property in condition to rent. Score two points if you can get it in shape for 5 percent or less of the purchase price. Score three points if the property is already in rental condition.[11]

Critical Activity #2: Funding

Once you have found a property that looks like a good investment, your next critical activity, says Allen, is to find a creative way to finance the purchase. Allen offers five techniques for purchasing properties with nothing down.

1. **Ultimate paper out:** The seller agrees to carry all of the financing at better rates than what the bank offers.
2. **The lease option:** You lease the property from the owner for several years, and part of the rental goes toward an agreed-upon purchase price should you decide to buy the property at the end of the lease.
3. **ABC (anything but cash):** You get the seller to agree to accept something other than cash as a down payment. For example, Allen says one of his students used a motorcycle as down payment. Another agreed to trade professional legal services to the seller in place of the down payment on a piece of property.
4. **Divide and conquer:** You raise the money to make the down payment by selling off pieces of the property you are purchasing. For example, Allen says he once raised the money for a down payment on a piece of property by selling off the back portion of the lot to a neighbor.[12]
5. **OPM (other people's money):** You find someone who agrees to provide the money for the down payment in exchange for a percentage of the profits when the property is sold.

Critical Activity #3: Farming

By "farming" Allen means "harvesting your profits."[13] Allen identifies two ways to harvest profits from real estate:

1. **Buy and hold:** You buy a piece of property and hold on to it for the long term, taking your profit from the rent your tenants pay. The critical skill you need for a "buy-and-hold" strategy, says Allen, is your ability to pick good tenants and retain them long-term.

2. **Flipping:** In this case, you have no intention of keeping the property very long. What you strive to do in flipping is to buy property at a price that is below its true market value and then resell it quickly for a profit. The key skills you need in flipping are the abilities to spot properties that are underpriced and to market the properties successfully once you have made the purchase. Allen says that if you want to be a successful real estate investor, you should plan to "buy at least one property per year to hold in your long-term portfolio, and flip at least one property per year for short-term profit."[14]

In short, if you want to invest in real estate, make sure you "find," "fund," and "farm" the way Allen recommends. Better yet, say other gurus, stick to stocks and bonds or be really safe and put your money in cash equivalents. That is the topic of our next section.

Cash Equivalents

As the name implies, cash equivalents are investments that can be quickly and easily converted to cash. They pay low interest compared with other investments but are relatively safe places to store cash you may need in the short term. Cash equivalents include savings accounts, CDs, U.S. Savings Bonds, and money market mutual funds. Here are some tips on the advantages and uses of cash equivalents, according to Olivia Mellan, coauthor of *Money Shy to Money Sure.*[15]

Savings Accounts

Savings accounts pay very low interest rates but, as Mellan notes, they are good places to stash cash you think you will need within a few months. She recommends you try to open such accounts at a credit union, if you qualify to join one, rather than a large bank, because savings accounts at credit unions usually pay a higher interest rate. She also recommends that you avoid specialty savings accounts such as Christmas Club accounts because they are basically just low-interest gimmicks.

Certificates of Deposit

CDs are also safe places to stash cash. You get a guaranteed interest rate for a given period (six months, one year, five years), and your investment is protected by the FDIC, just like your bank account. The downside to CDs is that you may have to forfeit interest and pay a penalty if you need access to the money before the CD matures. Mellan says CDs are especially useful in the following two circumstances:

1. You have suddenly come into possession of a chunk of money that you know you will need to use in the next two to three years and want a safe place to keep it where it might also earn some interest. For example, you have inherited money that you will need to tap to send your teenager to college in a year or two.
2. You are looking for a safe and secure investment that can offset the risks you have taken in purchasing stocks and bonds. CDs can cushion the blow should the rest of your investment portfolio suffer from market fluctuations and/or changes in interest rates.

U.S. Savings Bonds

U.S. Savings Bonds are guaranteed by the U.S. government and therefore are very secure investments, but our gurus say that their low interest rates make them better as gifts for children than investment for adults.

Money Market Mutual Funds

Money market mutual funds are pools of cash managed by a professional manager and invested in relatively safe investments such as short-term Treasury bills, CDs, and so on. Their chief advantages are that they pay a higher interest rate than savings accounts and they give you easier access to your money than you would have with a CD. You may even be able to write checks on your account.

Money market funds are not guaranteed by the U.S. government like CDs but generally have been relatively safe investments. In fact, notes Mellan, some people consider these funds to be so safe and convenient that they use them as the primary place to stash money that they will need in the short term.

Investments to Avoid

David and Tom Gardner call them the "Carnival of Freakish Delights."[16] Jane Bryant Quinn considers them "absolutely awful" and "the call of the wild."[17] Very few (make that none) of our gurus recommend any of the following for anyone who is not (1) so rich they can afford to lose their entire investment or more and not lose a minute's sleep, (2) very experienced and sophisticated (a true professional) when it comes to the specific form of investment, and (3) very lucky.

Despite these warnings, someone, somewhere, and at some time is going to swear to you that they know someone, somewhere, at some time who invested in one or more of these vehicles and made a killing. Don't believe it. Believe our gurus when they say that when you encounter one or more of these so-called investment opportunities, run away just as fast and far as you can.

Options and Commodities Futures

Options come in two varieties, as Ted Miller explains: "A *call* gives its holder the right to buy a particular stock at a specified price anytime before the option expires. Whoever sells (or 'writes') the call agrees to sell the stock at the specified price. A *put* gives its holder the right to sell a stock at a specified price within a specified time and obligates its seller to do the buying."[18]

You buy a call or sell a put if you think the stock will go up in price. You sell a call or buy a put if you think the stock will go down in price or stay the same. Commodities futures work in a similar fashion, but in that case what you are agreeing to buy or sell at a particular price are commodities such as soybeans, orange juice, cattle, pork, cotton, and so on.

Our gurus warn that when you are involved with options and futures, you aren't investing—you are just plain gambling. Peter Lynch, the highly successful manager of the Fidelity Magellan Fund, says that the odds are about 85 to 90 percent that you will lose. In fact, he thinks that options and futures are such a bad idea for the average investor, he refuses to even explain how they work for fear of enticing someone to actually buy some.[19]

IPOs (Initial Public Offerings) and Other Acronyms

Suppose your broker calls and tells you that the next Microsoft or Coca Cola is about to go public and he or she doesn't want you to miss the opportunity to get in

on the ground floor. Forget it, say our gurus. "The simple fact is that, if a broker is offering the stock, something is terribly wrong," says Mark Miller. "It's common knowledge on Wall Street that only the big boys (pension funds, institutions, mutual funds, and large traders on the floor) get the hot IPOs."[20] Whatever you are being offered is something they don't want, and if they don't want it why should you? IPOs are not for the typical or beginning investor—they are appropriate only for the big, rich, and very experienced. Mellan says that this is true of almost any investment "opportunity" that is known by an acronym, including ETFs, CMOs, UITs, LEAPs, SPDRs, and so on.[21] We are not going to tell you what these acronyms stand for. Our gurus say if you don't know already, you are NOT qualified to invest in them.

Collectibles

Coins, stamps, artwork, Japanese swords, baseball cards, rare books, comic books, antiques, clocks, photographs, vintage wine, watches, writing utensils, Tiffany lamps, you name it, and someone, somewhere is collecting it. Many collectors think their prized possessions are going to make them rich someday or at least provide a nice little inheritance for their kids. They are almost certainly wrong, say our gurus. The problems with collectibles as investments are almost endless, but here are just a few, courtesy of Eric Tyson and Ric Edelman:[22]

- **There is no buyer protection:** You may, and probably will, pay too much when you buy and get too little when you sell.
- **High maintenance costs:** You must invest considerable time and money keeping up your investment.
- **Your prize ceramic pig turns out to be in a poke:** Your prize find looked good until you got it home or in a different light and suddenly saw the nick, chip, scrape, scratch, or imperfection that makes it no longer such a prize.
- **The returns are low:** Tyson says that the best study he has seen that looked at the performance of collectibles over the past 20 years showed that only two—stamps and diamonds—beat inflation, and when the costs associated with buying and selling these items were factored in, even these didn't beat inflation. The problem, he goes on, is that the only way to get a decent return from collectibles is to be able to predict maybe 20 years in advance what is going to be popular.
- **You won't sell:** Ric Edelman says this is perhaps the biggest reason collectibles are a bad investment. You'll become so attached to whatever you are collecting, you will never think of parting with it.

The gurus don't want to discourage you from collecting; they just want you to collect something because collecting and owning it gives you pleasure.

Gold and Other Precious Metals

People think of gold, and to a lesser extent other precious metals such as silver, as a hedge against inflation. The gurus admit that there is a positive correlation between the price of gold and silver and inflation. During periods of hyperinflation, gold and silver do well, but over the long term, say our gurus, gold and precious metals are a "very silly investment."[23] In fact, Jane Bryant Quinn calls gold the "ultimate worry bead."[24] Generally speaking, our gurus say if you want to buy a few gold coins or silver pieces just in case inflation skyrockets or the U.S. government collapses, you can, but just don't think of them as an investment.

Penny Stocks

Penny stocks are cheap—very cheap. They sell for under $5 a share; often under $1. Robert Sheard, author of *The Unemotional Investor,* says they "represent the riskiest investments in the stock market."[25] Buy them, and it is very likely you and your money are going to be taken. Jane Bryant Quinn explains why:

Penny stocks come from mystery companies, with an untested business [plan]. . . .

If you're ever tempted by the pitch, here's what will happen. You'll buy the stock and, lo and behold, the price will rise. So you'll buy another stock and that will rise, too. It feels like luck (you genius, you), but actually the broker manipulates the price. You keep getting good news while the broker milks you for all the money he or she thinks you've got.

Then things change. Suddenly, one of your stocks goes down. You want to sell, but discover you can't. In penny-stock schemes, the brokers will not process your order unless you use your "profits" to buy another stock. They keep rolling your money into other ventures until they finally wipe you out.[26]

INVESTING IN MUTUAL FUNDS

Where is the best place to begin if you are a novice investor? Practically all of our gurus have one answer—mutual funds. Dee Lee and David Caruso, coauthors of *Let's Talk Money,* call mutual funds the mass transit of investing; "a way for people to climb aboard and leave the driving to someone else."[27]

Mutual funds are pools of stocks, bonds, CDs, and so on that are cared for by a professional manager or team of managers who decide when to purchase or sell investments in the pool. According to Ric Edelman, mutual funds themselves are not investments; they are a way for people to invest.[28] Instead of buying individual stocks or bonds, you and thousands of other investors purchase shares in the mutual fund money pool. You can then let the professional manager(s) who runs your mutual fund take care of all the researching, buying, selling, accounting, evaluating, and so on that non–mutual fund investors normally have to do themselves. Of course, there are disadvantages, as we shall see.

Types of Mutual Funds

Mutual funds come in a wide variety of flavors to satisfy just about anyone's investment tastes. Here is a list of some of the types of funds arranged in order from highest to lowest risk.[29]

Sector and Specialty Funds (most aggressive and risky)

- Gold and precious metals funds: Investments in gold and precious metal mining
- Micro-cap funds: Investments in very small companies

- Small company growth/value funds: Investments in small companies
- Sector funds: Investments in a specific industry

International Funds and Stock Funds

- Asset allocation funds: Investments in a mix of international and U.S. markets
- Aggressive growth funds: Investments in high-growth stocks
- International equity funds: Investments in foreign stocks
- Value funds: Investments in stocks undervalued by the market
- Growth funds: Investments in growth stocks
- Global equity funds: Investments in U.S. and foreign stocks
- High-yield bond funds: Investments in low-rated and/or junk bonds
- Mid-cap funds: Investments in medium-size companies
- Large-cap funds: Investments in large companies
- Stock index funds: Investments to match a specific stock index
- Fund of funds: Investments in other mutual funds
- Growth and income funds: Investments for both high dividends and growth
- Equity income funds: Investments in companies that pay high dividends

Balanced Funds

- Balanced funds: Seek a balance of stocks and bonds
- Income funds: Investments in bonds and dividend-paying stocks

Bond Funds

- International bond funds: Investments in bonds of foreign companies and countries
- Global bond funds: Investments in U.S. and foreign bonds
- Long-term tax-exempt bond funds: Investments in 15- to 30-year municipal bonds
- Long-term taxable bond funds: Investments in 15- to 30-year corporate or government bonds
- Intermediate-term bond funds: Investments in 5- to 15-year government or corporate bonds

Money Market Funds (least aggressive and least risky)

- International money market funds: Investments in foreign CDs and other short-term paper
- Tax-exempt money market funds: Investments in short-term municipal bonds
- Money market funds: Investments in CDs, short-term government treasuries, and so on

The Advantages and Disadvantages of Mutual Funds

Here are the advantages and disadvantages of mutual funds, according to our gurus.

Advantages of Mutual Funds

Our gurus name three primary advantages of investing through mutual funds.

1. **Instant diversification:** As we will explain in Chapter 9, one of the most important ways to reduce risk in investing is to own a wide variety of stocks and/or bonds. Because of their size, mutual funds can buy a much wider variety of stocks and bonds than any single individual can. As Eric Tyson notes, if you tried to go it alone, you would need to have several hundred thousand dollars to invest and would have to spread your investment across 8 to 12 securities to approach getting the kind of diversification that most mutual funds can offer.[30]

2. **Professional management:** This benefit is touted by all of our gurus. Rather than having to pick stocks, bonds, and other investments yourself, you can let a professional do the picking for you. Tyson says you can and should expect the best mutual fund managers to have five or more years of experience in analyzing and selecting investments and access to investment analysis and data that is simply not available to most people.[31] Finally, says Bambi Holzer, "[M]utual fund portfolio managers rely on reason, not emotion, to make investment decisions. . . . [Therefore, they] . . . keep people like you and [us] from making stupid mistakes with our money."[32]

3. **Low cost:** A big advantage of mutual funds over investing on your own, say our gurus, is that you can get started with a fund for an investment of as little as $500 to $1,000 and then continue to invest in small amounts or even by having your dividends reinvested. For a small fee, you not only get the benefits of having the costs of investment research spread across thousands of investors, but you also get to take advantage of substantial discounts when investments in the fund are bought or sold. As Tyson notes, mutual funds normally buy or sell thousands of shares of a security at one time. Consequently, their transactions fees are much less than you would pay for buying or selling a few shares on your own.[33]

Disadvantages of Mutual Funds

Our gurus identify the following disadvantages of mutual funds:

1. **Pseudo-diversification may cause a false sense of security:** As Jonathan Clements notes, you cannot assume that you have a diversified portfolio just be-

cause you are investing through a mutual fund. Some funds are so specialized that they offer little in the way of diversification.[34] The only way to know for sure is to check the investments of each fund you are considering.

As Terry Savage explains, you shouldn't rely on the name of the fund or a brief description. You need to review the actual stocks the fund holds, particularly its largest investments, to make sure that they are consistent with the fund's and your investment objectives. Savage also recommends going to http://www.morningstar.net/ to get an independent analysis of any fund you are considering. Finally, she cautions not to overdiversify by investing in dozens of funds because you'll just end up with a paperwork headache. Savage says that if you do your research right, you should be able to hold your investment to two or three mutual fund "families" and still be adequately diversified.[35]

By law a mutual fund cannot invest more than 5 percent of its assets in any one company; therefore, you are guaranteed at least some level of diversification.

2. **The professional manager may not be so professional:** There is no guarantee that a fund will be a superior performer just because a fund is managed by a "professional." In fact, says Arthur Levitt, most professionally managed stock funds fail to perform as well as their index during most years.[36] As James O'Shaughnessy, author of *How to Retire Rich,* says, you should not assume that a professional money manager is any less emotional about investing than most people:

Nearly every traditional mutual fund manager working today is subject to the same whims and passions and the same emotional decision-making process that makes regular investors underperform the S&P 500 [index of market performance.] Stocks are bought and sold on hunches, feelings, hope, and greed, not with underlying strategies that are consistently implemented. . . .

Professional fund managers live and breathe the market, minute by minute. If you think day-to-day market fluctuations can make you panic, think about what minute-to-minute movements must do to the emotions of professional managers! Moreover, it's a rare money manager who doesn't believe he or she is uniquely gifted in picking good stocks. They believe they have the ability to sift through each great story for the few that will lead to riches.

Unfortunately, the facts are against them. . . . They, too, are victims of their humanity—and, in many cases, their oversized egos.[37]

In addition, says O'Shaughnessy, the compensation system for fund managers may work against investors' long-term interest. For example, consider a fund manager who has a $1 million bonus tied to his or her fund beating the performance of a market index such as the S&P 500 Index. That manager might be encouraged to add some risky investments to the fund's portfolio if, for example, it is midyear and the fund's performance is trailing the index. This focus on short-term performance might be much too risky for you if you are a long-term investor.[38] Arthur Levitt says that most funds don't like to publicize their fund manager's compensation package, but you should ask about it anyway.[39]

3. **The low cost may not be so low:** Mutual funds are low cost only if you pick the right funds. In fact, some funds are very expensive. It all has to do with the fees you pay to invest through the particular mutual fund and the tax consequences of your investment. Let's look at the tax issue first.

- **Taxes:** A mutual fund can have an impact on your taxes by producing taxable distributions in the form of capital gains and dividends. Dividends are fund earnings that are paid out to shareholders on a periodic basis. Unless they are from a tax-free municipal fund, they are taxable income to you even if you reinvest them in the fund.

  Funds create capital gains when the fund manager(s) sell fund securities at a profit. Former Securities and Exchange Commission (SEC) Chairman Arthur Levitt warns that you could be incurring a large capital gain and not even know it when you buy a mutual fund if you aren't careful. As he says:

  When you buy into a fund, you are most likely buying into a tax liability. For example, say you buy $10,000 worth of Fund XYZ on December 20 at $10 a share. The next day, the fund calculates that its cap gains for the entire year came to $2.00 a share. You own 1,000 shares and therefore will receive a "distribution" of $2,000—taxable to you. Because you were a shareholder of record on December 21, you have to pay the same taxes as the guy who bought on January 1, except that he probably paid less for his shares. In the end, the total amount of money you have invested in the fund remains $10,000, so you may be tempted to view all of this as a wash. But you have now incurred a tax bill on $2,000 of your own money. Soon you will receive a Form 1099 from the fund, which states your share of the dividends and the short- and long-term capital gain.[40]

Levitt says that one way you can minimize taxes is to avoid buying shares late in the year; another is to pay attention to after-tax, rather than just pretax, profits.

As of February 2002, mutual funds are required to report their after-tax performance in their fund's prospectus, so be sure to check.

- **Charges and fees:** When it comes to costs, mutual funds have two types of charges and fees—loads and operating expenses:
  - ☐ **Loads:** Loads are commissions some funds (called "load" funds) charge you when you buy or sell fund shares. There are three basic types of loads:
    - ☐ **Front-end loads (A shares):** You pay a commission of 1 to 6 percent when you buy the shares.
    - ☐ **Back-end loads (B shares):** You pay a commission when you sell your shares. Usually the amount you have to pay is less the longer you hold the shares. For example, you might be charged a commission of 6 percent if you sell your shares within one year. The amount of commission would be reduced each year until it reaches zero at some time in the future such as in year six or seven.
    - ☐ **Level loads (C shares)**—You pay an annual commission (typically 1 percent of your account balance) each year for as long as you hold shares in the fund.
  - ☐ **Management fees and operating expense:** In addition to loads (which are charged by load funds), all mutual funds charge fees to cover the costs associated with managing the fund and providing shareholder services. These fees typically included the following:
    - ☐ **Management fees:** These fees cover the costs of compensating the fund manager(s). They are stated as a percentage of the fund's average assets.
    - ☐ **12b-1 fees:** These fees cover the fund's sales and marketing expenses and are also stated as a percentage of the funds assets.

In short, say our gurus, a mutual fund can be low cost or high cost depending on its operating expenses and whether it charges a load or is no-load. A big mistake many mutual fund investors make is failing to pay attention to the loads and operating expenses of the funds they are buying. Although the fees and charges sound low (1, 2, 3 percent, etc.), as Arthur Levitt notes, they can make a significant difference in your return on your investment over time.[41] For example, Gary Belsky and Thomas Gilovich compared the results of investing $10,000 in an average-cost mutual fund for 10 years with what they would obtain from investing in a low-cost fund for the same period. They found that the low-cost fund produced a 14 percent greater return over the entire period.[42]

Here's a trick that Arthur Levitt says will help you put mutual fund expense in the proper context:

Don't look at the 1 percent or 2 percent expense ratio in isolation, but rather as a percentage of what you expect your returns to be. [For example,] . . . if a fund advertises its expense ratio as 1.5 percent, and you are reasonably expecting the fund to return 7.5 percent after one year, the true expense ratio is 20 percent (1.5 divided by 7.5 = 20 percent). A thriftier fund with an expense ration of 0.5 percent eats up only 6.6 percent of your returns (0.5 divided by 7.5 = 6.6 percent).[43]

Index Funds

According to David and Tom Gardner, as well as most of the other gurus, index funds are not only killer competitive products in the mutual fund industry, they are "brainless and respectable" "first stop" choices for most investors.[44] Index funds simply attempt to match an underlying index such as the S&P 500 (an index of 500 large industrial, financial, utility, and transportation stocks), the Russell 2000 (an index of 2,000 small company stocks), the Wilshire 5000 (an index of the entire U.S. stock market), or the Lehman Brothers Aggregate Bond Index (an index of the overall bond market). Index fund managers don't try to second-guess or outwit the market. They simply buy stocks or bonds that are representative of the index. As Charles Schwab says, "With index funds, you don't play the odds, you play the averages, and you're not dependent upon a manager's expertise."[45]

Advantages of Index Funds

Our gurus identify the following advantages that index funds have over other mutual funds.

1. **Index funds outperform managed funds:** Since their inception in the mid-1970s, index funds have consistently outperformed managed funds. There are three reasons for this, says Jane Bryant Quinn.[46] First, managers of nonindex funds usually hold out a cash cushion as protection in the case of a market downturn. As a result, they are seldom fully invested and they can miss opportunities for gains in the market. In contrast, index fund managers are almost always fully invested. Second, even if a managed fund doesn't charge a load, it normally has higher operating expenses than an indexed fund. The index fund's lower cost gives it an advantage from the start. Finally, there is clear evidence that superstar fund managers are rarely superstar stock pickers for long. As our gurus suggest, compare the list of the top 10 performers last year with the top 10 this year—the odds are very good that few if any of last year's superstars will show up in this year's list. In fact, it is more likely that last year's champion will be this year's bottom-of-the-heap loser.

2. **Index funds are truly low cost:** Index funds don't have to hire superstar fund managers because the work of picking stocks or bonds can be done mostly by a computer. Therefore, the annual operating expenses of an index fund are much lower than those of a managed fund. In addition, because index fund managers aren't buying and selling securities constantly in a mad chase after making their return, you don't have to worry about being suddenly hit with large capital gains taxes, as can happen with managed mutual funds.

Selecting a Mutual Fund

All of our gurus offer advice on how you should go about selecting a mutual fund. We think Julie Stav, author of *Fund Your Future,* has one of the best approaches. The following is based on her ideas.[47]

Step #1: Narrow Your Search to Funds That Match Your Investment Objectives

More than 12,000 mutual funds are vying for your investment dollars, so your first challenge is to narrow your selection to a more manageable number by eliminating from consideration any funds that don't match your investment objectives. Stav suggests that you look at three criteria to narrow your choice.

1. **Long-term capital appreciation or short-term income:** Funds differ in their investment objectives. Some funds invest for *growth,* meaning that their managers invest primarily in stocks and are more interested in long-term capital appreciation than short-term income from dividends. Other funds invest for *income,* meaning that their managers invest primarily in bonds or in companies that pay large dividends. They are interested in generating current income. Finally, some firms invest for *growth and income,* meaning that their managers invest primarily in stocks that pay dividends. They are interested in short-term income along with respectable long-term capital appreciation.

Stav says the key question to ask yourself is this: "Do I want to invest so I can begin to receive income now, . . . or am I willing not to touch any of the money and just let it grow for a period of two years or longer?"[48] If you are interested in current income, you are a *income investor* and should look for mutual funds that invest for income. If you are investing for the long term and aren't interested in current income, then you are a *growth* investor and should look for mutual funds that invest for growth.

Mutual fund companies are required by the SEC to state their fund's objectives in the fund's prospectus. You can obtain a copy of the fund prospectus directly from the mutual fund company or by going to the SEC Web site at http://www.sec.gov/edgar/

searchedgar/prospectus.htm and entering the first few letters of the mutual fund company's name, such as "VAN" for Vanguard.

2. **Capitalization choice:** Capitalization refers to the size of company the fund invests in—large-cap (over $5 billion), mid-cap ($1 billion to $5 billion), small-cap ($250 million to $1 billion), and micro-cap (under $250 million). Remember that as a general rule, the stock of small companies tends to fluctuate more and therefore is riskier than the stock of larger companies. Again, check the fund prospectus for an indication of the capitalization choice of the fund.

3. **Investment style:** Finally, funds differ in the investment styles of fund managers. There are three basic styles of investing: *value, growth,* and *blend.* Fund managers with a *value* style seek to buy stocks that are selling for bargain prices. Fund managers with a *growth* style seek to buy stocks of companies that are growing rapidly. As the name suggests, fund managers with a *blend* style seek a balance between growth and value. As Stav notes, investment style matters because the stock market rewards and punishes different styles at different times. For example, in the 1990s growth stocks performed well, so growth funds did well. After 2000, growth stock fell out of favor and value funds started to do well. As a rule of thumb, Stav says that "growth stocks tend to do well when the stock market as a whole is rising. Value stocks tend to shine when the stock market is falling or just treading water."[49]

Check the capitalization choice and investment style of any fund you are considering by going to http://morningstar.com/ and requesting a Morningstar Quicktake® Report on the fund. Look for the "Morningstar Category" designation such as "Large Growth" or "Small Value" under the tab "Snapshot." Also, look for a style box on the report under the "Diagnostics" tab that shows the capitalization choice and investment style at a glance.

Step #2: Check the Fund's Total Return

Total return refers to the profit the mutual fund has made in the past. Stav says to look for the trailing total return table in the Morningstar Quicktake Report under the "Returns" tab. You are looking for the 1-year, 3-year annualized, 5-year annualized, and 10-year annualized returns. See Exhibit 8.1 for three examples.

When you compare the performance of these three funds, you can see some significant differences. For example, although all three funds had a negative return over the last year, the "annualized" or average return for Fund A and Fund B over 10 years was 9.8 and 14.6 percent, respectively. Fund C hasn't been in existence for 10 years, so there are no long-term results. However, Fund C's performance over the three-year and five-year periods has been negative and significantly worse than Fund A and Fund B.

EXHIBIT 8.1. **Examples of Total Return Percentages for Three Index Funds**

Fund A: S&P 500 Index Fund

Trailing Total Returns

	TOTAL RETURN %	+/− S&P 500	% RANK IN CAT
1-Year	−16.89	−0.03	43
3-Year Annualized	−12.00	−0.01	51
5-Year Annualized	0.66	−0.02	36
10-Year Annualized	9.80	−0.07	24

Fund B: Large Value Stock Fund

Trailing Total Returns

	TOTAL RETURN %	+/− S&P 500	% RANK IN CAT
1-Year	−4.37	12.49	3
3-Year Annualized	6.33	18.32	1
5-Year Annualized	8.19	7.51	1
10-Year Annualized	14.26	4.39	2

Fund C: Large Growth Fund

Trailing Total Returns

	TOTAL RETURN %	+/− S&P 500	% RANK IN CAT
1-Year	−21.67	−4.79	50
3-Year Annualized	−21.85	−4.99	50
5-Year Annualized	−18.76	−6.77	62
10-Year Annualized	—	—	—

How much credence should you give to the historical performance of mutual funds? Our gurus say you should keep in mind the warning printed in every fund's prospectus that past performance isn't an indicator of future performance. In particular, they say, you should ignore short-term (daily, weekly, monthly, and quarterly) results; as Bambi Holzer puts it, top funds for the quarter and even top funds for the year are usually nothing more than flukes.[50] You can give more credence to longer-term (3-year, 5-year, and 10-year) performance, say our gurus, but even then you should keep the results in perspective. Stav says the stability of the returns over a three-year or longer period are more important than the returns themselves because they give you some indication of how volatile and risky a fund is. The lesson, says Peter Lynch, is that you shouldn't "spend a lot of time poring over the past performance charts. That's not to say that you shouldn't pick a fund with a good long-term track record. But it's better to stick with a steady and consistent performer than to move in and out of funds, trying to catch the waves."[51]

Step #3: Check the Fund's Ranking

The fund's ranking tells you how the fund has performed in the past compared with other similar funds. Stav says you should look at two types of numbers. First, look at the column in the Morningstar Quicktake Report labeled "+/− S&P 500." These numbers show how the fund performed over different periods compared with the S&P 500 Index. As we explained earlier, the S&P 500 Index is a index of 500 large industrial, financial, utility, and transportation stocks and is generally accepted as a rough measure of the performance of the market in general. Most fund managers strive to beat the S&P 500; the "+/− S&P 500" column on the Morningstar report tells you how well the managers of the fund you are considering did over different periods. In our examples in Exhibit 8.2, Fund A, the S&P 500 Index Fund, has performed very close to the S&P 500 during each period, as we might expect. Fund B beat the performance of S&P 500 during each period and beat it by a substantial margin in the last three years. On the other hand, Fund C underperformed compared with the S&P 500.

The second set of numbers Stav says you should look at are found in the column labeled "% Ranking in Cat" (see Exhibit 8.1). These figures tell you the percentage rank of the fund compared to similar finds. The ranking ranges from 1 to 100. A ranking of "1" means the fund was in the top 1% of all similar funds in terms of performance. A ranking of "100" means it was beaten by all other similar firms. In our examples, you can see that Fund A was in the top quarter of funds over the last ten years while Fund C was in the bottom half. Fund B was a top performing fund ranking first over both three and five years and second over ten years.

EXHIBIT 8.2. **Morningstar Ratings for Three Index Funds**

Fund A
Morningstar Rating

3-Year	★★★
5-Year	★★★
10-Year	★★★★
Overall	★★★★

Fund B
Morningstar Rating

3-Year	★★★★★
5-Year	★★★★★
10-Year	★★★★★
Overall	★★★★★

Fund C
Morningstar Rating

3-Year	★★★
5-Year	★★★
10-Year	Not Rated
Overall	★★★

Step #4: Check the Fund's Morningstar Rating™

The category ranking tells you how the fund performed relative to other similar funds. The Morningstar Rating not only tells you how the fund ranked in terms of performance, but balances performance with the level of risk the fund manager took in generating those returns. Morningstar assigns stars based upon a fund's rating. A fund with a five-star (★★★★★) rating is rated in the top 10 percent of similar funds in terms of risk/performance, whereas a fund with a one-star (★) rating places it in the bottom 10 percent. Stav says you should look for funds with no less than a five-star rating. To find the Morningstar Rating, look under the "Ratings" tab in the Quicktake Report. As you can see in the examples in Exhibit 8.2, only Fund B has a five-star rating for all periods.

Step #5: Check the Fund's Beta

A fund's beta is a measure of the degree of volatility of the fund relative to the S&P 500 Index. A beta less than 1 indicates that the fund is *less* volatile—in other words, it has fewer up-and-down swings—than the S&P 500 Index. A beta greater than 1 indicates that the fund is more volatile. As Stav notes, "[T]here is no better or worse beta rating, but remember that the higher the beta, the higher the possible returns you may have in your fund when things are going well, but the bigger the losses will be during the inevitable lows."[52] To find the beta for any fund you are considering, check the "Ratings" tab in the Morningstar Quicktake Report for the fund. In our examples, because it is an S&P 500 index fund, Fund A has a beta of 1.00. Fund B has a beta of 0.68, indicating that it is less volatile than Fund A. Fund C has a beta of 1.15, indicating that it is more volatile.

Fees and Expenses

	FUND A	FUND B	FUND C
Maximum sales fees %			
Initial (front-end load)	0.00	0.00	5.75
Deferred (back-end load)	0.00	0.00	0.00
12b-1	0.00	0.00	0.25
Total expense ratio	0.18	0.54	1.16

Step #6: Check the Fund's Fees

Finally, says Stav, you want to check the fund's fees. What is the expense ratio? Does the fund charge a 12b-1 fee? As we noted earlier, fees are important because they can make a significant difference in your total return over time. Fees are listed in the Morningstar Quicktake Report under the "Portfolio—Fees and Expenses" tab. Loads are listed as "Maximum Sales Fees %—Initial (Front-End) and Deferred (Back-End)." The other numbers you want to look at are under the heading "Actual Fees %"—12b-1 and Total Expense Ratio. In our examples, Funds A and B charged no load whereas Fund C charged an initial or front-end load of 5.75 percent. Fund C also charged a 12b-1 fee of 0.25 percent. The total expense ratios of the three funds were 0.18 percent, 0.54 percent, and 1.16 percent for Funds A, B, and C, respectively. Notice that because of the front-end load, 12b-1 fee, and higher expense ratio, Fund C is by far the most expensive fund. Fund A is the least expensive, which is common for index funds.

Other Selection Criteria

The gurus say that in addition to finding funds whose investment objectives match your own, you want a fund with the following:

- A consistent and high 10-year total return
- Positive performance over time compared with the S&P 500
- A low percentage ranking in its category (10 percent or less, according to Stav)
- A five-star Morningstar Rating
- A low beta
- No load
- No 12b-1 fees
- A low expense ratio

Two other things to consider are the fund's turnover rate and the experience of the fund manager. A fund's turnover rate is a measure of how active the fund manager is in buying and selling stock. As Olivia Mellan notes, funds with high turnover rates can hurt you in two ways.[53] First, they generate trading costs from all of the buying and selling that don't appear in the fund's expense ratio but are deducted from your account as a kind of hidden charge. Second, funds with a high turnover rate can generate significant capital gains and therefore can subject you to additional taxes. The annual turnover rate for a fund is listed under the "Snapshot" tab of the Morningstar Quicktake Report. Mellan says you should consider a turnover rate of 50 to 75 percent as high and that anything over 100 percent is extremely high.

A final factor you may want to consider when selecting a fund, say our gurus, is the experience of the fund manager. David Teitelbaum, author of *The Procrastinator's Guide to Financial Security,* has the following recommendations:

- **Look for a long track record.** You want a manager who has a lot of experience. Ideally, the experience should be in running the fund you are considering. Teitelbaum says when you find a fund with a good long-term track record, check to see how long the current manager has been managing the fund. If the current manager is new, the long-term track record may be meaningless.
- **Be suspicious if you notice that the fund manager has changed his or her investment style.** As we noted earlier, some fund managers are *value investors;* others are *growth investors.* Teitelbaum warns that you should be concerned if a manager switches styles; that may be a sign that the manager is just trying to catch the segment of the market that is hot at the moment in order to make the fund look good. The problem with a manager who switches

back and forth between value and growth investing, says Teitelbaum, is that "in most instances, a value manager won't do well investing in growth stocks, and a manager who specializes in small-cap stocks won't do well picking large-cap stocks. [Therefore,] you should always avoid funds that have shifted strategies."[54]

- **Be cautious about investing with managers who have loaded their funds with stocks from one or two sectors such as technology, financial services, or energy services.** A fund manager who loads up on stocks from a hot sector can look like a genius. The problem, says Teitelbaum, is that all hot sectors eventually turn cold. Plus, a fund manager who constantly chases "hot" sectors eventually will guess wrong, and the fund will suffer. So, check the Morningstar Quicktake Report under the "Snapshot" tab for the "Sector Breakdown" of any fund you are considering. If the fund is heavily loaded with stocks from a particular sector such as health care or consumer goods or services and you are not committed to such sector investing, find yourself another fund.

- **Watch out for funds that have a large and sudden growth in assets.** The gurus warn that you should be careful about investing in funds that have grown too big; the excess cash may force the fund manager to have to change investment strategies and invest in less-favorable stocks and/or keep a larger-than-normal cash balance. When that happens, says Teitelbaum, you can expect the fund's performance to suffer.[55] Again, say our gurus, you should check the Morningstar reports and other sources.

We have referred frequently to the Morningstar Quicktake Report in this chapter. Similar information can be found from Value Line Publishing at its Web site at http://valueline.com/index.html/. Also check your local library for printed copies of Morningstar and Value Line reports.

In this chapter, we covered the five basic types of investment and provided the pros and cons of each. In our next—and last—chapter, we will cover investing for retirement and provide some key investment strategies. But first, let's revisit our key points about investing.

⚷ KEY POINTS

⚷ The major types of investments are stocks, bonds, real estate, and cash equivalents.

- When you buy stock, you are buying *equity* in a company; in other words, you are becoming a part owner of the company.

- You should consider stocks only when you are investing for a minimum of 5 years, and preferably 10 years or longer.

- One way to distinguish between types of stocks is according to the size of the company issuing them, from large-cap to micro-cap.

- You make money from stocks by receiving dividends and/or by profiting from capital gains.

- Growth stocks pay small dividends. You own them when you are looking to make profits through capital gains.

- Income stocks pay high dividends. You own them when you want a steady income.

- Value stocks are stocks that are considered undervalued by the stock market.

- When you buy bonds, you are lending money to a company or government.

- The average investor should avoid the following types of investments:
  - Options and commodities futures
  - Initial public offerings (IPOs)
  - Most investments known by an acronym such as ETFs, CMOs, LEAPs, and so on
  - Collectibles such as coins, rare books, artwork, and so on
  - Penny stocks

- Mutual funds are the best way for the novice investor to begin investing.

- Mutual funds come in a wide variety of flavors to satisfy just about anyone's investment tastes.

- The advantages of mutual funds include instant diversification, professional management, and low costs.

- One disadvantage of mutual funds is that they provide a false sense of security. Too, it's important to research who's running the fund and what fees they charge.

- Index funds largely eliminate the need for professional fund managers.

- The keys to selecting a mutual fund that is right for you are as follows:
  - Matching the fund to your investment objectives
  - Checking the fund's total return over a long period, preferably 10 years
  - Checking the fund's ranking on Morningstar

- Checking the fund's Morningstar rating
- Checking the fund's beta
- Checking the fund's fees
- Checking the fund's turnover rate
- Checking the experience of the fund's manager(s)

OUR GURUS

David Caruso, coauthor of *Let's Talk Money*

Ric Edelman, author of *New Rules of Money*

Robert Kiyosaki, author of *Rich Dad's Guide to Investing*

Dee Lee, coauthor of *Let's Talk Money*

Dwight Lee, coauthor of *Getting Rich in America*

Arthur Levitt, coauthor of *Take on the Street*

Peter Lynch, coauthor of *Learn to Earn*

Richard McKenzie, coauthor of *Getting Rich in America*

Suze Orman, author of *The 9 Steps to Financial Freedom*

Jonathan Pond, author of *Your Money Matters*

Jane Bryant Quinn, author of *Making the Most of Your Money*

Charles Schwab, author of *Charles Schwab's Guide to Financial Independence*

Eric Tyson, author of *Personal Finance for Dummies*

9

Investing for Retirement

People invest in stocks, bonds, real estate, cash equivalents, and things they shouldn't invest in for a wide variety of reasons. Regardless of the reasons people invest and save, almost everyone devotes at least part of their investment dollars to one very important goal—retirement. We conclude this book with a discussion of our gurus' recommendations for how to reach that goal. What are the special things you must know about investing for retirement? We'll start with the most basic retirement question: How big a nest egg will I need?

HOW MUCH MONEY WILL YOU NEED TO RETIRE?

All of our gurus offer methods for guesstimating how big an investment nest egg you will need to retire, but we think a method offered by Charles Schwab is one of the most enlightening.[1] Schwab says to begin by estimating how much you think you will need in annual income from investments once you retire. According to Schwab, financial planners normally suggest that you use an amount somewhere between 80 and 100 percent of your current income. You should use 100 percent if you think your expenses after retirement will be roughly the same as they are now. Use a number less than 100 percent if you think your expenses will be less because, for example, you will have paid off your mortgage or you no longer will have the expense of commuting to work. If you think you will have more expenses after you retire because you intend to travel extensively, for example, then Schwab says you should use an amount greater than 100 percent of your current salary.

Once you have an estimate of the retirement income you will need on an annual basis, then divide that number by 12 to get the income you need per month.

Although Schwab doesn't mention it in the discussion of his formula, if you expect to receive Social Security, a company pension, or income from another source such as rental property, and/or you plan to work during retirement, the income you need from your retirement investments may be less than the annual retirement income needed as shown in this formula. For example, if you currently make $100,000, and you estimate you'll need 80 percent of that after retirement, then the figure you're starting with is $80,000. But let's say you expect to receive $18,000 per year from Social Security ($1,500 per month) and $13,000 per year from your company pension. You could reduce your annual retirement income needed from $80,000 to $49,000, which would allow you to make do on a smaller investment nest egg.

Next, says Schwab, divide the monthly retirement income figure (in this example, $6,667, or 80,000 ÷ 12) by 1,000 and multiply by 230,000.[2]

$$(\text{monthly retirement income} \div 1{,}000) \times 230{,}000 =$$
$$\text{retirement nest egg you need.}$$
$$(\$6{,}667 \div 1{,}000) \times 230{,}000 = \$1{,}533{,}410$$
$$(\$\underline{\hspace{2cm}} \div 1{,}000) \times 230{,}000 = \$\underline{\hspace{2cm}}$$

If you want to factor in income you expect from a pension, contact your company's pension plan manager for an estimate of what your pension might be. Contact the Social Security Administration (SSA) for an estimate of what you might receive in Social Security benefits by writing to Social Security Administration, Office of Earnings Operations, P.O. Box 33026, Baltimore, MD 21290–3026, or going to the SSA Web site at http://www.ssa.gov/mystatement/.

If you want a more precise way of estimating how much you will need in retirement, consult Schwab's more detailed calculation formula in his book *You're Fifty—Now What?* Also see Schwab's automated retirement planning tools at http://www.schwab.com/.

Here are two other Web sites with useful retirement-planning tools:

Quicken's Retirement Planner at http://www.quicken.com/retirement/planner/
The CNBC Retirement Planner at http://moneycentral.msn.com/retire/planner.asp/

RETIREMENT INVESTMENT VEHICLES

In our previous example, if you wanted $80,000 in annual retirement income, you would have to accumulate a $1.5 million nest egg by retirement age, or slightly less than $1 million if you factor in Social Security, a company pension, or other income. Fortunately, you have a number of investment vehicles, many tax friendly, that you can use to build your nest egg. Here's a brief summary of some of the most popular options.

These are general descriptions. For complete information on any given plan, its detailed provisions and limitations, please consult your employer's pension plan administrator or your tax advisor.

Traditional Pension/Defined Benefit Plan

With traditional company pension or defined benefit plans, you work 20-plus years and retire with a fixed monthly income for the rest of your life. The benefits may not be enough to meet all of your needs, but they're a good base for reducing the amount of monthly retirement income you must generate from your investments and other sources. If you have this type of retirement benefit from your company, you are in luck; most companies no longer offer them.

401(k) and 403(b) Plans

The 401(k) is a retirement plan that allows you as an employee to contribute a portion of your pay to a tax-deferred retirement account. Your contributions are made on a pretax basis, so they reduce the amount of your W-2 taxable income. Your contributions and earnings aren't taxed until you start making withdrawals. In general, you cannot make withdrawals until age 59 1/2 without being hit by a 10 percent penalty; however, you can usually borrow against your 401(k) account. Your employer may make a matching contribution to your plan each year up to a pre-specified limit. Similarly, employees of nonprofit organizations such as public school systems, hospitals, and charitable organizations may contribute to 403(b) plans.

Our gurus say you should fund your 401(k) to the maximum, particularly if your employer makes a matching contribution. The 401(k) is an essential retirement investment tool, and it's important to keep track of its status. See Exhibit 9.1 for a list of 10 warning signs that your 401(k) might be in trouble, according to former SEC chairman Arthur Levitt.

Individual Retirement Accounts (IRAs)

Individual retirement accounts (IRAs) are individual retirement savings plans that you set up with banks, brokers, or mutual fund companies. If you have earned income, you are allowed to contribute up to $3,000 per year (as of 2002—$3,500 if you are 50 or older) to your individual retirement account. Your spouse can set up an IRA and also contribute up to $3,000 per year regardless of whether he or she has earned income. In most cases, you cannot withdraw funds from your IRA prior to age 59 1/2 without paying a substantial penalty.

EXHIBIT 9.1. Ten Warning Signs of 401(k) Trouble

Arthur Levitt says you should keep a watchful eye on your 401(k) plan. Here are his 10 warning signs that your funds might be in danger.

1. Your 401(k) or individual account statement is consistently late or comes at irregular intervals.
2. Your account balance does not appear to be accurate.
3. Your employer fails to transmit your contribution to the plan on a timely basis.
4. There is a significant drop in account balance that can't be explained by normal market ups and downs.
5. You receive account statements that do not show the contributions from your paycheck that were made.
6. Investments listed on your statement are not what you authorized.
7. Former employees are having trouble getting their benefits paid on time or in the correct amounts.
8. Your account statement or a letter from your employer reports an unusual transaction, such as a loan to the employer, a corporate officer, or a plan trustee.
9. There are frequent and unexplained changes in investment managers or consultants.
10. Your employer has recently experienced severe financial difficulty.

Source: Arthur Levitt with Paula Dwyer, Take on the Street (New York: Pantheon, 2002), p. 279.

There are two basic types of IRAs—traditional IRAs and Roth IRAs. Exhibit 9.2 contains a summary of the key differences between the two.

Simplified Employee Pensions (SEP-IRAs)

SEP-IRAs are retirement plans for small employers and the self-employed. If you are self-employed, you can contribute up to 15 percent of your net earnings to a SEP-IRA.

Keogh Plan

Keogh plans are for self-employed people and partnerships. They operate similarly to SEP-IRAs but are more complicated to set up. However, they allow you to contribute more of your earned income (up to 25 percent in 2002) than with a SEP-IRA. Keoghs essentially have the same provisions as a traditional IRA.

EXHIBIT 9.2. **Comparison of Traditional and Roth IRAs**

	TRADITIONAL IRA	ROTH IRA
Deductible contribution?	Contributions may be deductible.	Contributions are not deductible.
Tax-free growth	Money invested in the IRA grows tax free. Withdrawals are taxed as normal income.	Money grows tax free. Withdrawals are not taxed.
Deadline for withdrawals	Withdrawals must begin by age 70 1/2.	No deadline.
Eligibility	Anyone with earned income or who has a spouse with earned income.	Not available to persons with high incomes.

Savings Incentive Match Plans for Employees (SIMPLEs)

SIMPLEs are retirement plans for self-employed individuals, partnerships, and small businesses that employ fewer than 100 employees and don't have another retirement plan. SIMPLEs can operate like IRAs or 401(k) plans. Employees and the self-employed are eligible if they receive $5,000 of earned income from the employer (as of 2002). Eligible employees in 2002 could make a tax-deductible contribution of up to a maximum of $7,000 ($7,500 if 50 or older). In addition, employers are required to make a matching contribution up to a maximum of 3 percent of each employee's compensation. Like IRAs, there are substantial penalties for withdrawals prior to age 59 1/2.

THE KEY TO SUCCESSFUL RETIREMENT INVESTING

Regardless of the retirement investment vehicle you choose or are required to use by your employer, our gurus say that the key to success in investing for retirement is your ability to balance the risk and reward of your investments over time. Remember that risk and reward are related—investments that offer the greatest opportunity for return (reward) also carry the greatest risk. For example, small-company stock generally offers a greater potential for gains than large-company stock but also carries a greater potential for loss. In short, the various types of investments we have discussed fall along a risk-reward continuum that looks much like this:

Low Risk				High Risk
Cash equivalents	Bonds	Stocks	Real estate	Investments to avoid (IPOs, commodities, etc.)

In this case, we are talking about market risk or the risk of losing money on your investment. However, as Jonathan Pond notes, there is another kind of risk that can be equally damaging: the invisible risk of inflation, which can have a significant impact on your retirement income:

Someone who is planning to retire figures that, in addition to Social Security, he'll need $25,000 per year in income for living expenses. Now $25,000 happens to be just what his annual retirement income is expected to be, so he thinks he's in good shape. But consider how inflation can affect the purchasing power of his $25,000 over his retirement years. If inflation is 3 1/2 percent per year, after less than seven years our retiree has seen his purchasing power drop to $20,000. After 20 years, his purchasing power can be cut in half. So that $25,000 of income, which looked so good at the time he was planning his retirement, could be worth far less in terms of purchasing power later in life.[3]

In short, say our gurus, the twin risks of loss of investment due to market risks and loss of purchasing power due to inflation present a significant challenge to anyone planning for retirement. If you stick to safe and secure, low-market risk investments like CDs, you risk losing purchasing power to inflation. If you throw caution to the wind and load up on high-risk stocks, you might win big, but you also might be wiped out by a sudden market decline. Are there any ways you can minimize market risks while simultaneously protecting yourself from the ravages of inflation? Yes, say our gurus, there are.

RETIREMENT INVESTMENT STRATEGIES

In this section, we discuss five strategies for minimizing market risk and maximizing return on retirement investments. Although we are discussing these strategies in terms of retirement investing, they are good strategies to follow regardless of your investment goals. The strategies are asset allocation, diversification, dollar-cost averaging, buy and hold, and compounding.

Asset Allocation

The basic idea behind asset allocation is that you can minimize your risk and maximize your return by spreading your investments across a range of asset types. In other words, instead of putting all of your money in stocks and running the risk of a loss if the stock market declines, you invest only some of your funds in stocks and put the rest into bonds or cash equivalents such as money market funds or CDs.

The amount you should invest in stocks, say the gurus, depends on your age or, more precisely, how many years you have before retirement. The idea behind this answer is that from day to day, week to week, month to month, the market fluctuates, and history shows that over time it usually goes up, but short-term it can turn down. Consider, for example, what happened in the early 2000s. Asset allocation is designed to protect you from those inevitable short-term downturns particular when you are getting close to retirement. If you are in your twenties and investing for retirement and the market takes a sharp downturn, you have plenty of years left to make up your losses, but what happens if you are five years away from retirement and the bottom falls out? Like many investors in the early 2000s, you may find your nest egg wiped out, and the only choice you may have is to delay your retirement for years. Here is the asset allocation rule of thumb with some modifications from several of our gurus.

 To determine how much of your portfolio to invest in stocks, subtract your age from 100. Invest your age in bonds and/or cash equivalents and the balance in stocks.[4] For example, if you are 20, the amount you would invest in stocks and bonds/cash equivalents (CEs) would be:

$$\text{bonds/CEs} = \text{age} = 20 \text{ percent}$$
$$\text{stocks} = 100 - 20 = 80 \text{ percent}$$

If you are 50, the amount you would invest in stocks and bonds/cash equivalents would be:

$$\text{bonds/CEs} = \text{age} = 50 \text{ percent}$$
$$\text{stocks} = 100 - 50 = 50 \text{ percent}$$

Although many gurus use the 100-minus-age rule of thumb, a number offer their own variations. Here are two examples.

Eric Tyson's Asset Allocation Rule of Thumb

Tyson takes the standard asset allocation rule of thumb and adds in the additional factor of your risk tolerance.[5] He says if you are a risk adverse/play-it-safe kind of investor, use the 100-minus-age for stocks and your age for bonds and cash equivalents, but if you want to be a little more aggressive, then use the following:

$$\text{bonds} = \text{age} - 10$$
$$\text{stocks} = 110 - \text{age}$$

For example, if you are 20 years old,

$$\text{bonds} = 20 - 10 = 10 \text{ percent in bonds/cash equivalents}$$
$$\text{stocks} = 110 - \text{age (20)} = 90 \text{ percent in stocks}$$

If you want to be very aggressive, then use the following:

$$\text{bonds} = \text{age} - 20$$
$$\text{stocks} = 120 - \text{age}$$

Using the same example of a 20-year-old:

$$\text{age (20)} - 20 = 0 \text{ percent in bonds/cash equivalents}$$
$$120 - \text{age (20)} = 100 \text{ percent in stocks}$$

Charles Schwab's Asset Allocation Rule of Thumb

Charles Schwab offers a more elaborate asset allocation rule of thumb that involves your looking at your asset allocation and gradually moving from a heavy investment in stocks at age 50 or less to a more limited investment in stocks as you get older. See Exhibit 9.3 for his recommendations in five-year increments from age 50 to 80.

EXHIBIT 9.3. Charles Schwab's Investment Recommendations

AGE	% STOCKS	% BONDS	% CASH EQUIVALENTS
50	95%	0%	5%
55	90%	5%	5%
60	80%	15%	5%
65	70%	25%	5%
70	60%	30%	10%
75	50%	40%	10%
80	40%	45%	15%

Source: Charles R. Schwab, You're Fifty—Now What? Investing for the Second Half of Your Life (New York: Crown Business, 2001), p. 158.

Notice how aggressive Schwab is in his recommended asset allocation—he never recommends that you have less than 40 percent of your portfolio invested in stocks. Schwab makes this recommendation based on his "confidence in the growth potential of stocks, as both investments and as legacies to pass on to our heirs."[6] Other gurus have less confidence.

Who is right? How much should you have invested in stocks in your later years? Unfortunately, there is no definitive answer to that question. Ultimately, you have to decide which rule of thumb—the less-aggressive standard one or more-aggressive ones offered by Tyson and Schwab—is right for you.

Regardless of the investment strategy you choose, you will have to rebalance your asset allocation over time either to bring your portfolio back in line with your original allocation and/or to adopt a new asset allocation as you age. As Charles Schwab notes, when you are working with retirement accounts, rebalancing your asset allocations can get tricky because of government rules on such things as IRA withdrawals and transfers. Here are some general guidelines from Schwab to help you negotiate the asset allocation rebalancing act without triggering excessive taxes or penalties.

- **If possible, rebalance in your retirement account, rather than in your regular one.** . . . You have fewer tax considerations that way.
- **If you do rebalance in a regular account, make sure you understand the tax consequences of any trade you consider.** . . . The biggest thing to avoid is holding an investment for less than 12 months—if you do, your profits are taxed as ordinary income. The next biggest concern is capital gains. If, for example, you sell an investment in a regular account, you have a taxable transaction. If you've held that investment for a long time, chances are that you bought it for a substantially lower price than you sold it for—which means that you've probably made significant profit, and that amount will be taxed at capital gains rates.
- **If an asset class is high, consider buying more of what's low instead of selling what's high.** When you compare your current asset allocation percentages against your original percentages and you find that an asset class (meaning stocks, fixed-income, or cash equivalents) is higher than the percentage you chose, selling something from that group can seem like the easiest way to rebalance. . . .

  Although selling is the most obvious solution, . . . selling is really a last resort [in a regular account], thanks to capital gains taxes; if you sell, you may realize a capital gain, and that gain will be taxed. You've worked hard for this money, and you don't want it eaten away in taxes.

  So, instead of selling off some of the investment that's high, consider buying some of the investment class that's low, to bring its percentage up. . . .
- **Redirect dividends or regular investing money to the investment class that's low.** If you are investing regularly, you can also redi-

rect what you're buying each month or quarter so that you're buying investments in the under-weighted class.

- **Use withdrawals to rebalance.** Once you begin to withdraw from your accounts, you can use your annual withdrawals to rebalance by selling from the asset group you want to decrease. Or you can spread out your withdrawal amount among types of assets to bring them to the percentages you want.[7]

Diversification

Diversification is the first cousin to asset allocation. Whereas asset allocation is concerned with reducing risks by spreading your investments across a range of asset types (stocks, bonds, and cash equivalents), diversification is concerned with minimizing your risks by buying a range of investments within a given asset type. The reasoning behind diversification is that even within an asset type, risks vary greatly. For example, some stocks are riskier than others, and as Dwight Lee and Richard McKenzie, coauthors of *Getting Rich in America,* note, "Even if you are better than average at picking stocks, there is still a good chance that any one pick you make will be a loser."[8] Here is where diversification comes in. Instead of picking one stock or two, you can pick 50 or 100 stocks. You may pick some losers, but the hope is that your losses in a few stocks will be outweighed by your gains in others. It's like hedging your bets in gambling. Consider the following analogy that Lee and McKenzie provide:

> If you have a weighted coin that comes up heads 55 percent of the time (the probability that you pick a winning stock on any one choice), you would be foolish to bet everything you own on one toss (one stock). But if you bet, say, $10 on each toss (stock), then the probability that you will come out $100 ahead on every hundred tosses (stocks)—fifty-five wins and forty-five losses—approaches 100 percent as the number of tosses (stocks) increases.[9]

As Lee and McKenzie's analogy suggests, diversification works best if you invest in a large number of different stocks. The problem is that unless you are very rich, you may not have sufficient funds to purchase hundreds of different stocks. As we said earlier, this is one of the realities that makes mutual fund investing so attractive. Small investors can achieve a level of diversification in mutual funds that they could never achieve if investing on their own.

Despite its advantages, some of our gurus aren't fans of diversification. For example, Robert Kiyosaki argues that "the strategy of diversification is an investment strategy for 'not losing.' It is not an investment strategy for winning."[10] Kiyosaki prefers portfolio concentration over diversification because when you concentrate your investments, you become smarter and more intense in your thoughts and actions. He cites the famous investor Warren Buffet as an authority who agrees with his concentrate rather than diversify strategy.

Concentration may be a better strategy if you are a Warren Buffet or Robert Kiyosaki, but diversification is still good advice for most investors. Keep those Enron employees who had almost all of their 401(k) money tied up in their company's stock in mind when you make your decision. Many Enron employees lost much, if not all, of their retirement savings because they weren't diversified.

Dollar-Cost Averaging

Asset allocation and diversification seek to reduce risks by having you spread your investments across many different investments and asset types. Dollar-cost averaging seeks risk reduction through the timing of your investments.

The ultimate wisdom of all investing is "Buy Low and Sell High," but the trick has always been figuring out when low is truly low and high is truly high. Dollar-cost averaging takes the guesswork out of the process. Here is an illustration of how dollar-cost averaging works, courtesy of Ric Edelman.

In Edelman's example, he assumes that you have $100 dollars to invest each month. Over the course of a year, you make the monthly purchases shown in Exhibit 9.4.

Now, says Edelman, calculate two numbers. First, take the total amount you invested ($100 × 12 months = $1,200) and divide that by the number of shares you owned at the end of the year. Your answer is your average cost per share:

$1,200 invested ÷ 324,412 = $3.70 average cost per share

Next, calculate the average price of the shares you bought. You get that number by dividing the total of share prices ($68) by 12 (the number of months you made investments).

$68 ÷ 12 = $5.67 average price per share

Now, says Edelman, compare the two numbers. The average price of the shares you bought was $5.67, but the average cost of those shares to you was only $3.70. Therefore, over the course of the year, the price of the shares went down. As the price fell, you were able to buy an increasing number of shares. Does that look like a built-in profit? Absolutely, says Edelman, and that's the beauty of dollar-cost averaging. Edelman explains that dollar-cost averaging works very well as long as you adhere to four conditions:

EXHIBIT 9.4. **Edelman's Share-Purchasing Example**

Month	Share Price	Shares Purchased
January	$10.00	10.000
February	$ 9.00	11.111
March	$ 8.00	12.500
April	$ 7.50	13.333
May	$ 7.00	14/286
June	$ 6.00	16.667
July	$ 5.50	18.182
August	$ 5.00	20.000
September	$ 4.00	25.000
October	$ 3.00	33.333
November	$ 2.00	50.000
December	$ 1.00	100.000
TOTAL	$68.00	324.412

Source: Ric Edelman, Ordinary People, Extraordinary Wealth: The 8 Secrets of How 5000 Ordinary Americans Became Successful Investors—and How You Can Too (New York: HarperBusiness, 2001), p. 58.

1. you must invest a specific amount of money,
2. you must invest this money at a regular interval,
3. the money you are investing must be money you have only recently obtained, and
4. you must maintain this system for long periods of time.[11]

Fortunately, says Edelman, those conditions make dollar-cost averaging ideal for retirement investing for most people:

> Your paycheck is the same each pay period and the amount you place into your plan is the same each time, too. And because you get paid at regular intervals, your contributions are made at regular intervals as well. Third, the reason you are waiting to invest the money today is that you were only paid today; you didn't invest this money last week simply because you didn't have the money last week. And finally, you're going to be working for a very long time—for years and probably for decades. That's more than enough time for dollar cost averaging to ride the waves of the market's volatile performance.
>
> Thanks to dollar cost averaging, you don't have to worry whether the market is up or down. When the price is high (relative to other times), you

simply will not purchase many shares (relative to other purchases). But when the price is low, the system will automatically obtain for you a higher number of shares. Therefore, dollar cost averaging is certain to produce for you the lowest average cost, and that puts you in a great position to enjoy profits.[12]

You're even better off, says Edelman, if you have a 401(k) and your boss is matching your contribution—perhaps half of what you are buying at low average costs is with your boss's money.

Most of our gurus consider dollar-cost averaging a great way to reduce long-term risk. However, Jane Bryant Quinn notes that there are at least two circumstances under which dollar-cost averaging may actually work against you.

1. **When the market is moving steadily upward like it did in the late 1990s:** During such periods, says Quinn, "monthly investing gives you a higher average cost per share than if you'd been able to invest all your money at once."[13] Why is that? Well, let's look at how Edelman's example might have worked out under different conditions. Imagine that the trend in share price had been reversed. In other words, the share price started out at $1 a share in January and went up, ending at $10 per share in December. Let's further assume that you had the full $1,200 to invest in January. You could have bought 1,200 shares rather than 324.412, and your average cost per share would have been $1.00 instead of $3.70. You would have been much better off.

2. **When you receive a cash windfall, such as from a sudden inheritance:** Quinn argues that you are better off forgetting dollar-cost averaging and investing these funds all at once.[14] You run the risk that the market will go down after you make the lump-sum investment, but, Quinn argues, history shows that the odds are about two out of three that the market will go up rather than down.

Buy and Hold

Buy and hold means not trying to time the market but investing for the long term. It is essentially the premise underlying dollar-cost averaging and much of our gurus' advice about investing in general. It's the advice of practically all of the most famous investors who say that they can't outguess the market in the short term, so no one else should try.

What do investing experts like Warren Buffet, Peter Lynch, and Sir John Templeton know that most of us don't realize? Investments such as stocks are risky in the short term but much less risky the longer you hold them. Here are the facts. Jane Bryant Quinn cites a study conducted by Chicago's Ibbotson Associates in 1997 that looked at the historic performance of stocks held for different periods of

EXHIBIT 9.5. **Historic Performance of Stocks**

Holding Period	Chance of Earning 10% to 20% (Compounded Annual Return)	Chance of Suffering a Loss
1 Year	18%	28%
5 Years	51%	10%
10 Years	48%	3%
20 Years	62%	0%

Source: Jane Bryant Quinn, Making the Most of Your Money (New York: Simon & Schuster, 1997), p. 577.

time since 1926. The results are shown in Exhibit 9.5.[15] Quinn draws the following conclusions from this study:

1. In any one-year period, stocks are dicey. You get the biggest gains if you hit them right. But you also risk the biggest losses.
2. Over 5-year holding periods, your chance of loss is small. Over 10-year periods negligible. Over 20-year periods, zero.
3. The longer you hold stocks, the stronger the likelihood that you'll earn compound annual returns in the area of 10 to 20 percent (but it's much closer to 10 percent than 20 percent).
4. You probably won't earn more than 20 percent long term.[16]

Quinn's wisdom and that of our other gurus is simple—when it comes to money for retirement, invest for the long term.

Compounding

Einstein is said to have called compounding humankind's greatest invention.[17] Our gurus say it is the final and in many respects, the greatest secret of successful investing for retirement. Dee Lee and David Caruso provide a good example of how compounding works. (See Exercise 9.1.)

John is the big winner. Assuming a 10 percent return, Lee and Caruso calculate that John ends up at age 60 with over $658,000 in his retirement account. That's not a bad return for the $72,000 he has invested over 36 years.

Jane comes in second with $417,879 in her account, while Dick winds up with only $240,200. Jane invested less than half the money that Dick invested for less than half the amount of time, but she still ended up with nearly twice as much in the end. Because she started early, Jane was able to let the power of compounding work for her. And that's what our gurus want you to do. The ultimate secret to suc-

EXERCISE 9.1. The Power of Compounding

Instructions: Read these three scenarios and answer the questions that follow.

Scenario #1: Jane starts work at age 25, invests $2,000 per year in her retirement account until age 35, and then makes no further investments. She retires at the age of 60.

Scenario #2: Dick also starts work at age 25, but he doesn't start investing for his retirement until he is 35. From then on he puts in $2,000 per year up until the age of 60.

Scenario #3: Like Jane and Dick, John starts work at age 25 and like Jane he starts right away investing $2,000 per year in his retirement account. Unlike Jane, he doesn't stop investing. Instead, he continues putting in $2,000 a year every year until he is 60.

Who ends up with the LARGEST retirement nest egg? _____

Who ends up with the SMALLEST retirement nest egg? _____

Source: Dee Lee and David Caruso, Let's Talk Money: Your Complete Personal Finance Guide (Worcester, MA: Chandler House Press, 1999), pp. 87–89.

cessful retirement investing, they say, is to start early and invest a small amount consistently. Ideally, don't ever stop investing, like Jane did—let the power of compounding work for you. If you use dollar-cost averaging, you will be investing in such small amounts that you will hardly miss the money. And if you couple asset allocation and diversification with a buy-and-hold strategy, you are almost guaranteed to amass a tidy nest egg.

SOME CONCLUDING REMARKS

We chose this discussion of investing for retirement as our final chapter for two reasons. First, regardless of your retirement plans, whether they are to keep working till you drop or spend your time on the golf course or with your grandkids, having the peace of mind that you have the financial wherewithal to pursue your dream is a worthwhile life goal. Second, negotiating the pitfalls of retirement planning is no easy task and the tips from our gurus will help but you have to be "money smart," not just "retirement investment smart," if you are going to succeed. In a sense, then, everything that we have discussed before this chapter has been a kind of prologue to retirement investing. You can't do what our gurus suggest you do for retirement planning if you don't understand your relationship with money, haven't worked our financial and spending plans, haven't gotten your spending under control, don't know how to use debt and credit wisely, and so on.

We hope this book has given you many useful ideas on how to manage your money wisely. Now that you have finished reading it, we hope it is filled with underlined tips and techniques that you plan to incorporate into your daily life. Most of all, we hope that by reading this book, you are better fortified to do financial battle to protect your assets and achieve your dreams. In that regard, we send you our very best wishes for your money success.

🔑 KEY POINTS

- A basic rule of thumb is that you will need 80 percent of your current income in retirement.

- You need a retirement nest egg of roughly $230,000 for every $1,000 of monthly income you require in retirement in order for your retirement funds to last 40 years.

- The key to successful retirement investing is to balance risks with return.

- Asset allocation helps you to minimize risk by spreading out your investment dollars over a range of asset types.

- Diversification helps you minimize risks by having you buy a range of investments within any given asset type.

- Dollar-cost averaging helps you minimize the risk of buying high by spreading out your purchases over time. Usually, it enables you to make investments at the lowest cost per share.

- Buy and hold is the strategy preferred by most expert investors. The longer you hold stocks, the less likelihood you will suffer a loss.

- The greatest secret of successful investing for retirement is taking advantage of the power of compounding.

The Gurus

Robert Allen is a successful entrepreneur and author of the best-selling books *Nothing Down, Creating Wealth,* and *Multiple Streams of Income,* along with the more recent titles *The One Minute Millionaire,* written with Mark V. Hansen, and *Multiple Streams of Internet Income.* He is a frequent guest on radio and television shows, including *Larry King Live* and *Good Morning America* and has been featured in the *Wall Street Journal, People,* and *Reader's Digest.* Mr. Allen can be reached through his Web site www.robertallen.com.

Ginger Applegarth is president of Applegarth Advisory Group, a financial and investment management firm, and author of *Wake Up and Smell the Money* and *The Money Diet.* In addition, she has been a personal finance correspondent for NBC's *Today Show* and CNBC's *The Money Club* and has appeared on other television programs and networks, including *The Oprah Winfrey Show, Bloomberg Television,* and CNN. *Worth* magazine selected her as one of the top 60 financial planners in the United States. Ms. Applegarth can be reached through Applegarth Advisory Group, 10 Mount Vernon Street #225, Winchester, MA 01890.

Murray Baker, author of *The Debt-Free Graduate,* is a debt-free graduate of the University of Ontario, where he works as coordinator of First Year Programs. He is a recognized authority on student finance, debt, and loans and speaks frequently on university campuses. His work has appeared in numerous Canadian publications, including *The National Post, The Vancouver Sun, The Toronto Star,* and *Halifax Chronicle-Herald,* and he has made appearances on *Canada AM, CBC Newsworld,* BCTV's *Money Talks,* and *Global News.* Mr. Baker maintains a Web site at http://www.debtfreegrad.com.

Gary Belsky is an award-winning journalist who worked as a reporter for *Crain's New York Business,* wrote for *Money* magazine, served as a commentator on CNN's *Your Money,* and was senior editor at *ESPN The Magazine.* He is a graduate of the University of Missouri with a degree in political science and speech communication. His books include *Why Smart People Make Big Money Mistakes and How to Correct Them.*

Stacie Zoe Berg is a freelance journalist who contributes regularly to *The Washington Post, The Washington Times,* and various trade magazines. She is the author of *The Unofficial Guide™ to Investing in Mutual Funds* and *The Unofficial Guide to Managing Your Personal Finances.*

Jacqueline Blix is a proponent of life simplification and coauthor of *Getting a Life.* She earned a doctorate in communications from the University of Washington after working nine years in sales and marketing for AT&T. She lives in Seattle with her husband and coauthor, David Heitmiller.

Mark Bryan is a teacher, writer, and business consultant. He taught free enterprise in Russia, created the seminar "Business Creativity," and served as senior counselor at a New Mexico psychiatric hospital. He is a partner in Power and Light, Inc., which conducts workshops on a 90-day program for "money drunks" and on creativity. Mr. Bryan is a graduate of Harvard University with a master's degree in human development and psychology. He has appeared on *The Oprah Winfrey Show.* His books include *Money Drunk, Money Sober* and *90 Days to Financial Freedom,* which he coauthored with partner Julia Cameron. He can be reached through his Web site at http://www.markbryan.com.

Julia Cameron is a writer and filmmaker with credits in journalism, film, and television. Her work has appeared in the *New York Times, Washington Post, Chicago Tribune,* and *Los Angeles Times.* Along with her coauthor Mark Bryan, she teaches workshops on a 90-day program for "money drunks" and on creativity. Ms. Cameron's works include *Money Drunk, Money Sober* and *90 Days to Financial Freedom.*

David Caruso is a practicing Certified Financial Planner in Massachusetts. He has written articles for publications such as *The Boston Herald, The Boston Globe, The Boston Business Journal, Parenting,* and *Banker & Tradesman.* His books include *Let's Talk Money,* coauthored with Dee Lee, and *Decoding Wall Street,* coauthored with Robert J. Powell.

Nancy Castleman, along with partner Marc Eisenson, publishes and distributes books, software, audiotapes, and an assortment of other publications through their company Good Advice Press on such topics as saving money, managing debt, and living on less. Since 1990 they have published the *Pocket Change Investor* newsletter, which advises consumers on subjects like refinancing, taxes, and credit cards. The authors have appeared on *The Today Show, Dateline NBC, CBS Evening News, CBS This Morning,* and *Good Morning America,* and in the *New York Times* and *Washington Post.* Ms. Castleman's coauthored books include *Invest in Yourself* and *Slash Your Debt.* She can be reached at Good Advice Press, Box 78, Elizaville, NY 12523. She also maintains the Web site http://www.goodadvicepress.com.

Jean Chatzky is the at-large editor of *Money* magazine and a regular contributor to NBC's *Today Show.* Ms. Chatzky is a graduate of the University of Pennsylvania with a bachelor's degree in English. She worked as a research associate for Dean Witter before returning to journalism as a reporter/researcher for *SmartMoney.* In addition to her appearances on *The Today Show,* Ms. Chatzky has done extensive radio work and has appeared on *The Oprah Winfrey Show, Weekend Today,* and MSNBC. She is also the author of *Talking Money* and *The Rich and Famous Money Book.*

Jonathan Clements is an award-winning journalist who has worked for *Forbes* magazine and the *Wall Street Journal,* in which his "Heard on the Street" and "Getting Going" columns appeared. Mr. Clements was educated at Cambridge University. His books include *Funding Your Future* and *25 Myths You've Got to Avoid If You Want to Manage Your Money Right.*

Amy Dacyczyn published the newsletter *The Tightwad Gazette* from June 1990 until December 1996. In addition to her newsletter, she is the author of *The Com-*

plete Tightwad Gazette, The Tightwad Gazette II, and *Tightwad Gazette III.* She is now retired from her writing. Ms. Dacyczyn can be reached at R.R. 1, Box 3570, Leeds, ME 04263.

William Danko is associate professor and chair of the marketing department at the University at Albany, State University of New York. His works have appeared in the *Journal of Consumer Research, Journal of Business Research, Journal of Advertising Research,* and other leading research journals. He has collaborated with Dr. Thomas J. Stanley on academic and consulting studies and coauthored the bestselling *The Millionaire Next Door.* For more information, see his personal Web page at http://www.albany.edu/~danko.

Gerri Detweiler is a recognized authority on the credit and financial services industry. She is education advisor to the nonprofit Debt Counselors of America and former executive director of the consumer advocacy group Bankcard Holders of America. Ms. Detweiler has appeared on numerous radio and television programs including *The Today Show, Dateline NBC, CBS Evening News, CBS This Morning,* and *Good Morning America.* Her writing credits include articles in *Woman's Day* magazine and *Bottom Line Personal,* as well as authoring or coauthoring *The Ultimate Credit Handbook, Invest in Yourself,* and *Slash Your Debt.* Ms. Detweiler can be reached at Invest in Yourself, c/o Good Advice Press, P.O. Box 78, Elizaville, NY 12523 or through the Web site www.investinyourself.com.

Joe Dominguez was a successful Wall Street analyst. He was also coauthor of *Your Money or Your Life.* Mr. Dominguez died in 1997.

Ric Edelman is a financial advisor, educator, and author of five books: *The Truth about Money; Ordinary People, Extraordinary Wealth; Discover the Wealth Within; The New Rules of Money;* and *Financial Security in Troubled Times.* He also hosts weekly radio and television shows, writes a syndicated column for AARP's *Modern Maturity* magazine, and publishes a monthly newsletter. Edelman taught personal finance at Georgetown University and is a founder of Edelman Financial Services, Inc., and the nonprofit Edelman Center for Personal Finance Education. He can be reached through his Web site http://www.RicEdelman.com.

Marc Eisenson, along with partner Nancy Castleman, publishes and distributes books, software, audiotapes and other products through their company Good Advice Press, on topics such as saving money, managing debt, and living on less. Since 1990 they have published the *Pocket Change Investor* newsletter, which advises consumers on subjects like refinancing, taxes, and credit cards. The authors have appeared on *The Today Show, Dateline NBC, CBS Evening News, CBS This Morning,* and *Good Morning America,* and in the *New York Times* and *Washington Post.* Mr. Eisenson's coauthored books include *Invest in Yourself* and *Slash Your Debt.* He can be reached at Good Advice Press, Box 78. Elizaville, NY 12523. He also maintains the Web site http://www.goodadvicepress.com.

Debra Englander is a personal finance writer and editor. Her books include *Money 101* and *How to Be Your Own Financial Planner.*

Ron Gallen is the author of *The Money Trap* and a financial counselor. He has a background in business and addiction recovery. Gallen lives in New York City.

David Gardner is a cofounder of The Motley Fool, Inc., a Virginia-based company that focuses on personal finance management. He is a native of Washington, D.C., and a graduate of the University of North Carolina at Chapel Hill. He began his career as a writer for the newsletter *Louis Rukeyser's Wall Street* and then founded *The Motley Fool* newsletter with his brother Tom. The brothers are coauthors of *The Motley Fool Investment Guide* and several spin-off books. David Gardner also coauthored *The Motley Fool Money Guide* with Selena Maranjian. The Gardner brothers manage their nationally syndicated newspaper column and host *The Motley Fool Radio Show.* He can be reached at The Motley Fool, 123 North Pitt Street, Alexandria, VA. Also see the company's Web site, http://www.fool.com.

Tom Gardner is a cofounder of The Motley Fool, Inc., a Virginia-based company that focuses on personal finance management. Mr. Gardner graduated with a degree in English and creative writing from Brown University. In 1994, he and his brother David started *The Motley Fool* newsletter (see entry for David Gardner). Tom Gardner can be reached at The Motley Fool, 123 North Pitt Street, Alexandria, VA.

Thomas Gilovich is a professor of psychology at Cornell University. He holds a bachelor's degree from the University of California and a doctorate from Stanford University. His research has been published in such academic journals as the *Journal of Personality and Social Psychology* and *Cognitive Psychology,* as well as in his book *How We Know What Isn't So.* He is also the coauthor with Gary Belsky of *Why Smart People Make Big Money Mistakes and How to Correct Them.*

Ilyce Glink is a syndicated journalist, television correspondent, radio talk show host, and author who specializes in real estate and personal finance. She writes the twice-weekly syndicated column "Real Estate Matters" and contributes to *Woman's World* magazine and the *Los Angeles Times.* She has appeared on the Lifetime Networks' *Lifetime Life* and is the permanent guest host for the nationally syndicated *Clark Howard Show* on WSB Newstalk. Her books include *50 Simple Things You Can Do to Improve Your Personal Finances* and *100 Questions Every First-Time Home Buyer Should Ask.* Ms. Glink's company Think Glink, Inc., consults in the areas of real estate, personal finance, and business content solutions. She can be reached at Think Glink, Inc., P.O. Box 366, Glencoe, IL 60022. The company maintains a Web site at www.ThinkGlink.com.

Neale S. Godfrey, the former president of the First Women's Bank and founder of the First Children's Bank, is an acknowledged authority on family and children's finances. Ms. Godfrey appears regularly on television network programs like *The Oprah Winfrey Show, The Today Show, Good Morning America,* CNN, and CNBC. Her books include the best-selling *Money Doesn't Grow on Trees, Neale S. Godfrey's Ultimate Kids' Money Book, A Penny Saved, Making Change, Mom, Inc.,* and *Why Money Was Invented.*

Andrew Hacker teaches American politics at Queens College. He is the author of several books, including *Money: Who Has How Much and Why.*

Bob Hammond is a writer, consultant, and consumer advocate. He worked for *Taking Care of Business,* a weekly television program that highlighted the African-American business community. He was also an arbitrator for the Better Business Bureau, an investigator for the Fair Housing Council, and a consultant with Consumer Credit Counseling Services. His books include *How to Beat the Credit, Super Privacy, How to Get All the Credit You Want, Life after Debt, Credit Secrets,*

Life without Debt, Repair Your Own Credit, and *Credit Repair Rip-Off.* Mr. Hammond can be reached at P.O. Box 51581, Riverside, CA 92517.

Christopher L. Hayes is professor of psychology and chairman of the graduate program in gerontology at Long Island University's Southampton College. Professor Hayes is the author or coauthor of *Our Turn, Money Makeovers, Women in Mid-Life: Planning for Tomorrow,* and *Pre-Retirement Planning for Women.*

Christy Heady is the creator and founder of MoneyWhiz.com, a Web site designed to teach young adults how to save money and develop good personal money habits. She worked as a producer for CNN's *Moneyline* with Lou Dobbs and as a reporter for an ABC affiliate in Florida. Her articles have appeared in *Consumers' Digest, Chicago Tribune,* and *Los Angeles Times.* Ms. Heady is the coauthor of *The Complete Idiot's Guide to Managing Your Money.*

Robert Heady is a nationally syndicated columnist whose Tribune Media Services columns run in newspapers such as the *Chicago Tribune, Atlanta Journal, Cleveland Plain Dealer, Denver Post,* and the *Seattle Times.* He is also the founding publisher of Bank Rate Monitor, which surveys U.S. bank rates and averages in news media. Mr. Heady is a frequent speaker and has appeared on CNN's *Your Money* and *Moneyline, Good Morning America,* ABC's *20–20* and *World News,* CBS's *Morning News,* NBC's *The Today Show* and *Dateline,* and PBS's *Nightly Business Report.* He coauthored *The Complete Idiot's Guide to Managing Your Money* with his daughter, Christy Heady.

David Heitmiller is coauthor of *Getting a Life: Strategies for Simple Living, Based on the Revolutionary Program for Financial Freedom, Your Money or Your Life* and *Getting a Life: Real Lives Transformed by Your Money or Your Life* with his wife Jacqueline Blix.

Napoleon Hill was born in 1883 in Wise County, Virginia. Hill's *Think and Grow Rich* is the all-time best-seller among motivational books. His other works include *Success through a Positive Mental Attitude, Napoleon Hill's Keys to Success, The Law of Success in Sixteen Lessons, Master Key to Riches, Napoleon Hill's Positive Action Plan, Napoleon Hill's A Year of Growing Rich, Succeed and Grow Rich* *through Persuasion,* and *Grow Rich! With Peace of Mind.* For additional information, see http://www.naphill.org.

Bambi Holzer is senior vice president of investments for PaineWebber and coauthor of *Retire Rich: The Baby Boomer's Guide to a Secure Future* and *Getting Yours: It's Not Too Late to Have the Wealth You Want.* She also worked for Oppenheimer and Company as director of retirement services.

Clark Howard is the host of the consumer-advocacy radio show *The Clark Howard Show.* He is also a featured commentator on WSB-TV in Atlanta and a columnist with the *Atlanta Journal-Constitution.* After retiring from his successful chain of travel agencies at the age of 31, he opened the Consumer Action Center, which is staffed by volunteer researchers who answer consumer questions and research "raw deals" and "rip offs." Mr. Howard is the author of *Get Clark Smart* and *Clark Howard's Consumer Survival Kit.* He can be reached through his Web site at http://clarkhoward.com/.

Mary Hunt is the founder and publisher of the *Cheapskate Monthly* newsletter and is a recognized authority on spending and financial responsibility. She has appeared on such shows as *Good Morning America, The Oprah Winfrey Show,* and Fox TV's *The Crier Report.* She appears regularly on the home-and-garden network HGTV and has been featured in *USA Today, U.S. News and World Report, Newsday, Wall Street Journal,* and *Woman's Day.* Hunt's extensive publication list includes *Mary Hunt's The Complete Cheapskate,* plus several spin-offs, *Debt-Proof Your Kids, Mary Hunt's Debt-Proof Living, Debt-Proof Your Holidays, Tiptionary,* and *The Financially Confident Woman.* She can be reached through her Web site http://www.cheapskatemonthly.com/.

Mary Ivins responded to divorce from a 30-year marriage by earning her Certified Financial Planner designation. Two years later, she was accepted into the Registry for Financial Planning Practitioners, and she founded Ivins Financial Associates four years after that. She is the author of *Financial Security for Women.*

Azriela Jaffe is a recognized authority on entrepreneurial couples, business partnerships, and the concerns of small-business owners and home-based professionals. She also founded Anchored Dreams, a consulting firm that offers business assistance to individuals, couples, and partners; she produces the three newsletters *Entrepreneurial Couples Success Letter, The Best Ideas in Business,* and *Keeping in Touch;* and she writes the syndicated column "Advice from A–Z." Ms. Jaffe is the author or coauthor of *Create Your Own, The Complete Idiot's Guide to Beating Debt, Starting from "No,"* and *Honey, I Want to Start My Own Business.* She can be reached at Anchored Dreams, P.O. Box 209, Bausman, PA 17504. Her company also maintains a Web site at http://www.isquare.com/crlink.htm.

Jason Kelly began his career as a technical writer for IBM. He now writes the Neatest Little Guide series, which includes *The Neatest Little Guide to Stock Market Investing, The Neatest Little Guide to Making Money Online, The Neatest Little Guide to Mutual Fund Investing, The Neatest Little Guide to Do-It-Yourself Investing,* and *The Neatest Little Guide to Personal Finance.* Kelly currently lives in Ashikaga, Japan.

Mike Kidwell is a cofounder of Debt Counselors of America® and of Myvesta, a financial crisis and treatment center based in Maryland. Kidwell has appeared in print and on broadcast media for *USA Today, Consumer Reports,* MSNBC, ABC, and PBS. He and partner Steve Rhode cohost the nationwide, Web-cast radio program *MoneyHelp^sm with Steve and Mike* and are coauthors of *CheapMeals.com Cookbook, Get Out of Debt,* and *Ultimate Spending Plan Program Yearly Tracking Workbook.* He can be reached through the Debt Counselors of America Web site, http://www.dca.org/.

George Kinder has worked in the field of financial services for more than 30 years. After graduating from Harvard, he began his career as a tax advisor and later founded a tax and investment management firm. In 1991 he founded George D. Kinder Financial Services, Inc. Mr. Kinder has appeared on radio and television and has been featured in the *Wall Street Journal, New York Times, Newsweek, Fortune,* and other periodicals. He also conducts his The Seven Stages of Money Maturity™ workshops and seminars and is the author of *The Seven Stages of Money Maturity.*

Robert Kiyosaki is the author behind the best-selling Rich Dad, Poor Dad series. After founding his own successful entrepreneurial venture, he left the business

world in 1985 and established an international education company that taught business and investing principles. He retired at the age of 47 and began investing in real
estate and developing small-cap companies. He also joined the lecture tour with
other money and motivation gurus including Zig Ziglar and Tony Robbins. Mr.
Kiyosaki can be reached through the offices of Cashflow Technologies, Inc., 4330
North Civic Center Plaza, Suite 101, Scottsdale, AZ 85251. He also maintains the
Web site http://www.richdad.com/.

Deborah Knuckey is a freelance writer, speaker, and advice columnist. She earned
a master's degree in business administration from the University of California, Los
Angeles and has worked as a financial and political journalist, management consultant, and marketing consultant. Her books range from personal finance to adventure
travel and include *The Ms. Spent Money Guide* and *Conscious Spending for Couples*. She can be reached through the Web sites http://www.deborahknuckey.com
and http://www.MsSpent.com.

Phil Laut, author of *Money Is My Friend,* is a graduate of the U.S. Coast Guard
Academy and Harvard Business School. He has worked as a comptroller at a major
computer manufacturer. Mr. Laut can be reached through his Web site at
http://www.Phillaut.com.

Dee Lee is a Certified Financial Planner and a Registered Investment Advisor. She
is the founder of Harvard Financial Educators, which conducts financial workshops
focusing on educating and motivating financial consumers to take control of their
finances. She writes a weekly column for the *Sunday Boston Herald* and contributes to the interactive mutual fund site Brill.com. Her books include *The Complete Idiot's Guide to 401(k) Plans, Let's Talk Money, The Complete Idiot's Guide
to Retiring Early,* and *Everywoman's Money.* Ms. Lee can be reached at P. O. Box
304, Harvard. MA 01451, or through her Web sites http://www.deelee.net and
http://www.msmoney.com.

Dwight Lee has been the Ramsey Professor of Economics and Private Enterprise
at the University of Georgia since 1985. Professor Lee holds a bachelor's degree
in economics from San Diego State College and a doctorate in economics from
the University of California, San Diego. He has published more than 100 articles

in academic journals and over 200 articles and commentaries in magazines and newspapers. He is also the coauthor of eight books, including *Getting Rich in America, Failure and Progress, Managing through Incentives,* and *Quicksilver Capital.*

Mark Levine has been Stephen Pollan's collaborator for more than 15 years. He is the coauthor of *Starting Over, Lifescripts, Stephen Pollan's Foolproof Guide to Selling Your Home, Live Rich, Die Broke, The Die Broke Complete Book of Money,* and *Turning No into Yes.*

Arthur Levitt is former chairman of the Securities and Exchange Commission (1993 to 2001) and a Wall Street veteran. As a champion of investor rights, Mr. Levitt created the Office of Investor Education and Assistance and established the Web site http://www.sec.gov to provide free and easy access to corporate filings and investor education materials. Mr. Levitt is a Phi Beta Kappa graduate of Williams College, coauthor of *Take on the Street,* and author of *How to Make Your Money Make Money.*

Nancy Lloyd is the personal-finance commentator for National Public Radio's *Morning Edition,* a correspondent for ABC radio, and a contributing editor for *Family Circle* magazine. She has appeared on a variety of television shows, including the *CBS Evening News, Up to the Minute, The Today Show,* and *Good Morning America.* She is also editor-at-large of *Kiplinger's Personal Finance Magazine.* Her articles are syndicated by the *New York Times,* and she has written for the *Washington Post, Good Housekeeping, Reader's Digest,* and *Cosmopolitan.* Ms. Lloyd is the author of *Simple Money Solutions.* She can be reached through her Web site www.nancylloyd.com.

Marshall Loeb is an award-winning economic and financial journalist. He has worked as the economics editor at *Time* and the managing editor at *Fortune* and *Money* magazines. His daily program *Your Dollars* broadcasts on the CBS Radio Network, and his column "Your Money" runs in several newspapers. In addition to these duties, he was named editor of the *Columbia Journalism Review.* Mr. Loeb's books include *Marshall Loeb's Lifetime Financial Strategies, Leadership for Dummies®,* and *52 Weeks to Financial Fitness.*

Peter Lynch is now retired from the Fidelity Magellan Fund, which he managed from 1977 to 1990. He continues to serve as a member of the board of trustees of the Fidelity Group of Funds, writes a column for *Worth* magazine, and does non-profit work. His books include *One Up on Wall Street, Beating the Street,* and *Learn to Earn.*

Richard McKenzie is the Walter B. Gerken Professor of Enterprise and Society, Graduate School of Management, at the University of California, Irvine. Professor McKenzie is the author of more than 20 books and several hundred journal articles, policy papers, and commentaries. He has appeared in many national newspapers, including the *Wall Street Journal, Washington Post, New York Times,* and *Los Angeles Times.* His books include *Getting Rich in America, Managing through Incentives,* and *Trust on Trial.*

Deborah McNaughton is the founder of Professional Credit Counselors, a group that offers assistance in credit consulting, mortgages, automobile purchases, and financial planning. She also conducts "Credit and Financial Strategies" seminars and motivational workshops. Ms. McNaughton is a licensed real estate agent and has been featured in numerous publications including *Good Housekeeping, Woman's Day,* and *Your Money Magazine.* She writes for OnMoney.com and publishes a monthly newsletter, *Financial Victory.* Her books include *The Get Out of Debt Kit, The Insider's Guide to Managing Your Credit, Financially Secure, About Credit,* and *Destroy Your Debt!* Ms. McNaughton can be reached at 1100 Irvine Blvd., #541, Tustin, CA 92780, or through her Web site http://www.financialvictory.com.

Olivia Mellan is a psychotherapist in the field of money-conflict resolutions. She conducts seminars and appears regularly on television shows such as *20/20, The Oprah Winfrey Show,* and *The Today Show.* Ms. Mellan writes a monthly column for *Investment Advisor* and produces the *Money Harmony Newsletter.* Her books include *Overcoming Overspending, Money Shy to Money Sure,* and *Money Harmony.* Ms. Mellan can be contacted by mail at Olivia Mellan & Associates, Inc., 2607 Connecticut Avenue, NW, Washington DC 20008, or through her Web site http://www.moneyharmony.com.

Mark Miller has been a financial planner and stockbroker. In 1994 he launched the *$ensible $aver* newsletter, which is intended to help subscribers become better cheapskates. His books include *The Complete Idiot's Guide to Being a Cheapskate* and *The Sensible Saver.*

Ted Miller is Kiplinger's senior vice president for publishing. He is the author or editor of *Kiplinger's Practical Guide to Investing* and *Kiplinger's Practical Guide to Your Money.*

Edward Mrkvicka is a banking and financial columnist for *Bottom Line Personal* and the *National Enquirer.* He is also president and chief executive officer of Reliance Enterprises and author of *Your Bank Is Ripping You Off, The Bank Book,* and *J. K. Lasser's Pick Winning Stocks.*

Stephen Nelson is a certified public accountant and former financial columnist for *Inc.* and *PC Computing* magazines. He has also worked for Arthur Andersen as a senior consultant. Mr. Nelson's books include *The Millionaire Kit, QuickBooks 2002 for Dummies, Quicken 2002 for Dummies, Microsoft Outlook Version 2002 Plain and Simple, Quicken 2003 for Dummies,* and *MBA's Guide to Microsoft Excel 2000.*

Maria Nemeth is a licensed clinical psychologist, columnist, author, seminar leader, and speaker. Dr. Nemeth is the founder of You and Money, a personal and professional development/transformational seminar and is a former columnist for the *Sacramento Business Journal.* Her books include *The Energy of Money* and *You and Money.* Dr. Nemeth can be contacted at Maria Nemeth & Associates, 9070 Laguna Springs Way, Elk Grove, CA 95758. She maintains a Web site at http://www.marianemeth.com.

Holly Nicholson is president of Financial Planning Services, Inc., a firm that provides financial and investment advice and money management services. She is a Certified Financial Planner, Registered Investment Adviser, licensed stock broker, and author of *Money and You.* Ms. Nicholson can be reached at 700 Exposition Place Ste. #131, Raleigh, NC 27615. She also maintains a Web site at http://www.askholly.com.

James O'Shaughnessy is the founder and chairman of O'Shaughnessy Funds, a group of no-load mutual funds, and author of *What Works on Wall Street, How to*

Retire Rich: Time-Tested Strategies to Beat the Market and Retire in Style, and *Invest Like the Best.*

Suze Orman is a Certified Financial Planner and author of best-selling books on personal finance. In 1987 she founded the Suze Orman Financial Group, where she stayed until 1997. Ms. Orman is the personal finance editor for CNBC, a financial contributor to NBC's *Today Show,* and a contributing editor to *0: The Oprah Magazine.* She has been featured in *Newsweek, The New Yorker, The New Republic,* and *USA Today,* and she has appeared on *Larry King Live* and *The Oprah Winfrey Show.* Her books include *The Road to Wealth; The 9 Steps to Financial Freedom; Suze Orman's Financial Guidebook; The Courage to Be Rich; Where the Money Is; You've Earned It, Don't Lose It;* and *Money Cards: Words That Lead to Wealth.* She can be reached through her Web site http://www.suzeorman.com.

Greg Pahl is a freelance journalist who has written for numerous publications including *The Champlain Business Journal.* He is the author of *The Unofficial Guide to Beating Debt* and *Complete Idiot's Guide to Saving the Environment.*

Stephen Pollan has been a practicing attorney for 35 years. As a recognized financial expert, he works as a contributing editor to *Personal Finance* magazine and writes a column for *Working Woman* magazine. Mr. Pollan has appeared on television on PBS's *Nightly Business Report,* NBC's *Today Show,* ABC's *Good Morning America, CBS This Morning,* and *Wall Street Journal Reports,* and he was a personal finance correspondent for CNBC for five years. His best-selling books, all coauthored with Mark Levine, include *Starting Over; Stephen Pollan's Foolproof Guide to Selling Your Home; Live Rich, Die Broke; The Die Broke Complete Book of Money;* and *Turning No into Yes.* He can be reached through the Web site http://www.diebrokeliverich.com.

Jonathan Pond is president of the money management firm Financial Planning Information, Inc., and author of several books on personal finance management. He appears regularly on television, including segments of NBC's *Today Show* and PBS's *Nightly Business Report.* Mr. Pond is the author of *1001 Ways to Cut Your Expenses, Your Financial Future, Your Money Matters,* and *Jonathan Pond's Financial Management Guide.* He maintains a Web site at www.jonathanpond.com.

Jane Bryant Quinn is a columnist, author, and television personality. She writes a syndicated column for *New York Daily News* and regularly contributes to *Newsweek* and *Good Housekeeping.* Ms. Quinn has worked for the *CBS Morning News* and for *Evening News with Dan Rather.* She hosted a series called *Take Charge!* for public television and currently appears on ABC's *The Home Show.* Quinn, who holds a bachelor's degree from Middlebury College, is the author of the best-selling *Making the Most of Your Money.*

Dave Ramsey is the founder of Ramsey Investments, Inc., a real estate brokerage firm that specializes in foreclosure and bankruptcy real estate, as well as the Lampo Group, a consulting firm that offers financial counseling and seminars. He is the host of a talk radio show called *The Money Game.* Ramsey is author or coauthor of *Financial Peace, The Financial Peace Planner, How to Have More Than Enough, Priceless: Straight Shooting, No Frills, Financial Wisdom,* and *More Than Enough.* He can be reached through his Web site at http://www.daveramsey.com.

Steve Rhode is president and cofounder of the financial advisory firm Myvesta and cofounder of Debt Counselors of America. He is also coauthor of *The Path to Happiness and Wealth, CheapMeals.com Cookbook, Get Out of Debt,* and *Ultimate Spending Plan Program Yearly Tracking Workbook.* He can be contacted through the Web site http://www.dca.org.

Vicki Robin is a cofounder and president of the New Road Map Foundation, a nonprofit organization that promotes sustainability and reduced consumption. She has appeared on numerous radio and television shows, including *The Oprah Winfrey Show, Good Morning America,* and National Public Radio's *Weekend Edition.* She has also been featured in *People* magazine, *The Wall Street Journal, Mirabella, Woman's Day, Newsweek,* and the *New York Times.* Robin, who is a graduate of Brown University, is a coauthor of *Your Money or Your Life.* She can be reached at 5557 38th Ave NE, Seattle, WA 98105.

Terry Savage, author of *The Savage Truth on Money,* is a recognized financial authority, columnist, and regular guest on radio and television. She was a founding member and the first woman trader on the Chicago Board Options Exchange. She writes a syndicated column on personal finance for the *Chicago Sun-Times* and is a columnist for *Barron's Online.* She has appeared as a guest, commentator, or host on PBS's *Nightly Business Report, CNN Morning News, The Oprah*

Winfrey Show, and the *News Hour with Jim Lehrer.* Savage serves on the board of directors of McDonald's Corporation and Pennzoil Quaker State Company. She won an Emmy for a one-hour television special *Money—It Doesn't Grow on Trees!* Ms. Savage can be contacted at Terry Savage Productions, Ltd., 676 N. Michigan Avenue, Suite 3610, Chicago, IL 60611. Her Web site is located at http://www.TerrySavage.com.

Charles Schwab is founder, chairman of the board, and co-chief executive officer of The Charles Schwab Corporation, one of the largest financial services firms in the United States. He was selected by *Money* magazine as one of the seven people who most influence the economy. Schwab, who holds a bachelor's degree in economics and a master's degree in business administration from Stanford University, is a member of the board of trustees for his alma mater. He is also the founder and chairman of the nonprofit organization the Schwab Foundation of Learning. His books include *You're Fifty—Now What, It Pays to Talk,* and *Charles Schwab's Guide to Financial Independence.*

Robert Sheard was a writer and editor for *The Motley Fool.* As director for the *Foolish Workshops,* he covered topics ranging from particular stocks to investing in general. Mr. Sheard, who has a doctorate in English literature from Penn State University, is author of *The Unemotional Investor* and *Money for Life.* He is now a director for Sheard and Davey Advisors, Inc., and can be reached through their Web site at http://www.sdadvisors.com.

Don Silver is an estate-planning attorney and author of *The Generation Y Money Book, The Generation X Money Book, A Parent's Guide to Wills and Trusts,* and *Baby Boomer Retirement.*

Thomas Stanley is a lecturer, researcher, and the author or coauthor of the best-selling *The Millionaire Mind* and *The Millionaire Next Door,* as well as *Marketing to the Affluent* and *Selling to the Affluent.* He holds a doctorate in business administration from the University of Georgia and was formerly a professor of marketing at Georgia State University.

Barbara Stanny is the author of *Secrets of Six-Figure Women* and *Prince Charming Isn't Coming.* She holds a master's degree in counseling psychology and focuses on motivating women to become financially empowered. She has appeared on ABC's *Good Morning America, The View,* CNN, *The Maury Povich Show, Extra,* MSNBC, CNBC, and in the *New York Times* and *USA Today.* Ms. Stanny can be reached through her Web site http://www.princequiz.com.

Julie Stav is a financial planner, broker, and founder of Retirement Benefit Systems. She also runs a network of investment clubs and is the author of *Fund Your Future* and *Get Your Share.* Ms. Stav can be reached at Retirement Benefit Systems, 22231 Mulholland Hwy. #210, Calabasas, CA 91302. She maintains a Web site at http://www.juliestav.com.

Brooke Stephens is a registered investment advisor with her own firm and is a veteran of Wall Street. She appears regularly on CNBC, CNN, Bloomberg, and BET and is a member of the Financial Women's Association of New York and the National Black MBAs Association. Ms. Stephens began her career as an international trade officer with Chase and was later a senior investment consultant for Citicorp Investment services. She is the author or editor of *Talking Dollars and Making Sense* and *Wealth Happens One Day at a Time.* Stephens can be reached through her Web site at http://www.brookestephens.com.

Steven Strauss is a lawyer and recognized specialist in bankruptcy and Internal Revenue Service negotiations. He is also the author of the Ask a Lawyer series, including *Landlord and Tenant (Ask a Lawyer), Debt and Bankruptcy (Ask a Lawyer), Wills and Trusts (Ask a Lawyer),* and *Divorce and Child Custody (Ask a Lawyer).* His other books include *The Complete Idiot's Guide to Beating Debt, The Unofficial Guide to Starting a Home-Based Business,* and *The Business Start Up Kit.*

Howard Strong is a consumer advocate in the area of credit card protection. He is a former staff member of the U.S. Senate Committee on the Judiciary, Subcommittee on Antitrust and Monopoly. Mr. Strong is the author of *What Every Credit Card User Needs to Know, Credit Card Secrets That You Will Surely Profit From,* and *Credit Cards.* He can be reached at 6923 Geyser Avenue, Reseda, CA 91335.

David Teitelbaum is a personal financial planner and economist with the federal government. He writes articles on personal finance for various Washington,

D.C.–area publications and has appeared on local radio shows. Teitelbaum holds degrees in economics from the University of Michigan and mathematics from the University of Maryland. He is the author of *The Procrastinator's Guide to Financial Security*. He can be reached through his Web site at http://www.moneybalance.com.

Eric Tyson is a recognized personal finance author, lecturer, and advisor. The former management consultant has a bachelor's degree in economics from Yale University and a master's in business administration from the Stanford Graduate School of Business. He has been featured in *Newsweek, Kiplinger's Personal Finance Magazine,* the *Los Angeles Times, Chicago Tribune, Wall Street Journal,* and *Bottom Line/Personal* and has appeared on *The Today Show,* ABC, CNBC, PBS's *Nightly Business Report,* CNN, and Bloomberg Business Radio. Mr. Tyson's bestselling financial books include *Personal Finance for Dummies, Home Buying for Dummies, Mortgages for Dummies®, Mutual Funds for Dummies, Investing for Dummies®, Small Business for Dummies®, House Selling for Dummies,* and *Retirement Planning for Dummies.*

Notes

Chapter 1

[1] Suze Orman, *The Courage to Be Rich: Creating a Life of Material and Spiritual Abundance* (New York: Riverhead Books, 1999), p. 24.
[2] Suze Orman, *The 9 Steps to Financial Freedom: Practical and Spiritual Steps So You Can Stop Worrying* (New York: Three Rivers Press, 2000), p. 7.
[3] Ibid., pp. 7–8.
[4] Suze Orman, *Suze Orman's Financial Guidebook: Putting the 9 Steps to Work* (New York: Three Rivers Press, 2002), p. 89.
[5] Orman, *The Courage to Be Rich,* pp. 28–29.
[6] Ibid., p. 30.
[7] Ibid., pp. 30–31.
[8] Marc Eisenson, Gerri Detweiler, and Nancy Castleman, *Invest in Yourself: Six Secrets to a Rich Life* (New York: John Wiley & Sons, 1998), pp. 12–13.
[9] Ibid.

Chapter 2

[1] Thomas J. Stanley and William Danko, *The Millionaire Next Door* (Atlanta, GA: Longstreet Press, 1998), p. 96.
[2] Ibid., p. 13.
[3] Eric Tyson, *Personal Finance for Dummies* (Foster City, CA: IDG Books Worldwide, 1997), pp. 27–28.
[4] Jason Kelly, *The Neatest Little Guide to Personal Finance* (New York: Plume, 1999), p. 10.
[5] Suze Orman, *9 Steps to Financial Freedom,* p. 33.
[6] Mary Hunt, *Mary Hunt's Debt-Proof Living* (Nashville, TN: Broadman & Holman, 1999), p. 54.
[7] Ibid., pp. 54–55.

8 Jean Sherman Chatzky, *Talking Money: Everything You Need to Know about Your Finances and Your Future,* (New York: Warner Business Books, 2001), pp. 47–48.

9 Ilyce R. Glink,, *50 Simple Things You Can Do to Improve Your Personal Finances: How to Spend Less, Save More, and Make the Most of What You Have* (New York: Three Rivers Press, 2001), p. 24.

10 Dave Ramsey, *More Than Enough: Proven Keys to Strengthening Your Family and Building Financial Peace* (New York: Viking, 1999), p. 56.

11 Ginger Applegarth, *Wake Up and Smell the Money* (New York: Viking, 1999), p. 6.

12 Maria Nemeth, *The Energy of Money: A Spiritual Guide to Financial and Personal Fulfillment* (New York: Ballantine Wellspring, 1999), pp. 88–90.

13 Brooke Stephens, *Wealth Happens One Day at a Time,* p. 32.

14 Jane Bryant Quinn, *Making the Most of Your Money* (New York: Simon & Schuster, 1997), p. 954.

15 Tyson, *Personal Finance for Dummies,* p. 36.

16 Barbara Stanny, *Prince Charming Isn't Coming: How Women Get Smart about Money* (New York: Penguin, 1997), p. 160.

17 Tyson, *Personal Finance for Dummies,* pp. 48–49.

18 Chatzky, *Talking Money,* pp. 240–241.

19 Tyson, *Personal Finance for Dummies,* p. 47.

20 Ibid., p. 45.

21 Ibid., p. 46.

22 Ric Edelman, *The Truth about Money* (New York: HarperCollins, 1998), p. 612.

23 Tyson, *Personal Finance for Dummies,* p. 37.

24 Holly Nicholson, *Money and You* (Ft. Bragg, CA: Lost Coast Press, 1997), pp. 13–14.

25 Tyson, *Personal Finance for Dummies,* p. 382.

26 This list of questions was derived from Chatzky, *Talking Money.* pp. 245–247; Edelman, *The Truth about Money,* pp. 620–623; Christopher L. Hayes and Kate Kelly, *Money Makeovers: How Women Can Control Their Financial Destiny* (New York: Doubleday, 1998), pp. 353–355; Olivia Mellan and Sherry Christie, *Money Shy to Money Sure: A Woman's Road Map to Financial Well-Being* (New York: Walker, 2001), pp. 128–129; Nicholson, *Money and You,* pp. 13–19; Stephen Pollan and Mark Levine, *Die Broke: A Radical, Four-Part Financial Plan* (New York: Harper Perennial, 1998), pp. 175–176; Orman, *Suze Orman's Financial Guidebook,* pp. 126–127; and Tyson, *Personal Finance for Dummies,* pp. 379–383.

27 Edelman, *The Truth about Money,* pp. 617–618.

28 Tyson, *Personal Finance for Dummies,* pp. 40–43.

Chapter 3

1 Stephen Pollan and Mark Levine, *Live Rich: Everything You Need to Know to Be Your Own Boss, Whoever You Work For* (New York: Harper Perennial, 1998), p. 9.
2 Joe Dominguez and Vicki Robin, *Your Money or Your Life: Transforming Your Relationship with Money and Achieving Financial Independence* (New York: Penguin Books, 1999), pp. 3–4.
3 Ibid., pp. 226–227.
4 Robert T. Kiyosaki, *Rich Dad's Guide to Investing: What the Rich Invest in That the Poor and Middle Class Do Not!* (New York: Warner Books, 2000), p. 105.
5 Robert T. Kiyosaki, *Rich Dad's Cashflow Quadrant: Employee, Self-Employed, Business Owner, or Investor . . . Which Is the Best Quadrant for You?* (New York: Warner Books, 2000), p. 55.
6 Dominguez and Robin, *Your Money or Your Life,* p. 268.
7 Kiyosaki, *Rich Dad's Cashflow Quadrant,* pp. 54–55.
8 Robert T. Kiyosaki, *Rich Dad's Rich Kid, Smart Kid: Giving Your Child a Financial Head Start* (New York: Warner Business Books, 2001), pp. 193–194.
9 Robert G. Allen, *Multiple Streams of Income* (New York: John Wiley & Sons, 2000), p. 39.
10 Kiyosaki, *Rich Dad's Cashflow Quadrant,* pp. 66–67.
11 Ibid., p. 67.
12 Dwight R. Lee and Richard B. McKenzie, *Getting Rich in America: 8 Simple Rules for Building a Fortune and a Satisfying Life* (New York: Harper Perennial, 1999), pp. 168–170.
13 Joseph H. Boyett and Jimmie T. Boyett, *The Guru Guide™ to Entrepreneurship* (New York: John Wiley & Sons, 2001).
14 This discussion is based on Nancy Lloyd, *Simple Money Solutions: 10 Ways You Can Stop Feeling Overwhelmed by Money and Start Making It Work for You* (New York: Times Business, 2000), pp. 75–101. For convenience, we attribute all of these recommendations to Lloyd. In fact, in some instances she is referencing other experts. For example, the discussion of typical interview questions and smart responses to the questions is largely attributed by Lloyd to Barbara Collins, managing director of the New York office of Drake, Beam, Morin, an outplacement firm that helps laid-off workers.
15 Ibid., p. 75.
16 Ibid., pp. 75–76.

[17] Ric Edelman, *The New Rules of Money: 88 Strategies for Financial Success Today* (New York: Harper Perennial, 1998), pp. 12–13.

[18] Tyson, *Personal Finance for Dummies,* pp. 108–128.

[19] Robert Heady and Christie Heady, *The Complete Idiot's Guide to Managing Your Money* (New York: Alpha Books, 1995), p. 332.

[20] Tyson, *Personal Finance for Dummies,* pp. 121–124.

[21] Heady and Heady, *Complete Idiot's Guide to Managing Your Money,* pp. 332–334.

[22] Tyson, *Personal Finance for Dummies,* pp. 126–128.

[23] Heady and Heady, *Complete Idiot's Guide to Managing Your Money,* pp. 338–340.

[24] Edelman, *Truth about Money,* p. 62.

[25] Chatzky, *Talking Money,* pp. 63–64.

[26] Clark Howard, *Get Clark Smart: The Ultimate Guide for the Savvy Consumer* (Atlanta, GA: Longstreet Press, 2000), p. 56.

[27] Stacie Zoe Berg, *The Unofficial Guide to Managing Your Personal Finances* (New York: Macmillan General Reference, 1999), pp. 48–50.

[28] Kelly, *Neatest Little Guide to Personal Finance,* p. 109.

[29] Quinn, *Making the Most of Your Money,* p. 52.

[30] Ibid., p. 53.

[31] Berg, *Unofficial Guide to Managing Your Personal Finances,* p. 45.

[32] Stephens, *Wealth Happens One Day at a Time,* p. 141.

[33] Quinn, *Making the Most of Your Money,* pp. 144, 59–60.

[34] Berg, *Unofficial Guide to Managing Your Personal Finances,* pp. 45–47, 52–55; Chatzky, *Talking Money,* pp. 64–68; and Quinn, *Making the Most of Your Money,* pp. 144, 56–59.

[35] Quinn, *Making the Most of Your Money,* p. 63.

[36] Kelly, *Neatest Little Guide to Personal Finance,* p. 119.

[37] Quinn, *Making the Most of Your Money,* p. 63.

[38] Edward F. Mrkvicka, *Your Bank Is Ripping You Off* (New York: St. Martin's Griffin, 1999), pp. 203–204.

[39] Lloyd, *Simple Money Solutions,* p. 70.

Chapter 4

[1] Deborah Knuckey, *The Ms. Spent Money Guide: Get More of What You Want with What You Earn* (New York: John Wiley & Sons, 2001), p. 54.

[2] Ibid., pp. 64–65.

[3] Olivia Mellan and Sherry Christie, *Overcoming Overspending: A Winning Plan for Spenders and Their Partners* (New York: Walker, 1995), pp. 140–155.

[4] Ibid., p. 156.

5 Mary Hunt, *Mary Hunt's The Complete Cheapskate: How to Get Out of Debt, Stay Out, and Break Free from Money Worries Forever* (Nashville, TN: Broadman & Holman, 1998), pp. 94–100.

6 Ibid., p. 99.

7 Ibid.

8 Orman, *Suze Orman's Financial Guidebook,* p. 36.

9 Amy Dacyczyn, *The Complete Tightwad Gazette* (New York: Vaillard, 1999), p. 94.

10 The discussion on repooling is adapted from Orman, *Courage to Be Rich,* pp. 94–96.

11 Orman, *9 Steps to Financial Freedom,* p. 40.

12 Dominguez and Robin, *Your Money or Your Life,* pp. 195–197.

13 Glink, *50 Simple Things You Can Do to Improve Your Personal Finances,* pp. 32–33.

14 Andrew Hacker, *Money: Who Has How Much and Why* (New York: Touchstone, 1997), p. 43.

15 This discussion of the Fulfillment Curve is based on Dominguez and Robin, *Your Money or Your Life,* pp. 40–138.

16 Ibid., p. 117.

17 Jacqueline Blix and David Heitmiller, *Getting a Life: Strategies for Simple Living, Based on the Revolutionary Program for Financial Freedom, Your Money or Your Life* (New York: Penguin Books, 1997), pp. 260–261.

18 Orman, *Courage to Be Rich,* p. 45.

19 Quoted in Marshall Glickman, *Mindful Money Guide: Creating Harmony between Your Values and Your Finances* (New York: Ballantine Wellspring, 1999), p. 36. Original source: Henry David Thoreau, *Walden: The Writings of Henry David Thoreau, Volume 2* (Boston: Houghton Mifflin, 1910), p. 129.

Chapter 5

1 Allen, *Multiple Streams of Income,* p. 286.

2 Kelly, *Neatest Little Guide to Personal Finance,* p. 180.

3 Stephen L. Nelson, *The Millionaire Kit: Surprisingly Simple Strategies for Building Real Wealth* (New York: Times Business, 1998), p. 95.

4 Tyson, *Personal Finance for Dummies,* p. 327.

5 Quinn, *Making the Most of Your Money,* p. 341.

6 Insure.com, "What Happens When Your Insurance Company Goes Belly Up," <http://www.insure.com/gen/bellyup.html>, (February 26, 2001).

7 Charles R. Schwab, *You're Fifty—Now What? Investing for the Second Half of Your Life* (New York: Crown Business, 2001), p. 296.

8 Nelson, *Millionaire Kit,* p. 97.

9   Schwab, *You're Fifty—Now What?* pp. 295–296.

10 Quinn, *Making the Most of Your Money,* p. 416.

11 Edelman, *Truth about Money,* p. 514.

12 Quinn, *Making the Most of Your Money,* p. 417. Note that there are some limited exceptions to the strict definition of disability for the blind.

13 Don Silver, *The Generation Y Money Book: 99 Smart Ways to Handle Money* (Los Angeles: Adams Hall, 1998), p. 127.

14 Hunt, *Mary Hunt's Debt-Proof Living,* p. 287.

15 Quinn, *Making the Most of Your Money,* pp. 349–350.

16 Ibid., pp. 350–351.

17 See http://www.opensecrets.org/news/drug.

18 Lloyd, *Simple Money Solutions,* p. 181.

19 Orman, *9 Steps to Financial Freedom,* p. 87; and Orman, *Road to Wealth,* p. 209.

20 Orman, *9 Steps to Financial Freedom,* pp. 91–92.

21 Pollan and Levine, *Die Broke,* p. 194.

22 Orman, *Road to Wealth,* pp. 237–238.

23 Lloyd, *Simple Money Solutions,* p. 191.

24 Adapted from Howard, *Get Clark Smart,* pp. 154–157; Lloyd, *Simple Money Solutions,* pp. 190–198; Orman, *Road to Wealth,* pp. 237–249; Pollan and Levine, *Die Broke,* pp. 193–198; Quinn, *Making the Most of Your Money,* p. 454; and Tyson, *Personal Finance for Dummies,* pp. 367–368.

25 Quinn, *Making the Most of Your Money,* p. 454.

26 Adapted from Kelly, *Neatest Little Guide to Personal Finance,* p., 188; Lloyd, *Simple Money Solutions,* pp. 195–196; Pollan and Levine, *Die Broke,* pp. 196–198; Quinn, *Making the Most of Your Money,* 470–471; and Stephens, *Wealth Happens One Day at a Time,* p. 311.

27 Quinn, *Making the Most of Your Money,* p. 470.

28 Howard, *Get Clark Smart,* p. 151.

29 Pollan and Levine, *Die Broke,* p. 127.

30 Howard, *Get Clark Smart,* p. 152.

31 Ibid., p. 151.

32 These money-saving ideas are adapted from Berg, *Unofficial Guide to Managing Your Personal Finances,* p. 116; Heady and Heady, *Complete Idiot's Guide to Managing Your Money,* pp. 315–316; Howard, *Get Clark Smart,* pp. 151, 153; Kelly, *Neatest Little Guide to Personal Finance,* p. 185; Lloyd, *Simple Money Solutions,* pp. 187–188; Ted Miller, *Kiplinger's Practical Guide to Your Money: Keep More of It, Make It Grow, Protect It* (Washington DC: Kiplinger Books, 1998), pp. 157–163; Orman, *Road to Wealth,* p. 336; Pollan

and Levine, *Die Broke,* p. 129; and Quinn, *Making the Most of Your Money,* pp. 440–444.

[33] Howard, *Get Clark Smart,* p. 151.

Chapter 6

[1] Knuckey, *Ms. Spent Money Guide,* p. 250.

[2] Adapted from Steven D. Strauss and Azriela Jaffe, *The Complete Idiot's Guide to Beating Debt* (Indianapolis, IN: Alpha Books, 2000), pp. 5–8.

[3] Tyson, *Personal Finance for Dummies,* pp. 21–23.

[4] Greg Pahl, *The Unofficial Guide to Beating Debt* (Foster City, CA: IDG Books Worldwide, 2000), pp. 170–171.

[5] Ibid., p. 169.

[6] Bob Hammond, *Life without Debt: Free Yourself from the Burden of Money Worries Once and for All* (Franklin Lakes, NJ: Career Press, 1995), p. 141; and Orman, *Road to Wealth,* p. 174.

[7] Dave Ramsey, *Financial Peace* (New York: Viking Penguin, 1997), p. 90; Mark. W. Miller, *The Complete Idiot's Guide to Being a Cheapskate* (New York: Alpha Books, 1999), p. 43; Hunt, *Mary Hunt's The Complete Cheapskate,* p. 67; and Hunt, *Mary Hunt's Debt-Proof Living,* p. 89.

[8] Dacyczyn, *Complete Tightwad Gazette,* p. 77

[9] Hunt, *Mary Hunt's Debt-Proof Living,* p. 32.

[10] Nelson, *Millionaire Kit,* pp. 84–87.

[11] Gerri Detweiler, Marc Eisenson, and Nancy Castleman, *Slash Your Debt: Save Money and Secure Your Future* (Kalamazoo, MI: Financial Literacy Center, 1999), p. 35.

[12] Ron Gallen, *Money Trap: A Practical Program to Stop Self-Defeating Financial Habits So You Can Reclaim Your Grip on Life* (New York: Harper Resource, 2001), p. 7.

[13] Pond, *Your Money Matters,* p. 87.

[14] Howard, *Get Clark Smart,* p. 65.

[15] Pond, *Your Money Matters,* p. 72.

[16] Howard, *Get Clark Smart,* p. 69.

[17] Lloyd, *Simple Money Solutions,* p. 47.

[18] Howard Strong, *What Every Credit Card User Needs to Know: How to Protect Yourself and Your Money* (New York: Henry Holt, 1999), p. 45.

[19] Federal Reserve Board, "Shop: The Credit Card You Pick Can Save You Money," <http://www.federalreserve.gov/pubs/shop/>, (October 30, 2002).

[20] Strong, *What Every Credit Card User Needs to Know,* p. 49.

[21] Hunt, *Mary Hunt's Debt-Proof Living,* p. 215.

[22] Strong, *What Every Credit Card User Needs to Know,* p. 54.

[23] Federal Trade Commission, "Credit, ATM, and Debit Cards: What to Do If They're Lost or Stolen," <http://www.ftc.gov/bcp/conline/pubs/credit/atmcard.htm>, (October 30, 2002).

[24] Steve Rhode and Mike Kidwell, *Get Out of Debt: Smart Solutions to Your Money Problems* (Rockville, MD: Debt Counselors of America, 1999), p. 70.

[25] Hunt, *Mary Hunt's Debt-Proof Living,* pp. 202–211.

[26] Ibid., p. 203.

[27] Ibid., p. 204.

[28] Rhode and Kidwell, *Get Out of Debt,* p. 61.

[29] Hunt, *Mary Hunt's Debt-Proof Living,* p. 208.

Chapter 7

[1] Howard, *Get Clark Smart,* p. 7.

[2] Ibid.

[3] Ibid., p. 8.

[4] Adapted from Heady and Heady, *Complete Idiot's Guide to Managing Your Money,* p. 174.

[5] Eisenson, Detweiler, and Castleman, *Invest in Yourself,* p. 264.

[6] Howard, *Get Clark Smart,* p. 8.

[7] Heady and Heady, *Complete Idiot's Guide to Managing Your Money,* p. 174.

[8] Quinn, *Making the Most of Your Money,* p. 286.

[9] Heady and Heady, *Complete Idiot's Guide to Managing Your Money,* p. 174.

[10] Quinn, *Making the Most of Your Money,* p. 267.

[11] Dwight R. Lee and Richard B. McKenzie, *Getting Rich in America: 8 Simple Rules for Building a Fortune and a Satisfying Life* (New York: Harper Perennial, 1999), p. 81.

[12] Hunt, *Mary Hunt's Debt-Proof Living,* p. 297.

[13] Edelman, *Truth about Money,* p. 336; and Kelly, *Neatest Little Guide to Personal Finance,* pp. 98–99.

[14] Hunt, *Mary Hunt's Debt-Proof Living,* p. 302.

[15] Murray Baker, *The Debt-Free Graduate: How to Survive College without Going Broke* (Franklin Lakes, NJ: Career Press, 2000), p. 21.

[16] Stanley and Danko, *Millionaires Next Door,* p. 68.

[17] Tyson, *Personal Finance for Dummies,* p. 285.

[18] Quinn, *Making the Most of Your Money,* p. 478.

[19] Ric Edelman, *New Rules of Money,* p. 63.

[20] Ibid.

[21] Orman, *Courage to Be Rich,* p. 203.

22 Adapted from Orman, *Road to Wealth,* pp. 134–135.

23 Quinn, *Making the Most of Your Money,* p. 487.

24 Ibid.

25 Tyson, *Personal Finance for Dummies,* p. 302.

26 Tyson, *Personal Finance for Dummies,* p. 302; and Quinn, *Making the Most of Your Money,* pp. 487–488.

27 Quinn, *Making the Most of Your Money,* p. 482.

28 Ibid., pp. 481–482.

29 These questions are taken from Quinn, *Making the Most of Your Money,* pp. 483–486, except where indicated.

30 Orman, *Road to Wealth,* pp. 157–158.

31 Ibid., p. 156.

32 Mrkvicka, *Your Bank Is Ripping You Off,* p. 104.

33 Quinn, *Making the Most of Your Money,* p. 486.

34 Eisenson, Detweiler, and Castleman, *Invest in Yourself,* p. 245.

35 David F. Teitelbaum, *The Procrastinator's Guide to Financial Security: How Anyone over 40 Can Still Build a Strong Portfolio—and Retire Comfortably* (New York: AMACOM, 2001), pp. 93–94.

36 Jonathan Clements, *25 Myths You've Got to Avoid If You Want to Manage Your Money Right: The New Rules for Financial Success* (New York: Simon & Schuster, 1998), pp. 174–179.

37 Lloyd, *Simple Money Solutions,* pp. 255–256.

38 Bob Hammond, *Life without Debt,* pp. 62–65.

39 Chatzky, *Talking Money,* p. 204.

40 Strauss and Jaffe, *Complete Idiot's Guide to Beating Debt,* pp. 94–97.

Chapter 8

1 Heady and Heady, *Complete Idiot's Guide to Managing Your Money,* p. 246.

2 See Chatzky, *Talking Money,* pp. 69–87; Ric Edelman, *Ordinary People, Extraordinary Wealth: The 8 Secrets of How 5000 Ordinary Americans Became Successful Investors—and How You Can Too* (New York: HarperBusiness, 2001), p. 138; Dee Lee and David Caruso, *Let's Talk Money: Your Complete Personal Finance Guide* (Worcester, MA: Chandler House Press, 1999), p. 119; Peter Lynch and John Rothchild, *Learn to Earn: A Beginner's Guide to the Basics of Investing and Business* (New York: Fireside, 1995), pp. 112–113; and Tyson, *Investing for Dummies,* p. 149.

3 David Gardner and Tom Gardner, *The Motley Fool Investment Guide: How the Fool Beats Wall Street's Wise Men and How You Can Too* (New York: Fireside, 2001), p. 92.

4 Quinn, *Making the Most of Your Money,* p. 735.

5 Marshall Loeb, *Marshall Loeb's Lifetime Financial Strategies* (Boston: Little, Brown, 1996), p. 169.

6 Orman, *Road to Wealth,* p. 423.

7 Edelman, *Truth about Money,* p. 143.

8 Allen, *Multiple Streams of Income,* p. 121.

9 Quinn, *Making the Most of Your Money,* p. 820.

10 Allen, *Multiple Streams of Income,* p. 126.

11 Ibid., p. 136.

12 Ibid., p. 147.

13 Ibid., p. 150.

14 Ibid.

15 Mellan and Christie, *Money Shy to Money Sure,* pp. 56–58.

16 Gardner and Gardner, *Motley Fool Investment Guide,* p. 289.

17 Quinn, *Making the Most of Your Money,* p. 789.

18 Miller, *Kiplinger's Practical Guide to Your Money,* p. 384.

19 Peter Lynch, *One Up on Wall Street: How to Use What You Already Know to Make Money in the Market* (New York: Penguin, 1990), p. 278.

20 Miller, *Complete Idiot's Guide to Being a Cheapskate,* p. 268.

21 Mellan and Christie, *Money Shy to Money Sure,* p. 94.

22 Edelman, *Truth about Money,* pp. 149–151; Tyson, *Personal Finance for Dummies,* p. 204.

23 Edelman, *Truth about Money,* p. 109.

24 Quinn, *Making the Most of Your Money,* p. 807.

25 Robert Sheard, *The Unemotional Investor* (New York: Fireside, 1998), p. 30.

26 Quinn, *Making the Most of Your Money,* pp. 792–793.

27 Lee and Caruso, *Let's Talk Money,* p. 185.

28 Edelman, *Truth about Money,* p. 166.

29 Adapted from Quinn, *Making the Most of Your Money,* pp. 605–608.

30 Tyson, *Personal Finance for Dummies,* p. 206.

31 Ibid.

32 Bambi Holzer, *Retire Rich: The Baby Boomer's Guide to a Secure Future* (New York: John Wiley & Sons, 1998), p. 162.

33 Tyson, *Personal Finance for Dummies,* p. 206.

34 Clements, *25 Myths You've Got to Avoid If You Want to Manage Your Money Right,* p. 72.

35 Terry Savage, *The Savage Truth on Money* (New York: John Wiley & Sons, 1999), p. 127.

36 Arthur Levitt with Paula Dwyer, *Take on the Street* (New York: Pantheon, 2002), p. 55.

37 James O'Shaughnessy, *How to Retire Rich: Time-Tested Strategies to Beat the Market and Retire in Style* (New York: Broadway Books, 1998), pp. 77–78.

[38] Ibid., p. 83.

[39] Levitt with Dwyer, *Take on the Street,* p. 54.

[40] Ibid., p. 52.

[41] Ibid., p. 47.

[42] Gary Belsky and Thomas Gilovich, *Why Smart People Make Big Money Mistakes and How to Correct Them: Lessons from the New Science of Behavioral Economics* (New York: Fireside, 1999), p. 123.

[43] Levitt with Dwyer, *Take on the Street,* pp. 49–50.

[44] David Gardner and Tom Gardner, *The Motley Fool: You Have More Than You Think—The Foolish Guide to Personal Finance* (New York: Fireside, 1998), p. 83.

[45] Charles R. Schwab, *Charles Schwab's Guide to Financial Independence: Simple Solutions for Busy People* (New York: Crown, 1998), p. 89.

[46] Quinn, *Making the Most of Your Money,* p. 702.

[47] Julie Stav, *Fund Your Future* (New York: Berkley Books, 2001), pp. 76–133.

[48] Ibid., pp. 89–90.

[49] Ibid., p. 86.

[50] Holzer, *Retire Rich,* p. 163.

[51] Peter Lynch, *Beating the Street* (New York: Simon & Schuster, 1993), p. 68.

[52] Stav, *Fund Your Future,* pp. 101–102.

[53] Mellan and Christie, *Money Shy to Money Sure,* p. 98.

[54] Teitelbaum, *Procrastinator's Guide to Financial Security,* p. 242.

[55] Ibid.

Chapter 9

[1] This discussion is based on Schwab, *You're Fifty—Now What?* pp. 46–49.

[2] Schwab's method assumes that you will live 40 years in retirement and takes into account expected inflation. The factor of 230,000 is based on research conducted by the Schwab Center for Investment Research and is explained in detail in the appendix to Schwab's book *You're Fifty—Now What?* It represents the amount you would need to have at the start of retirement for every $1,000 you would withdraw from your retirement fund over a 40-year period. The figure is adjusted for inflation and assumes a moderately aggressive asset allocation. It is based on historical data for the period 1950–1999.

[3] Pond, *Your Money Matters,* p. 99.

[4] Some gurus talk about dividing your nonstock allocation roughly equally between bonds and cash equivalents. Others would have you hold cash equivalents to the minimum you need for current expenses and place all of your nonstock allocation into bonds or bond mutual funds.

[5] Tyson, *Investing for Dummies,* p. 180.

6 Schwab, *You're Fifty—Now What?* p. 159.

7 Ibid., pp. 160–161.

8 Lee and McKenzie, *Getting Rich in America,* p. 164.

9 Ibid.

10 Kiyosaki, *Rich Dad's Cashflow Quadrant,* p. 43.

11 Edelman, *Ordinary People, Extraordinary Wealth,* p. 59.

12 Ibid., pp. 59–60.

13 Quinn, *Making the Most of Your Money,* p. 600.

14 Ibid.

15 Adapted from Quinn, *Making the Most of Your Money,* p. 577.

16 Ibid.

17 Mellan and Christie, *Money Shy to Money Sure,* p. 48.

Bibliography

Allen, Robert G. *Multiple Streams of Income.* New York: John Wiley & Sons, 2000.

Applegarth, Ginger. *Wake Up and Smell the Money.* New York: Viking, 1999.

Baker, Murray. *The Debt-Free Graduate: How to Survive College without Going Broke.* Franklin Lakes, NJ: Career Press, 2000.

Belsky, Gary, and Thomas Gilovich. *Why Smart People Make Big Money Mistakes and How to Correct Them: Lessons from the New Science of Behavioral Economics.* New York: Fireside, 1999.

Berg, Stacie Zoe. *The Unofficial Guide to Managing Your Personal Finances.* New York: Macmillan General Reference, 1999.

Blix, Jacqueline, and David Heitmiller. *Getting a Life: Strategies for Simple Living, Based on the Revolutionary Program for Financial Freedom, Your Money or Your Life.* New York: Penguin Books, 1997.

Bryan, Mark, and Julia Cameron. *Money Drunk, Money Sober: 90 Days to Financial Freedom.* Los Angeles: Lowell House, 1992.

Chatzky, Jean Sherman. *Talking Money: Everything You Need to Know about Your Finances and Your Future.* New York: Warner Business Books, 2001.

Clements, Jonathan. *25 Myths You've Got to Avoid If You Want to Manage Your Money Right: The New Rules for Financial Success.* New York: Simon & Schuster, 1998.

Dacyczyn, Amy. *The Complete Tightwad Gazette.* New York: Vaillard, 1999.

Detweiler, Gerri, Marc Eisenson, and Nancy Castleman. *Slash Your Debt: Save Money and Secure Your Future.* Kalamazoo, MI: Financial Literacy Center, 1999.

Dominguez, Joe, and Vicki Robin. *Your Money or Your Life: Transforming Your Relationship with Money and Achieving Financial Independence.* New York: Penguin Books, 1999.

Edelman, Ric. *The New Rules of Money: 88 Strategies for Financial Success Today.* New York: Harper Perennial, 1998.

———. *Ordinary People, Extraordinary Wealth: The 8 Secrets of How 5000 Ordinary Americans Became Successful Investors—and How You Can Too.* New York: HarperBusiness, 2001.

———. *The Truth about Money.* New York: HarperCollins, 1998.

Eisenson, Marc, Gerri Detweiler, and Nancy Castleman. *Invest in Yourself: Six Secrets to a Rich Life.* New York: John Wiley & Sons, 1998.

Englander, Debra Wishik. *How to Be Your Own Financial Planner: Your Step-by-Step Guide to a Worry-Free Future.* Roseville, CA: Prima, 1995.

Gallen, Ron, *Money Trap: A Practical Program to Stop Self-Defeating Financial Habits So You Can Reclaim Your Grip on Life.* New York: Harper Resource, 2001.

Gardner, David, and Tom Gardner. *The Motley Fool: You Have More Than You Think—The Foolish Guide to Personal Finance.* New York: Fireside, 1998.

———. *The Motley Fool Investment Guide: How the Fool Beats Wall Street's Wise Men and How You Can Too.* New York: Fireside, 2001.

Glickman, Marshall. *Mindful Money Guide: Creating Harmony between Your Values and Your Finances.* New York: Ballantine Wellspring, 1999.

Glink, Ilyce R. *50 Simple Things You Can Do to Improve Your Personal Finances: How to Spend Less, Save More, and Make the Most of What You Have.* New York: Three Rivers Press, 2001.

Godfrey, Neale S. *Making Change: A Woman's Guide to Designing Her Financial Future.* New York: Simon & Schuster, 1997.

Hacker, Andrew. *Money: Who Has How Much and Why.* New York: Touchstone, 1997.

Hammond, Bob. *Life without Debt: Free Yourself from the Burden of Money Worries Once and for All.* Franklin Lakes, NJ: Career Press, 1995.

Hayes, Christopher L., and Kate Kelly. *Money Makeovers: How Women Can Control Their Financial Destiny.* New York: Doubleday, 1998.

Heady, Robert, and Christy Heady. *The Complete Idiot's Guide to Managing Your Money.* New York: Alpha Books, 1995.

Hill, Napolean. *Think and Grow Rich.* New York: Fawcett Crest, 1960.

Holzer, Bambi. *Retire Rich: The Baby Boomer's Guide to a Secure Future.* New York: John Wiley & Sons, 1998.

Howard, Clark. *Get Clark Smart: The Ultimate Guide for the Savvy Consumer.* Atlanta, GA: Longstreet Press, 2000.

Hunt, Mary. *Mary Hunt's Debt-Proof Living.* Nashville, TN: Broadman & Holman, 1999.

———. *Mary Hunt's The Complete Cheapskate: How to Get Out of Debt, Stay Out, and Break Free from Money Worries Forever.* Nashville, TN: Broadman & Holman, 1998.

Ivins, Mary F. *Financial Security for Women: Using Your Head and Heart to Achieve It.* Chicago: Symmetry, 1999.

Kelly, Jason. *The Neatest Little Guide to Personal Finance.* New York: Plume, 1999.

Kinder, George. *The Seven Stages of Money Maturity: Understanding the Spirit and Value of Money in Your Life.* New York: Delacorte Press, 1999.

Kiyosaki, Robert T. *Rich Dad's Cashflow Quadrant: Employee, Self-Employed, Business Owner, or Investor . . . Which Is the Best Quadrant for You?* New York: Warner Books, 2000.

————. *Rich Dad's Guide to Investing: What the Rich Invest in That the Poor and Middle Class Do Not!* New York: Warner Books, 2000.

————. *Rich Dad's Rich Kid, Smart Kid: Giving Your Child a Financial Head Start.* New York: Warner Business Books, 2001.

Knuckey, Deborah. *The Ms. Spent Money Guide: Get More of What You Want with What You Earn.* New York: John Wiley & Sons, 2001.

Laut, Phil. *Money Is My Friend.* New York: Ballantine Wellspring Books, 1999.

Lee, Dee, and David Caruso. *Let's Talk Money: Your Complete Personal Finance Guide.* Worcester, MA: Chandler House Press, 1999.

Lee, Dwight R., and Richard B. McKenzie. *Getting Rich in America: 8 Simple Rules for Building a Fortune and a Satisfying Life.* New York: Harper Perennial, 1999.

Levitt, Arthur with Paula Dwyer. *Take on the Street.* New York: Pantheon, 2002.

Lloyd, Nancy. *Simple Money Solutions: 10 Ways You Can Stop Feeling Overwhelmed by Money and Start Making It Work for You.* New York: Times Business, 2000.

Loeb, Marshall. *Marshall Loeb's Lifetime Financial Strategies.* Boston: Little, Brown, 1996.

Lynch, Peter. *Beating the Street.* New York: Simon & Schuster, 1993.

————. *One Up on Wall Street: How to Use What You Already Know to Make Money in the Market.* New York: Penguin, 1990.

Lynch, Peter, and John Rothchild. *Learn to Earn: A Beginner's Guide to the Basics of Investing and Business.* New York: Fireside, 1995.

McNaughton, Deborah. *The Insider's Guide to Managing Your Credit.* Chicago: Dearborn Financial, 1999.

Mellan, Olivia, and Sherry Christie. *Money Shy to Money Sure: A Woman's Road Map to Financial Well-Being.* New York: Walker, 2001.

————. *Overcoming Overspending: A Winning Plan for Spenders and Their Partners.* New York: Walker, 1995.

Miller, Mark W. *The Complete Idiot's Guide to Being a Cheapskate.* New York: Alpha Books, 1999.

Miller, Ted. *Kiplinger's Practical Guide to Your Money: Keep More of It, Make It Grow, Protect It.* Washington DC: Kiplinger Books, 1998.

Mrkvicka, Edward F. *Your Bank Is Ripping You Off.* New York: St. Martin's Griffin, 1999.

Nelson, Stephen L. *The Millionaire Kit: Surprisingly Simple Strategies for Building Real Wealth.* New York: Times Business, 1998.

Nemeth, Maria. *The Energy of Money: A Spiritual Guide to Financial and Personal Fulfillment*. New York: Ballantine Wellspring, 1999.

Nicholson, Holly. *Money and You*. Ft. Bragg, CA: Lost Coast Press, 1997.

Orman, Suze. *The Courage to Be Rich: Creating a Life of Material and Spiritual Abundance*. New York: Riverhead Books, 1999.

———. *The 9 Steps to Financial Freedom: Practical and Spiritual Steps So You Can Stop Worrying*. New York: Three Rivers Press, 2000.

———. *The Road to Wealth*. New York: Riverhead Books, 2001.

———. *Suze Orman's Financial Guidebook: Putting the 9 Steps to Work*. New York: Three Rivers Press, 2002.

O'Shaughnessy, James. *How to Retire Rich: Time-Tested Strategies to Beat the Market and Retire in Style*. New York: Broadway Books, 1998.

Pahl, Greg. *The Unofficial Guide to Beating Debt*. Foster City, CA: IDG Books Worldwide, 2000.

Pollan, Stephen, and Mark Levine. *Die Broke: A Radical, Four-Part Financial Plan*. New York: Harper Perennial, 1998.

———. *Live Rich: Everything You Need to Know to Be Your Own Boss, Whoever You Work For*. New York: Harper Perennial, 1998.

Pond, Jonathan. *Your Money Matters: 21 Tips for Achieving Financial Security in the 21st Century*. New York: G. P. Putnam's Sons, 1999.

Quinn, Jane Bryant. *Making the Most of Your Money*. New York: Simon & Schuster, 1997.

Ramsey, Dave. *Financial Peace*. New York: Viking Penguin, 1997.

———. *More Than Enough: Proven Keys to Strengthening Your Family and Building Financial Peace*. New York: Viking, 1999.

Rhode, Steve, and Mike Kidwell. *Get Out of Debt: Smart Solutions to Your Money Problems*. Rockville, MD: Debt Counselors of America, 1999.

Savage, Terry. *The Savage Truth on Money*. New York: John Wiley & Sons, 1999.

Schwab, Charles R. *Charles Schwab's Guide to Financial Independence: Simple Solutions for Busy People*. New York: Crown, 1998.

———. *You're Fifty—Now What? Investing for the Second Half of Your Life*. New York: Crown Business, 2001.

Sheard, Robert. *The Unemotional Investor*. New York: Fireside, 1998.

Silver, Don. *The Generation Y Money Book: 99 Smart Ways to Handle Money*. Los Angeles: Adams Hall, 1998.

Stanley, Thomas J. *The Millionaire Mind*. Kansas City, MO: Andrews McMeel, 2000.

Stanley, Thomas J., and William Danko. *The Millionaire Next Door*. Atlanta, GA: Longstreet Press, 1998.

Stanny, Barbara. *Prince Charming Isn't Coming: How Women Get Smart About Money*. New York: Penguin, 1997.

Stav, Julie. *Fund Your Future*. New York: Berkley Books, 2001.

Stephens, Brooke. *Wealth Happens One Day at a Time: 365 Days to a Brighter Financial Future.* New York: Harper Books, 1999.

Strauss, Steven D., and Azriela Jaffe. *The Complete Idiot's Guide to Beating Debt.* Indianapolis, IN: Alpha Books, 2000.

Strong, Howard. *What Every Credit Card User Needs to Know: How to Protect Yourself and Your Money.* New York: Henry Holt, 1999.

Teitelbaum, David F. *The Procrastinator's Guide to Financial Security: How Anyone over 40 Can Still Build a Strong Portfolio—and Retire Comfortably.* New York: AMACOM, 2001.

Tyson, Eric. *Investing for Dummies.* New York: Hungry Minds, 1999.

———. *Personal Finance for Dummies.* Foster City, CA: IDG Books Worldwide, 1997.

Index